Memory, Meaning, and Resistance

BOOKS BY FRAN LEEPER BUSS

La Partera: Story of a Midwife

Dignity: Lower Income Women Tell of Their Lives and Struggles

Journey of the Sparrows

Forged under the Sun/Forjada bajo el sol:
The Life of Maria Elena Lucas

Moisture of the Earth:
Mary Robinson, Civil Rights and Textile Union Activist

Memory, Meaning, and Resistance:
Reflecting on Oral History and Women at the Margins

Memory, Meaning, and Resistance

REFLECTING ON ORAL HISTORY AND WOMEN AT THE MARGINS

Fran Leeper Buss

University of Michigan Press
Ann Arbor, MI

Published in the United States of America by
The University of Michigan Press
Manufactured in the United States of America
♾ Printed on acid-free paper

2020   2019   2018   2017   4   3   2   1

A CIP catalog record for this book is available from the British Library.

Library of Congress Cataloging-in-Publication Data

Names: Buss, Fran Leeper, 1942- author.
Title: Memory, meaning, and resistance : reflecting on oral history and women at
  the margins / Fran Leeper Buss.
Description: Ann Arbor, MI : University of Michigan Press, [2017] | Includes
  bibliographical references and index.
Identifiers: LCCN 2017012623 | ISBN 9780472053599 (pbk. : alk. paper) |
  ISBN 9780472073597 (hardcover : alk. paper) | ISBN 9780472123056
  (e-book)
Subjects: LCSH: Women--United States--Biography.
Classification: LCC CT3260 .B88 2017 | DDC 920.720973--dc23
LC record available at https://lccn.loc.gov/2017012623

To David, Pat, Jacky, Barbara, Madeline, and Sandy

Contents

Acknowledgments

I want to especially thank the Coordinating Council for Women in History for awarding me the first Catherine Prelinger Prize for Women in History in 1998. The prize helped finance interviews for this book. I am grateful to the Ford Foundation for its support; full transcripts of many of these interviews have been placed in the Schlesinger Library at the Radcliffe Institute for Advanced Study at Harvard University. The Tucson-based Amazon Foundation also funded some interviews.

Professors Dana Wilbanks, Karen Anderson, and Hermann Rebel contributed to my intellectual training, and I want to acknowledge an intellectual debt to the philosopher Shari Stone-Mediatore for her book *Reading across Borders: Storytelling and Knowledges of Resistance*. LeAnn Fields, my editor at the University of Michigan Press, has believed in my work for many years and given me critical feedback. I cannot thank her enough for both her backing and her belief in the importance of working-class women's lives. The independent editor Amy Smith Bell worked diligently with me on the manuscript, going beyond expected assistance when I had serious problems with my eyesight. Miriam Davidson assisted me with some additional material. The late Florence Davis, Jacky Turchick, and University of Arizona history professor Susan Crane read earlier versions of this manuscript. The members of my writing group—Kaymarie Peterson, Gerry Barton, and Marge Pellegrino—motivated me for many years. Teresa Hager transcribed interviews and offered encouragement.

Many friendships sustained me as I did this work, and I thank Pat Manning, Jacky Turchick, Teri Robinson, Delle McCormick, Barbara Clarihew, Mary Robinson, Maria Elena Lucas, Margaret Buss, Agate Nesaule, Josefina

Castillo, Madeline Kiser, Miriam Davidson, and Sandy Peterson. There is no way to express my gratitude to the women I have interviewed, whose experiences make this book what it is, especially Jesusita Aragon, Maria Elena Lucas, Mary Robinson, Rose Augustine, and Pat Manning. Finally, I thank my husband, David Buss, for his loving support and profound belief in my work. Our children—Kimberly, Lisa, and Jim—have inspired me throughout their lives.

Preface

This book is a result of seven sets of interviews, including those collected for an unpublished project about border and peace activists in Tucson, Arizona. I estimate that in all I have interviewed in depth more than a hundred working-class women from around the United States, beginning in 1976 and continuing through 2016. These women are from multiple racial and ethnic backgrounds. A few of them I interviewed just one time, but the transcripts from many of my interviews are much longer, representing multiple interviews spanning years. The transcripts from my interviews with Maria Elena Lucas, a Mexican American farmworker and labor organizer, are thirteen hundred pages long (in addition to nine hundred pages of her own writing). Those from Mary Robinson, an African American textile union leader, are fifteen hundred pages long. So far, peace and border activist Pat Manning, a white woman, and I have a thousand-page transcript. All the transcripts and my indexes for them are (or ultimately will be, upon completion) housed in the Schlesinger Library of American Women at the Radcliffe Institute for Advanced Study at Harvard University. My personal journals, kept from 1970 through today, are also located there and include the stories of many interviews.

To compare the transcripts, I indexed them and artificially imposed a linear chronology upon each narrative, beginning with the woman's childhood, often including together her memories given to me on several occasions. Michael Frisch, a leading expert in oral history supports this approach: "I advance the notion that a relatively aggressive, even manipulative approach to the 'actual' text may be the best way to faithfully convey its real meaning and essence."[1] Because conversation has its own rhythm, he continues, it is important to record and preserve the entire interview.[2] I agree with Frisch's approach and have tried to preserve the exact interview for each narration. In reorganizing the stories in a chronological fashion, I worked through each narrator's life and ended up with her own account of the meaning of her life, her belief system, and her observations of the situation in which she lived. By the time Mary Robinson and I started to work together, I was trying to reproduce the text in roughly the same proportions to the transcripts. For example, the transcripts refer seventy-eight times to Mary's mother's work when Mary was a child, so we gave much emphasis to that aspect of Mary's own story. Also, Mary spoke seventeen times about the murders of black prisoners by white sheriffs, so we included several segments on that.

I clarified pronouns and excluded my prompting in order to shorten the narratives. With Maria Elena and Mary, I had perhaps asked a thousand questions apiece, so the questions were impossible to include with any coherency. I also eliminated many of the verbal repetitions, such as "ah," "well," and "you know." Exact transcripts of spoken text include many such false starts and to include them all is to make the narrator sound ineffective. On a whole, however, I kept standard spelling, following Frisch: "Speech that sounds articulate and coherent to the ear tends to read, when too-literally transcribed in print, like inarticulate stage mumbling; such transcription becomes an obstacle to hearing what the person in the interview is trying to say."[3]

The biggest disruption I made to the actual transcribed tapes concerned Mary Robinson. We had done our research over twenty-three years, and yet I wanted her story to read as a contemporary narrative. I therefore combined old transcripts and more recent ones into one single, linear story. I also included brief introductions for each woman at the outset of each work. The introductions grew increasingly complex as I studied history myself, and it is easy to follow my intellectual and political development between those written in 1976 and the more recently written introductions to Maria Elena's and Mary's work. The introduction to the unpublished manuscript "Spiritual Visions/Border Lives: Progressive Women Activists at the U.S.-Mexico Border" was written with my coeditor, Josefina Castillo.

After I completed first Maria Elena's, then Mary's narrations, I took the stories to them so that they could review them. By this time, Maria Elena's eyesight was poor and she couldn't read, so I went through the manuscript with her, prioritizing those sections I thought would be most problematic for her and reading these passages out loud. When we had completed about half the manuscript, however, Maria Elena asked me to stop. She was going through too many emotions, she said. Likewise, I took the transcript to Mary Robinson, but she chose not to read it. She said she trusted my judgment. I think the feelings were just too strong. After I had worked on this project for so many years with these women, they both felt they could trust me.

My guiding research questions have been the following. How are the working-class women I interviewed situated or embedded within structures of race, class, and gender? How were the women exploited by the dominant culture and its web of structures? How do the women construct memories that give them strength and meaning and fuel their resistance? How do the women's lives express knowledge from beneath middle-class explanations of behavior? How do the ideas of the women resist dominant cultures, and how can others aid in the power of this resistance? Accordingly, each chapter in this book addresses a theme: situated locations, agency, memory construction, interrelationships, meaning, knowledge from below, activism and social movements, and activism and spirituality.

I adapted my questions to the person I was interviewing. Some of my primary questions with Maria Elena, for example, were: Why had someone of her brilliance been repressed before she had even begun to get access to education? Why had no one taken her seriously except as a laborer and a reproducer of workers? How did she represent other girls in her life situation? With Mary Robinson I asked: How could someone who loves her community and land so completely never have been considered in the allocation of resources? Her life situation had denied her family the land they had worked and loved. Why had a reversal of that condition never been seriously contemplated by the dominant powers? Who makes such decisions? How do they enforce them? How is violence ultimately used to ensure results? What particular kinds of exploitation do African American women face? In the interviews with border activists, such as Pat Manning, I asked such background questions as: Who benefits from the enormous work undocumented laborers perform as stigmatized service workers in the United States? Who is enriched from the created poverty in their home countries? What are the unique dangers undocumented women face? All these questions involve the interactions of race, class, and gender.

Working-class women from a variety of racial and ethnic backgrounds tell stories about their lives to express the meanings they have experienced. These narratives are shaped by cultural constrictions, values, memories of real events, interpretations of those events, storytelling traditions, and the women's own sense of agency. In the process of telling these stories, the women create meaning. By sharing their narratives, the women reveal and reshape the meaning these experiences hold for themselves, their cultural context, and the dominant culture. As part of the process, the women resist the constrictions on their lives and help create historical change. Such essential storytelling adds critical dimensions to democratic debates about social priorities and the future.

I interviewed some women who claimed their identities as lesbian, although the women with the longest interviews included here identify primarily as heterosexual. There are probably two reasons for this. First, my own social connections have been primarily heterosexual. Second, during the 1970s and 1980s, when I began interviewing a large number of women, lesbian, bisexual, and transgender women often had to live hidden lives. That included women in well-known resistance groups. More recent interviews of mine have included openly lesbian women, but to date I have not interviewed any transgender women.

A note on methodology: There are other ways to do oral history than those I have used. I investigated individual women's life stories, concentrating on the many details such a focus can bring; however, many other oral historians explore in depth "particular social, categorical, or positional location[s]."[4] For example, they might interview a number of gays and lesbians who participated in the Stonewall Inn protests in 1969. The protests were a series of spontaneous demonstrations by the gay community in reaction to police arrests at a nightclub. They are widely considered to have led to the public emergence of the gay rights movement.[5] Likewise, oral historians might examine the Sanctuary movement, a religious and political crusade begun in the 1980s, which provided safe haven to refugees fleeing the violence in Central America.[6]

Each chapter highlights an analytical concept, such as situated location, agency, memory construction, and meaning, as illustrated by excerpts from the women's oral histories. Generally, the interpretation is presented first, followed by the oral history segments that illustrate it, then further analyzed and refined. Each chapter builds on themes that came earlier, and in the final chapter, notions of women's spirituality build on many of the analytical concepts in previous sections, especially meaning.

I have been conducting oral history interviews for forty years now, and, like the women I interviewed, am no longer young. I hope that a younger generation of readers will be inspired by the stories of those who have gone before and will find the insights in this book useful as they perform their own research and analysis on their lives and those of others.

Many of the issues the women in this book faced have not gone away, in fact have worsened, including the problems of poverty and growing inequities in our social system. Increasingly people of color face the threat of physical harm from the police and incarceration from our criminal justice system, leading to contemporary resistance movements like Black Lives Matter. Similarly, young people are hampered by an unfair immigration system, which denies them legal recognition. Several of the women in the book have personal experience with domestic violence and sexual assault, problems that still persist. I have been impressed by the way survivors of college sexual assault have been fighting back, working to take care of themselves and make their campuses safer for all.

I have written this book because I believe the stories herein will give other women insights and strength. I am seventy-five years old, and it seems time to delve into my past work and present what wisdom I have gained from it. Perhaps my mother's experience in an orphanage, which she described to me in so much anguish so many years ago, led me to search out women's stories. Over my lifetime, I have developed emotionally and intellectually as I undertook the work described throughout this book. I hope that is reflected.

Mary Robinson and Fran Leeper Buss in Dubuque, Iowa, in 2002. (Photo by Barbara Jennings)

Introduction

> To be able to live and understand the drama we call our lives, people give meaning to their experiences by telling stories.
>
> —TINEKA A. ABMA

Lilly Baker (a pseudonym) came from a Kentucky coal-mining family of thirteen and went through school only to the fourth grade, but as a child she helped her mother care for others. At fifteen, she began working with a mountain nurse, and from then on Lilly walked throughout the mountains and hollows where people lived. She stayed with and nursed the sick, cared for their families, and comforted their kin. She served as a midwife when necessary. Lilly married a coal miner and gave birth three times. She remembers cradling her "blue baby" with a heart defect in her arms until the baby died. She cared for her husband throughout his life until his death from black lung.

I stayed with Lilly when I interviewed other women in Appalachia in 1980. Lilly, then a tiny and slightly stooped seventy-six-year-old, had an oval face, dark brown eyes, fair skin, and heavy black and white eyebrows. She had told me, her face glistening: "I got baptized in the creek when I was fourteen. God came down in a cloud and said, 'Lilly, visit the sick and the afflicted. It's your holy mission.'" Six decades later, Lilly had not forgotten her charge. She told me she would take me to one of the afflicted, and we climbed up the hollow.

Just about thirty years later, I sat in my office in Tucson, Arizona, and talked to Lupe Castillo. Lupe had grown up in a working-class family in a segregated Mexican American section of the city. She had a different idea from Lilly's about her mission in life. It did not involve a call from God, but instead she felt a commitment to the Chicano movement. As a young woman, Lupe became a political activist. She marched with the early anti–Vietnam War demonstrators and helped develop the Mexican American rights movement in the 1970s. She fought for immigrant rights and planned movement strategies. We talked in depth several times, during which she described Arizona's contemporary attacks on the Ethnic Studies' Mexican American program in the Tucson schools. Lupe taught Ethnic Studies at the college level.

On May 3, 2011, she was arrested because of her activism. The Tucson Unified School District's governing board held a tumultuous, four-hour meeting about ending the Mexican American Studies program in the schools. It took place in front of a tense, standing-room-only audience. About three hundred people gathered outside, listening to the speakers. Armed police guarded the board members. When Lupe and another woman tried to speak after the call-to-the-audience part of the meeting had ended, the board ordered them out. They protested, and police in tactical gear arrested them. Other protestors objected, and the police arrested five more women.

"I wanted to say a few words," Lupe said afterward. "I wanted to read from Dr. Martin Luther King Jr.'s 'Letter from Birmingham'!" She was "horrified at the level of police presence." Police issued a citation for criminal trespass and ordered the arrested to appear in the city court. The school district's governing board decided to hold a community forum before anything could be settled.[1]

Lilly's and Lupe's stories are among the many oral histories I have collected during my forty years as a historian of working-class women. Oral histories are interviews that record the life experiences of a narrator for cultural or historical purposes. To understand my oral history work and the conclusions I have made about the process, the reader must know something of my background and the reasons for my actions. The following narrative about my life is just one version of my history. Here I have included incidents and ideas that are important to understanding the oral histories that appear in this book. The historian Anthony Le Donne has written that the "very act of thinking requires interpretation."[2] My own history has informed my skills and thinking over the years as I conducted these oral histories.[3]

I was born in 1942, soon after the bombing of Pearl Harbor, which signaled the entry of the United States into World War II. I grew up along the beautiful Mississippi bluffs of Dubuque, Iowa, wandering among the hills, closely observing my community. Although we were Protestants, we lived among Catholic institutions—a convent, churches, and diocese head-quarters. Meat-packing factories followed the river bottom. When I was ten years old, my mother called me to sit next to her as she lay in her bath, where she soaked her emaciated body. She was tense and rapidly losing weight. The bathtub helped her relax. Her words, confusing to me, burst out: "She pulled me away from my sister. The only person I had. She gave me the doll of dead Virginia, then knocked it out of my hands. She said I had to replace Virginia, but that I wasn't worthy."

My mother was mentally ill and, even as an adult, she carried great anger toward her foster mother. She had experienced extreme periods of agitation and depression throughout her life. She had lived with her older sister in an orphanage as a child, and during the Great Depression, my mother had been taken in by poor farmers who wanted my mother only to replace a dead child of their own. The traumatic experience contributed to my mother's illness. As a child, I learned acute listening skills in an attempt to prevent my mother's mood swings.

My parents were white and working class, and my father worked two jobs to meet our family's needs. A seminary bookstore was located near my grade school, and the employees used to allow me to leaf through books of maps. In that way, I knew there was such a place as college. My parents had always embraced the myth that if you worked hard, you would succeed. There were few people of color in our small city, but we lived on the edge of an impoverished, rural neighborhood. As soon as I was conscious of difference, I was aware of economic hierarchies. The community was fiercely divided between its Catholic majority and its Protestant minority, and we were part of the minority so I learned some about that status.

I was a child during the communist scare of the 1950s, when adhering to a dominant, singular vision of the white citizen left almost no room for non-conformity.[4] As part of my socialization, I learned a language and symbol system of "whiteness." White stood for purity, darkness for pollution. White skin was to be cherished, but even among the whites, being blond was preferable to having dark hair. Racial language was everywhere, embedded in our daily lives. When I was about thirteen I joined the Rainbow Girls, an offshoot of the Masons. There we worked through the colors of the rainbow, learning a virtue with each color. For example, orange stood for religion, green for immortality, blue for fidelity, and violet for service. A Rainbow Girl's highest achievement was to "become white"—the culmination of all the learned qualities and a representative of purity. One year a girl who had achieved that goal became pregnant, and she was promptly whisked away from the group. I gave up on the Rainbow Girls and eventually graduated from high school.

I came of age at the beginning of the 1960s, and the Cold War continued to chill much American dissent. The civil rights movement clashed with the white caste system in the South, however, and the Vietnam War cast its long shadow.[5] Soon, people in the civil rights and antiwar movements protested throughout the land.[6] Writing about the 1960s, the historian Howard Zinn stated: "Never in American history had more movements for change been concentrated in so short a span of years."[7]

I began working part time when I was ten, and when I was eighteen, I started to work my way through college. I was the first person in my family to attend. I married young to escape the family situation. I worked full time as a nurse's aid and took evening classes. I gave birth to a daughter and later learned of a baby who needed a home. She was of mixed race, African American and white. Naively, I thought that if we could adopt her, I could save another child from some of the suffering my mother had endured. Not long after the adoption, I gave birth to a son. Adopting my daughter changed my life. I became involved with racial justice issues and could never again ignore how race interplays with social structures. Also, I was forced to confront my own biases in language. Lightness could no longer stand for higher spiritual understanding; darkness could no longer indicate benighted thinking.

Still, I did not demand equality and respect from my husband. He ignored my exhaustion from working full time and caring for three little children. I was yearning for meaningful work, but I continued to put him through college and graduate school. One afternoon while ironing other people's clothing for money, I watched television while my children played on the floor. A pregnant woman appeared on a TV panel. Talking about women's inequality and the discrepancy in pay, she said that women deserved equal rights and should be considered when family decisions were being made. The other panelists attacked her. This caught my undivided attention. Several members from the TV audience accused the woman of being outrageous. I thought, *There must be something to this if it makes other people so mad.*

I bought a copy of Betty Friedan's *The Feminine Mystique.* She talked about "the problem that has no name"—and then she named it: women's desire to contribute something with meaning to the world through their work. Friedan did not include issues for working-class women or women of color in her book, but her thesis shook me deeply. I thought of my own circumstances and cried for three days.[8]

When my husband graduated, we moved to Fort Collins, Colorado. In May 1970, as campuses exploded in reaction to the shootings at Kent State, my husband asked for a divorce and then relocated across the country. He only sporadically sent child support to the children, who were then ages five, three, and two. I read *The Feminine Mystique* again, and this time its hopefulness thrilled me. For a while I worked four part-time jobs, trying to earn a living and pay for day care, but the children and I went under financially. I applied for food stamps and welfare, or Aid to Families with Dependent Children (AFDC), a program that had originally been part of Franklin Roosevelt's New Deal of the 1930s. The program had been greatly expanded under Lyndon Johnson's War on Poverty, first introduced in 1964.[9] The assistance gave us enough income to barely survive.

While on AFDC, I met other poor women who provided my children and me with more love than I'd ever experienced in my life. We decided as a group that we had been through about all a woman in Colorado could go through. Inspired by "women's liberation," we formed a Women's Crisis and Information Center—one of the first in the country. I became the center's director and spent several years immersed in all sorts of issues concerning poor women: homelessness, difficulty getting adequate food, problem pregnancies, rape, violence against women, discrimination, and unsympathetic treatment by the community's social service system. This gave me insight into social hierarchies that I never forgot. The program eventually developed into one of the first shelters for abused women.

Although we did not know it at the time, we were part of what has been called the second wave of feminism, a movement that began in the 1960s and lasted until about the 1980s. As compared to the earlier women's suffrage movement, this wave dealt with such issues as sexuality, violence against women, reproductive rights, pay equality, poverty, and the opening of male-dominated professions to women.[10] A National Welfare Rights organization had been formed in 1967. Probably we had not heard of it because we were primarily white women, while the earlier organization consisted of many African Americans.[11]

Despite my work on behalf of other poor women, I couldn't protect myself against some of the greatest vulnerabilities for women. At that time in my community, only one gynecologist would see women on welfare. I went to him because of irregularity with my periods, and he convinced me that I needed an emergency hysterectomy. I was going off welfare the next week, so the surgery had to be rushed in order for it to be paid for. I arranged for child care and had the surgery. It turned out that my doctor was on drugs during the procedure. He cut me up. I had three more major surgeries to try to repair the damage and about a dozen minor surgeries without anesthetic because I could not afford it. The original surgery caused permanent damage in my bladder and bowels. Seven or eight times a day, I have to deal with my body's reminder of my extreme economic vulnerability back then. Police arrested the offending doctor while I was in his waiting room. He pulled a gun on the officers but was led away. I shook for days. I don't know what became of him, but I learned I was too poor to sue him. I had to pay for the other surgeries on my own—I was no longer on welfare—and went deeply into debt. These surgeries cut into my self-confidence. I now believe that for years I had a version of post-traumatic stress disorder.

Not all in my life was that hard, however. In late 1971, I met David, my husband of forty-four years. He formed a loving relationship with my children, our children, and in many ways I have lived a wonderful life. However, my firsthand knowledge of poor women's vulnerability has never left me. This understanding has been a driving force professionally and personally my whole life.

In 1972, I helped form an early women's conscious-raising group, a major organizing technique of second-wave feminism. In our group we dissected male-oriented language and symbols. At that time, inexperienced as we were, we believed that women were more loving and peace oriented than men; we assumed that women could bond together across racial and class divisions. I began to believe that if I'd had a female medical practitioner instead of the welfare doctor I had for my hysterectomy, I wouldn't have been injured so badly.

I had worked my way through college by then, and with the help of scholarships and loans, I entered seminary. I hoped to do religiously based social action work. While in seminary, I studied liberation theology—a Marxist-influenced belief system that calls for activists to view the world from the vantage point of the poor. Liberation theology saw the presence of God in marginalized people, people who live on the edges of society with few resources and little representation in powerful places. This view emphasized the experience of the everyday world and a recognition of the world's injustices. Its adherents called for radical social action, as well as reflection, and for followers to look at life and plan their activities taking into consideration those on the edges of society.

I also studied early feminist theory, primarily the work of the Marxist philosopher Shulamith Firestone, the theologian and philosopher Mary Daly, and the Christian theologian Rosemary Radford Reuther.[12] In my thesis I combined their thinking with my experience and articulated a feminist version of liberation theology that I called "an ethic of sisterhood." The writings of Gustavo Gutierrez, a major theorist of liberation theology, introduced me to Third World, Christian, Marxist analysis.[13] The presence of my biracial daughter had already politicized me, and in a class, the Christian theologian Vincent Harding taught ideas of liberation for African Americans. I also drew from the Brazilian educator and philosopher Paulo Freire, who saw liberation as a spiritual event that created "new space" and called for "conscientization"—consciousness raising with an activist component.[14] Freire inspired his followers to create tools with which the poor and marginalized could analyze their condition.

Now, with this education, both my lived experiences as a woman and my participation in a vibrant intellectual system informed all my decisions. I tried to write poetry describing the lives of the women I had known. Burdened by my earlier medical debt, my husband, children, and I lived a frugal life. After David graduated from seminary, we took a combination campus-community position in the small town of Las Vegas in northeastern New Mexico, where we both were active politically. Shortly after we moved, I heard of Doña Jesusita Aragon, an old Latina midwife still practicing her skills. She had delivered several of my friends' babies, and one friend said to me: "Somebody should do her story." I suddenly pictured a book written in the same style as Theodore Rosengarten's *All God's Dangers: The Life of Nate Shaw*.[15] That was the only oral history book that I had read at the time. I did not picture myself writing Jesusita's story; I envisioned finding someone from the Mexican American community to work on it as a community development project. I met Jesusita and shared the idea. She was excited.

For more than a year, I tried to find a community member to do the project, but it did not work out. Eventually, in 1976, Jesusita asked me to do it myself. "But I can't do it in Spanish," I said. "No, we will do it in English," she responded. Thus commenced my first oral history project. I had known about the discrimination by whites of Latinos in Las Vegas, and I knew that whites had cheated nearby Latino farmers and ranchers out of their land, but I had been naive about much of the region's racism and economic oppression. I had thought that as women, Jesusita and I could reach each other despite our racial and ethnic differences. I became convinced that under the primary care of someone like Jesusita, my entire medical nightmare years earlier would not have happened.

Researching her story, I learned about the presence of female public health workers who had begun working with the Latina midwives in the 1930s. The public health workers were all Anglo, except for one African American. Together, I thought, midwives and public health workers brought an all-female medical system to the impoverished mothers of northeastern New Mexico. I romanticized much of the interaction, however, and did not examine the real class, racial, and ethnic differences between the two groups of women. I began working with Jesusita, recording her story with my old reel-to-reel tape recorder. I watched her births and other medical practices and drove her to the places where she'd lived and worked throughout her long life. I knew that as an educated white woman, I had both a class and racial advantage over her, but still the community honored her and gave her a high status within her specific situation.

When the funding for David's and my work in Las Vegas ran out, we felt we needed to relocate to stable positions as our children went to junior and senior high school. We thus took a campus ministry position in Whitewater, Wisconsin. The move was especially hard on me because I had felt I was doing the work I was meant to do in Las Vegas. While in Wisconsin, I found a publisher for Jesusita's story, which was ultimately published as La Partera: Story of a Midwife.[16] I knew I had found my passion. I had been inspired by Studs Terkel's work interviewing people, especially his collection Working: People Talk about What They Do All Day and How They Feel about What They Do.[17] I thought I could do a similar project interviewing working-class and poor women, including not just their work conditions but other ways in which they got the economic necessities. For example, I would ask about their experiences with welfare, child support, or old-age pensions. I would try to racially balance the women I interviewed, though not according to a strict statistical breakdown.

With Jesusita's book in hand, which gave me a kind of authenticity, I began to ask poor and working-class women if I could interview them. I found them through friends of friends and through social justice programs with unions and churches. I told these women that I wanted to show how hard they worked for their precarious economic resources. I asked for general information about their lives. I explained that the interviews would be included in a book designed for college students. I revealed some of my own working-class background so that, with my higher education, I wouldn't seem so alien to them. Despite talking about economics with the women, I gradually realized we were talking about life's meaning.

In all, for the project I interviewed seventy-two women from a variety of ethnic, geographic, and economic situations. I typed up interviews, paid other transcribers for their help, and took extra jobs to pay the costs. The work eventually resulted in the book *Dignity: Lower Income Women Tell of Their Lives and Struggles*, which included the stories of ten women.[18] The book was meant to be a supplemental work for college classes, but I wrote it in clear language, and the women profiled throughout *Dignity* began to use it as an organizing tool. They took their own stories to other people in similar situations.

I realized throughout the process for that book that I had more power than the women I interviewed. I was white, had an education, and by this time we lived in a middle-class neighborhood. I had a book proposal and a probable publisher. I could give these women a chance to make their stories known. Almost everyone I interviewed began with the statement, "I don't know why anybody would want to know about my life," but as the interviews went on, even the women themselves began to see the importance of their accounts.

While working on *Dignity*, I met two women who would be important to me for the rest of my life: Maria Elena Lucas (Ortega) and Mary Robinson. Maria Elena was a laborer in the fields of Onarga, Illinois, and an organizer with the United Farm Workers. For days I followed her as she worked with distressed, often undocumented farmworkers. She shared some of her own writing with me, and I realized I had met someone who could give voice to their suffering. I went to the town where she lived when César Chávez dedicated a service center that she headed. I traveled to Onarga frequently, and Maria Elena and her children and I became friends. Her story is told in the final chapter of *Dignity*.

At this point in my writing career, I had some of the language necessary to talk about racial, class, and gender issues. I saw these categories as interwoven in specific historical situations. I was well aware that I came from a radically different background from Maria Elena's, and I knew I carried biased assumptions and prejudices as a result of this position of privilege, despite how I'd been shaken by my own earlier circumstances. However, I did not have enough intellectual or life experience to clarify all the connections between my privilege and Maria Elena's suffering. Later, in my research and through my friendship with her, I would learn the specifics of how trapped the migrant community is in an economic system that uses racial difference and gender to determine who will do some of the most demanding labor in the United States. I came to understand that I benefited from this class/gender/racial system through the food I ate and the education I received. I was part of a basic supposition that some would be advantaged in the system as others were discarded and considered unworthy of society's benefits.

In 1980, I traveled south and met Mary Robinson, an African American textile worker and union organizer in Montgomery, Alabama. She worked at one of the dangerous and notoriously anti-union J. P. Stevens plants. I made contact through the National Amalgamated Clothing and Textile Workers Union in New York. As the daughter of sharecroppers, Mary told me about the problems of being black and poor in the South. One heartbreaking memory she shared was trying as a young girl to kill a black doll because it wasn't white. She was willing to open up a whole world of understanding for me. I included Mary's stories in *Dignity*. Over the years, we have visited each other many times. I tape-recorded her stories—I wanted her experiences to be known to the world.

I began doing oral histories with poor women during the changeover from President Jimmy Carter to the Reagan-Bush era, a time that brought sharp cuts in benefits to poor people, the reduction of taxes for the wealthy, and an increase in military spending.[19] These policies continued in the Clinton years with his policy of "welfare reform," which forced economically disadvantaged mothers to work at poorly paid jobs and get off government assistance. And the rhetoric against the poor as "lazy" and "dangerous" has only increased in subsequent years.[20]

Throughout the 1980s, I continued to be politically active with women's and poverty issues, my children graduated from high school, and my husband and I moved to Tucson, Arizona. I began graduate school in history. I hoped to gain more understanding of the resilience many women showed in the face of racial, class, gender, and sexual oppression. I majored in U.S. history, with an emphasis on women's and racial and ethnic history. I minored in comparative women's history, emphasizing colonialism and the development of modern sexism, racism, and economic exploitation. As part of my studies, I read Marx again. Our children grew up to become loving and functional adults.

On March 3, 1988, a crop-dusting airplane sprayed Maria Elena with poison while she was working in South Texas. Her heart stopped several times, and when she got to medical care the doctor revived her. Her children called me, and within two weeks I went to see her, my tape recorder in hand. We began doing the in-depth oral history, which resulted in *Forged under the Sun/Forjada bajo el sol: The Life of Maria Elena Lucas*.[21] I understood that I came from a position of extraordinary privilege in comparison with Maria Elena. She was overwhelmed when she visited me later and saw all my books. She is brilliant, but her formal education had ended after about three full years of grammar school. After that, she worked full time in the fields. Her experience stood in stark contrast to mine: now, as I worked on my PhD, I understood the political realities that had allowed me to go to school and kept her from it. Today, Maria Elena and I talk on the phone once a week. She tells me details of her life, especially of her continuing struggles with poverty and illness. She also tells me of her prolific writing of poetry, songs, and prose describing the circumstances of the poor. "Save those writings," I tell her whenever we talk. "They are important."

The gap in inequality in the United States is much greater, however, than the discrepancy between Maria Elena's income and lifestyle and my own. Inequality started rising about 1973, shortly before I did many of my interviews, rose steadily in the 1980s, and continues today. Economist Anthony B. Atkinson reported that the top 1/10,000th of the American population currently receives 1/25th of the total income. Atkinson states:

> The official poverty rate in the U.S. fell from 33% in 1948 to 19% at the time Lyndon Johnson launched the War on Poverty in 1964. Poverty continued to fall until the late 1960s, but since then there has been little overall improvement in the poverty rate, and the absolute number has increased as the population has grown; today some 45 million Americans live below the official poverty line.[22] Young people today are in danger of falling into poverty, even if they attend college and do what policy makers suggest. Over the last 25 years, the wages of a typical college graduate working full time have risen only 1.6 percent, adjusting for inflation, while the burden of student debt has increased 163.8 percent. In 1990 a typical graduate with a bachelor's degree had incurred debt equal to 28.6 percent of her annual income; 25 years later, the percentage rose to 74.3 percent. Research suggests that the burden of student debt is responsible

for delayed home purchases, failure to obtain proper medical care, and deferring small business startups.[23]

The whole time I was working on Maria Elena's narrative, I was also think-ing of Mary Robinson and the stories that she told when we were together. Although it was twenty-three years in the making, the actual, focused work on Mary's book, *Moisture of the Earth: Mary Robinson, Civil Rights and Tex-tile Union Activist*, began when she had planned to come to Tucson on a sight-seeing trip.[24] Two weeks before she was to arrive, I nearly died because of complications from my disabilities. Consequently, I was too sick to sight-see, so when Mary arrived, she and I sat in front of my fireplace from 8:00 a.m. to 8:00 p.m. for eight days straight. During those hours, she narrated the basics of what would become the book.

Mary and I talked about race constantly. I studied everything I could on white racism, the power dynamics of the South, and the attempted union organizing that had taken place there. I visited her many times between 1981 and 2004 as we worked on the book. We traveled to courthouses and his-torical family sites; we interviewed people in the countryside; we crawled across the remnants of the dynamic black community of Mary's childhood. We talk on the phone every few days, and we still visit back and forth.

After *Moisture of the Earth* was finally published in 2009, I began to wonder if we could turn the tape recorder around, if Maria Elena and Mary could interview *me* about my personal history. We began to travel to see each other again, and this time I told them my own stories, recording our discussions. Neither Maria Elena nor Mary knew how to ask me questions to keep the process going, so I wrote out stories from my life, read them to each woman, then recorded their responses. It was a workable process, but I never tried to get the resulting manuscript published. My story was not as compelling as theirs. This process, during which they learned more about me, affected us all in several ways. It definitely increased our affection for each other and gave both women insight into some of the struggles in my own life. Mary accompanied me to the places of my childhood, as I had ac-companied her. I give an example of those trips in the epilogue. I showed videotapes of those visits to Maria Elena. We all got greater insight into the workings of an interrelated economy. I found the process immensely thera-peutic. The pain of traumas in my life lost their sting in Maria Elena's and Mary's love, which they expressed to me freely.

Despite the limits and struggles of my own working-class childhood and my mother's mental illness, though, our struggles were not comparable. The racism Mary and Maria Elena endured bound them to structures I never had to challenge. Nevertheless, these interviews anchored our relationships and opened our eyes to each other's worlds. We experienced what Shari Stone-Mediatore, a philosopher and feminist theorist, has described.

> Storytelling provides a means other than "universal principles" for resist-ing the objectification of people. When we share stories, we speak not from "above" but from within a community of storytellers. We address our audience as fellow storytellers, people who have perspectives of their own to contribute to the ongoing narrative. When we exchange stories, we also learn about how we both resemble and differ from one another. We therefore resist ideologies that absolutize and demonize human dif-ferences. A community of storytellers thus learns to listen to one another as individuals and cannot so easily categorize one another or impose on one another a predetermined agenda.[25]

While working on the oral histories, I tried to deal ethically with the women I interviewed. For me, this meant keeping in touch with them all and sharing royalties with Jesusita, Maria Elena, and Mary. But I wanted more for them; I realized that merely telling about injustice was not going to change it. For many years I tried to spend roughly equal hours between working on the books and working for specific political actions I hoped would help change the power dynamics. As I have become older, however, that is no longer feasible, and I now concentrate on the writing of the oral histories. I have been quite honored to become an important person in the lives of many of the women I've interviewed over the years. I saw four of the women through to their deaths.

The spirits of these women stayed with me when David and I moved to Tucson. My life there led to a manuscript on the U.S.-Mexico border, which I compiled and edited with my friend Josefina Castillo, "Spiritual Visions/ Border Lives: Progressive Women Activists at the U.S.-Mexico Border." We asked progressive women activists who work on border issues what spiri-tual and political ideas underlay their work. The power dynamics for this project have been somewhat different. While all the women included in this manuscript come from working-class backgrounds, some have received as much education as I have. Like Maria Elena Lucas and Mary Robinson, these women are leaders in their communities. Recently, I interviewed the poet Pat Manning, a white peace and border activist. She works with un-documented women in detention.

Life history narratives like I have done over my career take an enormous amount of time and energy. In my case they have taken nearly my whole adult life. I never was part of a formal oral history program, although I would suggest young oral historians participate in such a program if possible. I came late to the academic give-and-take that is important for oral historians, but, with some exceptions, such as my family and certain friends, the women I have interviewed and their causes became almost my entire life.[26]

These women's narratives have brought me many insights. Their stories are their own interpretations of their lives, and a number of interpretive systems can be used in their analysis. Much work has been done on the literary techniques involved in oral history collections. For example, a psychologist or sociologist could give her perspectives. Linguists could analyze the language and symbols. My interpretation rests on my training as a historian, on my long identity as a feminist, and as someone who analyzes and often advocates on behalf of resistance movements. Ultimately, I am concerned with making a world in which all people—especially those on the margins, the edges of society—can participate in political discussions and decision making and have access to the basic necessities of life. Stories of marginal women can help readers analyze power relations and see where we are complicit in their suffering. With such knowledge, we can begin to construct bonds of solidarity that will empower us all.

The women I have interviewed all began their lives as children in working-class homes, although a few were able to access higher education later in life. I define "working class" as the social group that is employed for wages, especially in manual or industrial work. Workers in manufacturing, farm laborers, waitresses, housekeepers, hospital workers, and miners are typically part of the working class. According to the Center for Working-Class Studies at Youngstown State University, "Americans like to believe that we are all middle class. But in a national survey, about 45 percent of Americans identified themselves as working class, and some economists say as many as 62 percent of Americans are working class."[27] People who are working class also have other identities (such as race/ethnicity, gender, sexuality, and nationality) that interweave with their working-class experiences. I have tried to address these interconnections throughout the women's narratives.

I often use the term "dominant culture" to refer to dominant Anglo-American (white) capitalist culture with all its arbitrary ideas and standards of behavior. When I refer to "nondominant" ideas or experiences or ethnic groups, I am talking about the beliefs and experiences of those not represented by the dominant (white) middle-class culture. These would include, among others, many poor African Americans, Native cultures, the values and needs of poor whites, Mexican Americans, and some lesbian, bisexual, and transgendered people. At times, such people are also labeled as "marginal," and I occasionally use that term. However, these women do not necessarily *feel* marginal. Instead, many of them feel like they are holding up the whole world. See the discussion on agency in chapter 2 for more on these issues. I occasionally use the term "inner" or "internal colonialism." This refers to the economic exploitation of a group within a society in which the workers' labor is sold cheap and the resources of that area are appropriated for the enrichment of other regions, usually those most closely associated with the state. In the United States, the Mexican American Southwest and Appalachia have been treated as colonies. Outside of the country, so has Puerto Rico. Such colonies are "made poor" by policies of the nation-state.

The concept of *intersectionality* has proven enormously useful in understanding the overlapping and magnifying effects of factors such as race, class, gender, sexuality, and religion.[28] Works by women of color, including Gloria Anzaldúa, Audre Lorde, bell hooks, Barbara Smith, and Patricia J. Williams, were foundational to my own thinking, and critical to the formation of the concept of intersectionality.[29] Vivian M. May defines "intersectionality" as follows.

> Intersectionality is an analytical and political orientation that brings together a number of insights and practices of Black feminist and women of color theoretical and political traditions. First, it approaches living identities as interlaced and systems of oppression as enmeshed and mutually reinforcing: one aspect of identity and/or form of inequality is not treated as separable or superordinate.[30]

These interlaced systems of oppression run through the lives of my interview subjects. Consuela Tafolla, mentioned in chapter 1, immigrated with her family from Puerto Rico to Milwaukee. As a schoolgirl, she experienced severe poverty, was treated as a subordinate by the males in her family, and simultaneously endured cruel treatment at the hands of racist teachers. The factors of poverty, gender, and race were then inextricably enmeshed and mutually reinforcing; she was not primarily a girl or primarily a person of color or primarily economically disadvantaged.

The political scientist Ange-Marie Hancock has said that intersectionality has two analytic projects. The first is to understand the relation between categories (such as that between race/ethnicity, class, and gender in Consuela's life) and second, "to render visible and remediable primarily invisible, unaddressed material effects of socio-political locations of Black women and women of color." Such invisible effects run through the lives of many of the women in this book, including Mary Robinson, who in chapter 9 tells the story of her murdered black doll. The concept of intersectionality is an enormously useful one, and I only wish it has been in my vocabulary earlier.[31]

CHAPTER I

Situated Locations
"Eight Girls, Trying to Have a Boy"

At the time of our first interview, in 1976, Doña Jesusita Aragon, then a sixty-eight-year-old Latina midwife from Las Vegas, New Mexico, moved forward in her rocking chair. I sat on her bed, looking toward her. Her soft hands patted my knee with emphasis. Her brown and white hair was short and curly, her face lined by years in the sun. Short and stocky, she wore a blue-and-white housedress, a full apron, and sturdy shoes. The fifteen-foot-square, aqua-colored room served as both a sitting room for her patients and a bedroom for herself and her granddaughter. The room held a dresser topped with doilies, family photos, and a multitude of religious objects and paintings, including a statue of San Antonio. A chest of drawers held records of her births. While Doña Jesusita and I talked, a woman in labor in an adjoining room rested.

Jesusita came from a specific time and place: twentieth-century rural New Mexico. Like all of us, she was *situated*—part of a specific historical and cultural context. Her unique historical, cultural, economic, gender, sexual, and national/racial/ethnic realities shaped her experience. These categories shape the retelling of stories. The stories told in this chapter—the experiences of Jesusita, Josephine Hunter, Helen Drazenovich Berklich, Lupe Castillo, Maria Elena Lucas, and Conseula Tafolla—illustrate this idea of situated interactions. They are culturally and historically specific and deal with memories of real events, as well as the women's later interpretations of these events. In the retelling of their experiences, the women use storytelling techniques (covered more extensively in chapter 3 on memory construction). A more detailed discussion of values is in chapter 5 on meaning. In the conclusion I talk more about the women's memories as compared to more traditional historical data. The stories told in this chapter involve agency, that life force that enables women to resist the constriction on their lives. But first here are three stories about poor, older women trying to remember and reassess the consequences of their mothers' deaths when they themselves were young.

One afternoon in 1976, when doing my first oral history with Jesusita, I learned about her mother's death in the flu epidemic of 1918. Las Vegas, New Mexico, had been part of Mexico until it was conquered by the United States in 1846. The community already had a Latino population with deep roots in the land, so it took decades for Anglos to impose their culture and achieve domination in economic and political affairs. Before that, many of the Latinos around Las Vegas lived in villages in the mountains, where they farmed and herded animals. The expanding Anglo capitalist economy, treating the area almost as a colony within the United States, drained resources and land from these mountain communities and surrounding areas. To cope with the breakdown of the older social and economic order, the Latinos developed a migratory pattern in which some of them maintained their residences in the village and other family members migrated for a period of time to work in Colorado mines or as laborers on sugar beet farms.[1]

The women were key to the survival of the home villages. They gardened, farmed, and kept animals; served in religious roles; and cared for the physical and social needs of the community. A key figure in the community was the *partera*, the midwife, who functioned at the gates of life and death.[2] While white people continued to appropriate land, newly landless villagers, including Jesusita Aragon's family, moved to nearby towns or tried to homestead on the plains. It was 1918, and Jesusita was ten years old.

> *My mother got pregnant again, her eighth baby. All girls. Eight girls, trying to have a boy. Only three girls lived. I was the first that lived. Then my two little sisters. There was a lot of death then 'cause they don't have any doctors here. Just do something that you think is good for it, to try and cure that people. My five sisters died when they were little. Between four, two, and one. From different kinds of sickness. There was much death and much sorrow.*
>
> *Then in 1918, when I was ten, the bad flu came. A lot of people die on that time. 1918. One of my uncles. And little ones too, my relatives' little ones. But I didn't get it, and I help take care of everybody. They ask for some water, something to eat, but they never touch it. They couldn't.*

My mother was pregnant when she got sick. And she last three days,
and she couldn't talk no more. She start with a pain in her back, and it
come through her chest so she couldn't talk. She writes to my grandmother
when she wants something. And her tears run. I cry, and she cries. I was
scared, and I stayed with her.

She was about seven months with the baby. The doctor took care of her
and said it was better for her to have the baby than to die with the baby in
because she was not going to last too long. And the doctor gave her some-
thing to make her have the baby. She could still talk a little then, and she
knew she was to have the baby, so she said, "Jesusita, call your aunt, tell her
that I have my baby," 'cause my grandmother was at the ranch. But that day
my grandmother come. My grandmother delivered it by herself, nobody was
with her, just the neighbors, right here in Upper Town.

It was another girl, the last one. I heard that baby cry. The baby girl
last about an hour, I think, and then she die. I think my mother didn't feel
anything; she was so sick. And in a few days my mother die. She was thirty-
four.

I was ten years old when my mother died, and the other sister was five,
and the little one, the little sister, was three years old. We cried and cried
and were sad, but my grandmother and aunts were with us.[3]

Jesusita's story is based on an actual event, her mother's death, but the
idea that her mother died after trying to have a son could be said to be Jesusita's interpretation. The events surrounding this belief had far-reaching
effects in Jesusita's life. After the death, the family moved back to a ranch on
the plains of eastern New Mexico, and because there were no sons to do the
ranch work, Jesusita had to take over the traditional role of oldest son. She
had to leave what she saw as the security of a girl's role in the family and herd
goats and sheep off by herself.

Sometimes I think they never care, even before I have my babies. You
know why, I used to work outside, taking care of the sheep and every-
thing. Back then we're not supposed to get wet when you're in your period.
Well, the girls don't care anymore; they always are getting wet and every-
thing, but then they weren't supposed to. But my family didn't care about
me. I get wet everywhere I was, and the next month I didn't feel any pain
nor nothing; it come on the right time. But they don't care; they make me
stay in the rain.[4]

Jesusita's story is a combination of historical and cultural settings, real events, and an interpretation that uses storytelling techniques. It is a *construction* formed by Jesusita at the time of my interviews out of different components. She recounts from her memory, not as a literal transcript of what actually happened. As a construction, she creates her story in an effort to explain its deepest meaning. Her family went against cultural traditions that said it hurt women to get wet during their menstruation. To Jesusita, this proved that they did not care about her well-being.

In 1979, while I was compiling the stories for my book *Dignity*, a seventy-two-year-old African American, Josephine Hunter, sat next to me on a sofa in front of a window. We were in a poor, predominantly African American section of Milwaukee, Wisconsin. Josephine had been part of the great exodus of blacks from their birthplaces in the South to the North in what is known as the Great Migration. Beginning in World War I and not ending until the 1970s, six million blacks fled the violent world into which they had been born.[5] Then in her late thirties, Josephine went north with a white family for whom she worked as a maid, one of the few occupations available at that time to black women in both the South and the North.

Josephine had moved into her apartment after the wave of "urban renewal" in the 1960s swept across the country, destroying stable minority communities. The city housing authorities demolished the home Josephine and her husband had owned and lovingly cared for. Now she had no savings and was forced to rent and live on Social Security. Nevertheless, Josephine's apartment was cheerful, and pots of African violets bloomed throughout. A short, stout disabled woman who walked stiffly with a cane, she had a freckled face and wore her white and gray hair pulled back in a bun. During several interviews, Josephine told me her stories. This first one involved the death of a mother. When Josephine was still young, her mother gave birth to another baby. A terrible fever followed.

> For two weeks . . . [she] was in bed and the baby was near her. Then the baby died one morning and she died in the afternoon. Who knows what the baby died of? They didn't have a doctor, just a midwife who was very old. We called the midwife Grandma Bates. All Grandma Bates knew [was] that my mother had a fever. They put jimsonweed on her. It was a weed that grew out in a field and had a white bloom on it like a morning glory, only the bloom was much larger. The weed had an awful odor, something

similar to horse manure. They would gather these weeds, bruise them, and put them in a towel or a rag and tie them 'round your head, and it would draw the fever out. So they put them around my mother's head, and they put them across her belly.

The next thing I knew, the undertakers came and took my mother away. She was dead, but nobody told me. I guess she died on a Monday, and they brought the body back on Wednesday evening. At that time her people had what they call a wake. It was at the home, and on the door there was a long piece of white ribbon tied up in a bow. . . .

They put my mother in a white coffin across the bay window in the front room. The house was full of people, going in and out, in the backyard as well as the front yard. It was September and very, very warm. They sang, they prayed, and they told jokes and drank coffee all night. When I got sleepy, one of the neighbors told me to go lay down on the daybed in the same room as my mother's coffin. Well, I laid on the daybed, and my mother was laying over there in this box, as I called it. I didn't know what it was.

One of the neighbors came to me when I woke up the next morning, and she said to me, "Now you better get a good look at your mother. You'd better look until the time for us to take her body to the church because you won't see her anymore."

And I said, "Why? And why is she in that box and don't talk?"

Well, the neighbor just patted me on the shoulders and said, "Just look," and she went away from me.[6]

Josephine's mother's death was a real event, retold at the time of our meetings in 1979 through memory and situated in a specific historical location. As such, the telling of her story was an interpretation of what happened, made vivid by Josephine's observations from the perspective of a child. Her memories had been shaped by her subsequent long struggle to find food and a place to sleep as she raised herself without the love of a family and in the charged racial locations of the South. After I interviewed Josephine, she told me she wanted to show me something. She opened a box that contained her own blue burial clothes. I felt dizzy in the intimacy of the moment and vowed that I would stay close to her in any way she chose. She eventually asked me to serve as her next of kin during her long, and final, illness.

Sixty-five-year-old Helen Drazenovich Berklich talked to me in 1980 in Hibbing, Minnesota. The daughter of white Yugoslavian immigrants to the

Mesabi Iron Range in northern Minnesota, Helen had grown up in Hibbing, the largest source of iron ore throughout the early twentieth century. The range had been mined in huge, open pit mines and worked by Slavic, Italian, and Scandinavian immigrants. It had a largely unionized labor force. The region was a land of difficulty and harsh winters. While the men worked in the mines, the women took in boarders and worked at nearly subsistence levels, rearing children. Helen, a short, wide woman with a booming voice, greeted me at her door, grabbed my arms, pulled me close to her, and said, "Frances, I'm going to tell you just how it was, just how it is, Frances." She proceeded to feed me while she talked for six hours. Again, we begin with memories of a mother.

> *My mother's family was very poor when they raised her, and they were strict, strict, strict. There was none of the premarital stuff with those old honkies. If you came home with a baby, you were dead. She was fifteen when she came to marry my father, and, of course, she'd never seen him.*
>
> *They were married in 1914 and my father worked on the ore docks and my mother took in boarders. And she had babies every year, nine by the time she was twenty-nine. The first died, and then I was the oldest. She also had a store and bootlegged. And she ate. I think eating was her outlet for her unhappiness because when she was married she was a beautiful, tall, thin lady, and then she got to over four hundred pounds. She weighed all that and was six feet tall, so people called her Big Mary.*
>
> *Her boarders were lumberjacks who would come out of the woods. They came like every three months for a vacation of two or three days. They'd come to the boardinghouses, and then they'd get moonshine and they'd get drunk and eat well and just lay around, and then they'd go back to the woods. I can remember it so well. She also had to take care of the store, so she had to learn to read and write in English.*
>
> *In Yugoslavia they have this idea about prestige for men. To this day, those women over there carry bundles on their head, and they're carrying the pails of water or whatever, and they're way out here pregnant, and the men are walking behind them carrying nothing. When I visited Yugoslavia I said to the man I was with, "Why isn't that guy helping his wife carry all that?"*
>
> *And he said, "Ohhh, that's a shame. A woman has to be worthy of her man, so she has to do all that kind of work." And sure enough, this is true. And let me tell you, my father was kingpin. God, he had prestige like you wouldn't believe. Because his wife was real worthy. [Laughs hard]. . . .*

I took care of all the little kids while my mother ran the store. And I'd take lickings for them. The kids would lie like hell and say I'd done things, but I'd rather take the lickings than let them get them. . . .

My mother had all of us children at home except for the last baby. She was very sick by then, and she had her in the hospital. Afterwards, the baby, Katherine, was taken to a children's home in Duluth, and the rest of us were sent to the St. James Orphanage. My mother died when she was twenty-nine years old. [Begins to cry.] She had nine children, a store, and twenty boarders. My father was up here working on the iron range at the time. . . .

The day before my mother died, Emil [her oldest brother] and I went to see her at St. Luke's Hospital. I was twelve, and Emil was ten. We took the streetcar, and when we got there she was dying. We didn't know it, though. She said, "You kids go on back. I don't want to see you; it hurts me." Then the last words she ever said to me were, "Helen, take care of your brothers and sisters." She was so sick. I can still see her. Then she died that night.

The next day the sister let me call the hospital, and I asked, "How is Mrs. Shebly?"

They had no idea I was the daughter, and they said, "She died."

I went down to the playroom of the orphanage and just hollered and screamed. [Cries hard]. So I took my brother Emil, and we went by streetcar to Crawford's Mortuary. That's where she was. They had her laid out on the couch; they hadn't put her in the coffin yet. We stood and looked at her.

Poor thing. She didn't have nobody with her. A baby every year and all that hard work. Her kidneys failed from all that bull work. My father was working at the ore docks and mines, and she always had everything ready for him. That was the prestige thing again. When I think of it, there couldn't have been love and helping each other with them.[7]

At the time of the interviews, Helen's memory had been constructed by events told to her by others, her interpretation of what she had experienced as a child, and conversations she had reconstructed over the years. Above all, the memories are flavored by what Helen remembers as her mother's last instruction: "Helen, take care of your brothers and sisters." That memory determined the rest of her life. Four years later, when she was sixteen, Helen married a Yugoslavian immigrant who was fifty-one, a man she barely knew, because he promised to take her brothers and sisters out of the orphanage. It was a loveless match, and Helen rapidly had four boys. Her husband got sick in his lungs because of iron dust, and Helen supported the whole family. She worked nearly as hard as her mother.

Much of second-wave feminism (the period beginning in the 1960s that focused on women's rights) talked about women's experience as a source of truth. Certainly, Jesusita, Josephine, and Helen—in their storytelling—were vehement about the truth of their experience. But subsequent thinkers, such as the historian Joan Wallach Scott, have questioned whether we can even find a real "truth" by examining experience.[8] Experience is so laden with interpretations because of the constructed nature of memory, Scott contends, that it is impossible to ascertain what really happened. Although I agree with her that memory is constructed, I also believe, like the philosopher Shari Stone-Mediatore has written, that to throw out the seriousness of women's experience is to "throw out the baby with the bath water."[9] Deaths do occur. Rapes do occur. A historian makes judgments about the stories she is told, but she takes the basis of those stories seriously.

My life's work as an oral historian has consisted of interviewing women because I believe they are especially vulnerable and because of the depth of my commitment to the women of my past. In keeping with that, I first look at the ways in which the women were situated by their sex and visions of sexuality both at the time of the interviews and at the times when they were living their "told" stories. These working-class women did not experience life the same way; they encountered life as unique individuals, each coming from historically specific gender relationships that are part of a unique and simultaneous racial, class, and sexual orientation. As such, each woman had many social and cultural groups with which she was aligned.[10] Let's dig deeper by examining the experiences of two other women, Maria Elena Lucas and Lupe Castillo.

Maria Elena Lucas, the subject of my book *Forged under the Sun/Forjada bajo el sol: The Life of Maria Elena Lucas,* has become one of my closest friends. Her history begins with Native cultures in the southwestern United States and the sixteenth-century Spanish conquest that decimated the Aztec Empire. In the process, Spanish colonists raped the Native women, and the mestizo (mixed) Mexican people resulted. Generations after this, Maria Elena was born in the Lower Rio Grande area of Texas. Like the rest of the Southwest, it had been part of Mexico for hundreds of years. Nevertheless, when Mexico won its independence from Spain, the new government in Mexico City opened its northern frontier to foreign settlement, and thousands of Anglo-American land speculators and settlers poured into Texas, "carrying with them a vision of empire, racial superiority, and economic process."[11]

Fighting broke out between Mexicans and Anglos in 1835. In 1844 the United States formally annexed Texas, resulting in the Mexican-American War, which ended with the Treaty of Guadalupe Hidalgo in 1848. At that point, Anglo-Americans rushed into much of the Southwest, and Mexicans were displaced from their lands, where they ultimately became an impoverished working class. Planning to be gentlemen farmers, Anglos from the North bought up the land, incurring steep land payments. These would-be gentlemen farmers faced labor problems. The kind of large-scale, commercial farming they planned "required cycles of intense, rapidly mobilized labor, especially during peak periods of planting and harvest."[12] At the same time, the new farmers had to keep wages low because of their land payments. The impoverished Mexican heritage residents of the Rio Grande Valley seemed a logical choice for workers. They had lost their lands, and their families were nearly starving.

This new farm order, with Anglo owners and exploited Mexican workers, defended itself through increasing racism and violence. The large Mexican population worked the fields seasonally and were segregated from Anglo life. The resulting migrant labor system gradually spread north to the Colorado sugar beet fields and then farther.[13] Mexican workers were kept in debt so they would never save enough to drop out of the system. Wages for adult workers were lower than their subsistence needs. Consequently, many Mexican workers depended on the labor of their children, who also brought in income. To create the large families that were necessary for survival, women gave birth frequently, perhaps every year. Maria Elena came from such workers. The oldest of seventeen migrant working children, she was forced as an adult to take her seven children to the fields to work with her.

Born in 1941, Maria Elena is dark haired and striking. I first interviewed her for my book *Dignity*, and then, after her near death from pesticide poisoning in 1988, the two of us began working on a full-length book. She had stored a trunk containing her writings among other rubble in the back of an old red truck that was partially buried close to the Rio Grande River. Eventually, when she was well enough, we located the trunk and took it back to the tiny recreational vehicle (RV) where she lived with three others. As chickens stepped in and out of the door, we sifted through the writing, finding poems she'd written about her childhood in Brownsville, Texas. There, during the winter, Maria Elena had worked selling things in the streets and going through garbage. Later she would accompany her large family north as migrant labor in the summer. She describes her "training" as a girl.

> I really loved my hat, and it was so worthless. I adored my blue straw hat 'cause I could put my braids up and mask, disguise myself. I would cover my face whenever I didn't want to see something or I didn't want somebody to see me. Whenever somebody was looking at me real weird, I'd pull my hat down. I even refused to take it off in school. . . .
>
> Daddy usually didn't allow us to work the streets, but I was very sneaky, and sometimes he was gone to work. I always dressed as a little boy on the streets, always. I wore my straw hat with my hair up, and I hung around with boys. Whatever we had, whether it was shoes, clothes, vegetables, or fruits or cactuses, I'd be in the street selling. You meet a lot of people in the streets, and you see and learn a lot of bad things, too. . . .
>
> You don't see any girls in the streets, but people couldn't tell the difference with me because I was too little. The first time I smoked was with the Indian girls, when we were working the crops, but I smoked more in the streets, and while some of the boys went to steal bread and food, I'd sit there and wait and take care of the shoeshine boxes or whatever they were selling, so they could do it. I took my share, too. Also I learned how to say bad words, and I saw other bad things, like men who'd rub against girls. Sometimes we'd be all crowded on a bus, and I could see that older men would hurt and bother a girl, then they would just sit very innocent like they hadn't done nothing. I learned how to take care of myself in these things, like how to bite. . . .
>
> I dressed like a boy to be safe, but deep down inside me, I was a little girl, and some of the kids in the crowd knew it, so they kind of protected me. The only problem I had was going to the rest room, and when anybody wanted to pee, I had to play dumb. . . . I worked in the streets to about age nine or ten, when I began to grow into a girl.[14]

Maria Elena told me about learning a very complicated and situated gender role: she was to act as a girl during certain times and as a boy during others. The fact that she needed to work in the streets like a boy was because of her family's position in a complex racial and economic hierarchy. She learned other details of that hierarchy when the family was working as migrant laborers, under the supervision of her father.

I remember overhearing the talking between the ranchero and the workers. It was always the men. Women were not included, and, of course, children had to stand aside and listen. If my mom was pregnant or had just had a baby, the grower would say, "Great, Manny." My dad's name was Manuel. "Another baby. That's good," the grower would say. "Keep it up. Eat a lot of mayonnaise and onions and give your wife a lot of it too." Then he'd laugh.

Onions and mayonnaise were considered to be something good for the woman to keep on having kids, and the kids were prohibited from eating onions and too much mayonnaise because that was considered to be sexual. The grower would also recommend it to the guys in the camp. He'd say, "Give your wives a lot of mayonnaise and onions." But I was the one who had to carry the load from all of Mama's babies, so I hated mayonnaise and onions because I thought that's what gave Mom all those kids.

The bigger families were better [for work in the fields] because that way the mom and dad were responsible for their own kids and could have better control, and that meant better-quality work, more labor for the grower. When my dad would go talk to the ranchero, Dad would say, "I have seven or eight kids or ten or eleven kids and so many working hands." The ranchero would say, "The bigger, the better." That way the grower wouldn't have to worry about hiring a whole bunch of different people. . . . There was also less of a problem in housing, in fights, with drinking, with garbage and all that. . . . That's how come Mama had a whole lot of kids. If each kid made five dollars a day, it's not the same as one person or two or three persons making five dollars a day.[15]

According to Maria Elena, then, the bodies of Latino women and children were being used by white growers for direct financial gain, a vicious form of racism based on a class system. Maria Elena's father at least partially colluded in this process, with the brazen use of his wife's most intimate being, a form of gender and sexual exploitation. Maria Elena's mother, in turn, exerted her power over the only one in the family with less power than she had: her girl child. These relationships demonstrate how power and privilege operate on multiple levels at once, further demonstrating the theory of intersectionality. This combination of racial, economic, and gender oppression kept women and girls in tightly locked boxes through issues of sexuality and vulnerability. In addition, most women in these circumstances were married young and had multiple births. There was no flexibility or cultural vision that would give these women space for questioning the overwhelming heterosexism of the situation. Maria Elena herself did not question this system until well into her adulthood.

The experiences of Lupe Castillo, from Tucson, Arizona, also illustrate this idea of various situated locations. Like Texas, much of Arizona was ceded to the United States after the Mexican-American War, but the desert community of Tucson, with its large Mexican and Native population, was not. With the Gadsden Purchase of 1854, the United States finally annexed Tucson and its vicinity. Today its population is still more than 30 percent Latino. Lupe's father worked as a copper miner in a nearby company town until his lungs got so bad that the family moved to the city. Southern Arizona was like southern Texas. Both were areas where wealthy Anglos exploited impoverished Mexican workers who were paid less than Anglo workers.[16] However, Lupe's father belonged to a labor union and fought for better working conditions; Lupe learned some of her militancy from him.

Like many people from Tucson, Lupe is especially active in immigration issues. Because of oppressive government policies, many undocumented migrants crossing into the United States are funneled through the beautiful but deadly Sonoran desert. Despite a similar cultural heritage to Maria Elena's, Lupe grew up situated in a different gender, racial, and economic setting. Her working-class family had more economic security than Maria Elena's, and Lupe did not have to work as a child. She has been a political organizer for most of her life, taking leadership in the Chicano movement, a movement of Mexican Americans, and promoting and teaching in Ethnic Studies. Today Lupe is disabled by arthritis but continues to be politically active. She and I have known each other for fifteen years. In 2009 we met in my office to record her story.

> Tucson was a segregated town when I grew up in the barrio downtown. There were blacks and Chinese, but we didn't see white people unless we went downtown. It was a distant world for us.
>
> I didn't intellectualize it as being segregated. That's just the way we lived. . . . Every few years my family would go to Magdelena in Mexico for the pilgrimage that was held there every October. I always had a sense when we were coming to the border. Everybody got uptight. I had an aunt who would always say, "I'm not crossing because they're not gonna let me through again." This happened even though she was already in her seventies. . . . So

we had a sense, as we got closer to the border or coming back in, that we were outsiders. I think that's where I began to get a sense of injustice, even though at that age I couldn't articulate it.

My mother had gone through tenth grade at Tucson High School, then she had to drop out during the Depression. She went to work with a business college working as a janitor. It was there that she managed to get an education in bookkeeping. She never worked outside of the home in it, but people would look to her for information.

My father was involved in his unions. He had been a copper miner. When he got sick in his lungs, he came into town. He started working in construction with my mother's relatives and then joined the Laborers' Union. So we knew about going to political rallies. He would talk about his work in the mines, and he would always have stories to tell us at dinner about his experiences.

My father got all the labor newspapers at home, and I would read them. I was just a voracious reader from when I was really young. I took everything in. . . .

I never felt that I was being pressured to get married or to not go to school or to start working. On the contrary, I was always encouraged to continue my studies. Within school, I was very free. I had strong models of women in my family—my grandmother, my mother, and others, and there were positive relationships between men and women. I don't know if that was what freed me from the sense that I was very limited as a woman.[17]

Lupe's gender role as a child, her sense of having no limits—so different from Maria Elena's—was partly the result of her family having a much more secure economic status. Also, within Lupe's Mexican community, she was buffered from some of the racism toward Mexican Americans in Tucson. But it was also because of the attitude of Lupe's parents toward her and their ideas about their daughter's possibilities. Somewhere in the growing-up process, Lupe imagined a different sexual orientation for herself. She has lived for many years as part of a couple with another woman.

The Dreamers is an organization of young undocumented immigrants who were brought to the United States as children and have grown up in this country and consider it their own. The Dreamers have no Social Security numbers, no proof of residency or driver's licenses. They are also ineligible for scholarships and financial aid that would help them in higher education. As part of a civil disobedience action, a group of nine Dreamers, five women and four men, some of whom had already been deported, met in Mexico in 2013 and tried to come back to the United States legally through a border crossing, where they knew they would be arrested. The women included Lizbeth Mateo, Lula Martinez, Adriana Diaz, Maria Penside, and Claudia Amaro.

Margo Cowan, Lupe's wife, a public defender in Pima County, Arizona, helped plan their defense, which consisted of applying for humanitarian visas or asylum. The Dreamers were prepared to be locked up in a detention center. On June 22, dressed in graduation caps and gowns and smiling broadly, the Dreamers linked arms and approached the Nogales border crossing. Supporters marched with them, chanting, "Undocumented and unafraid!" News reporters surrounded them. Border Patrol officers handcuffed the "Dreamers 9" and took them away, and they were imprisoned with fifteen hundred other detained immigrants. Community pressure supporting the Dreamers grew, and on August 7 they were offered temporary asylum and released. The Dreamers have continued to organize and protest, especially fighting for those already deported. Rather than hiding and working quietly at home or at poorly paid labor, the women Dreamers have learned to speak up and assert themselves, transcending the larger culture's expectations for them based on their race, class, and gender. In the process, they stand up for one of the most abused segments of our social system.[18]

Like the Dreamers, the women I interviewed learned their specific gender and sexual roles, roles that take place in concrete hierarchies; they also acquired class and racial/ethnic loyalties. I learned about Consuela Tafolla (a pseudonym) in 1981 when she was quoted in the *Milwaukee Journal* speaking about the importance of ethnic sensitivity among the officials of her sons' school. I called Consuela, introduced myself, and asked if we could meet. She agreed, and we began our work together.

Consuela's class and ethnic commitments lay in her poor Puerto Rican heritage. Puerto Rico is an unincorporated territory of the United States. Possessed by Spain for more than four hundred years, the United States seized it during the Spanish-American War in 1898. Sugar was the main product in this colonial rural economy. In the late 1940s, tax benefits for mainland companies and the promise of low wages for workers lured mainland industries to the island, and the poor or subsistence rural residents became an industrial working class. In recent years, many U.S. and foreign-owned factories have moved to lower-wage countries in Latin American and

Asia, leaving unemployment behind in Puerto Rico. Beginning especially after World War II, many poor Puerto Ricans emigrated to the United States
in search of a better life. Puerto Ricans passionately debate the island's political status, including the possibility of statehood or independence.[19]

At the time of my interviews with Consuela, most traditional Puerto
Ricans perceived of the family as primary. The emphasis was on the group
rather than the individual. Consuela, like many other Puerto Ricans, had a
deep sense of family obligation and often stressed this belief. She considered
herself able to fit in with other traditional Puerto Rican gender roles. The
psychologist Norma I. Cofresí has studied gender roles and notes that many
Puerto Rican woman are in transition: "Specifically, the traditional gender-
role ideal demands Puerto Rican women to be self-sacrificing mothers and
submissive, subservient, and sexually passive wives, with exclusive responsibility for domestic duties. The importance of safeguarding women's sexual
honor is extended into other spheres of their lives as well. . . . Needless to say,
these values may be at odds with the current reality of Puerto Rican wom-
en's lives."[20] Consuela was trying desperately to live up to these traditional
roles, but, as she told me, strict adherence to this social code was impossible
for her because of her husband's serious illness. She could not count on him
to fulfill traditional Puerto Rican male roles.

Consuela's parents had emigrated from the Puerto Rican mainland, leaving her in Puerto Rico with her grandmother. When Consuela was five, her
parents came to take her to Milwaukee, Wisconsin, with them. Terrified
that she was about to be separated from her beloved grandmother, Consuela fought to keep from leaving the only home she had ever known. So her
grandmother traveled with her. Eventually, the extended family in Puerto
Rico moved to Milwaukee as well. During one period, Consuela's family
lived with forty people in their household. After her arrival on the mainland, Consuela remembers the family's long series of accommodations to
the dominant culture. They met these adjustments with a great desire to
maintain their identity as Puerto Ricans and to continue the fiercely strong
cohesion of the family unit. Consuela's functioning within this group and
her loyalty to it, she told me, has been a recurring theme throughout her life.
Even when I met with her in 1981, years after her emigration to the United
States, the majority of her extended family still lived within a few blocks of
each other in an older, racially and ethnically mixed neighborhood on Milwaukee's north side.

Entering Consuela's home for the first time, I was greeted by smells of cleaning materials and Puerto Rican cooking. Consuela welcomed me warmly with a clear, assertive, and kind voice. She was a small woman in her late twenties then, with short, dark hair, a gentle face, and large brown eyes with heavy lashes. Her two small boys, with enormous eyes like hers, stood close by. Consuela talked openly and with animation while preparing our meal. She told me many details about her childhood in Puerto Rico and especially described her love for her grandmother. She talked about her husband's suffering with what was then called Vietnam syndrome, an early name for post-traumatic stress disorder, which changed his personality and made him aggressive and unable to work. According to Consuela, her husband had acquired the condition when he killed a child while fighting in the Vietnam War.

By the time of our last interview, several weeks later, Consuela's eyes had dark shadows, and she appeared to be very tired. The steady deterioration of her husband's condition deeply worried her and he had been hospitalized. As in the past, she turned to her extended family for both economic help and moments of laughter and relief from tension, but she was forced to deal by herself with much of the outside world. Nevertheless, Consuela kept her moments of deepest despair to herself, turning to her memories of her grandmother and her grandmother's ability to accept one's fate to help her bear the pain. Consuela told me stories about her childhood, with its specific class, racial/ethnic, gender, and geographic locations.

> When my parents first come to America, they suffered so much that my father didn't want to bring us here. My parents were hungry. They were turned away from houses because the people didn't rent to Puerto Ricans. They lived in a room and shared a toilet among four families. They couldn't get repairs done on the house. The winters were severe at that time, and somebody without a jacket or boots really suffered. It was so hard for them that my father didn't want to bring us here, but my mother wanted us close. She would have visions of us starving to death or crying for food because we didn't have money over there.
>
> They came for us, and we had to learn how to live here. We didn't know English when we first went to school, and learning it right away was hard. At that time the feelings for Puerto Ricans and Mexicans were real negative. I went to a public school where I had a teacher who was very prejudiced. She used to make me go through agony. She'd hit me and manhandle

me in class and knock me against the sink, saying, "This is the way you people are supposed to wash."

The winters were hard on us when we first came. We didn't have snow-shoes, slacks to wear, or mittens. We didn't even know what they were. We only had a woolen scarf and a coat, if we could afford it. Sometimes we'd go to school with a summer jacket. There were mountains of snow. We walked about a mile and a half to school and were afraid of freezing to death. American kids taunted us and said, "If you don't walk fast enough, you're going to freeze and stay that way until you die." So we rushed and hurried. The little ones cried, and since we older ones were supposed to take care of them, we took off our sweater, or whatever we would get from our church, and we wrapped them up so they wouldn't freeze and die.

Also, our parents were strict with us four girls as we grew. Sex was taboo at home. There were times when the boy relatives were segregated from us, even my brother. We weren't allowed to sit on our uncles' laps, hug our uncles, or anything like that because something could happen. We were raised not to talk to boys in the street. If any of the boys wanted to talk with us, he had to ask my father's permission to come upstairs and talk with us in front of the family. So we couldn't say hi to a boy because that would mean a lecture. We were well protected, like bodyguards. In fact, my father more or less told us that when a guy came and asked for our hands we had to marry him. Lucky for me, I didn't have to go through all that painful process of saying, "I don't want that guy." That would be hard. Still, I feel loyal to being Puerto Rican; that and my family are the most important things in my life.

It's hard for my children sometimes because they're caught between the Puerto Rican and the American culture. They'll have to learn to adjust to the two cultures, though, because I'm going to bring them up Puerto Rican and teach them Puerto Rican values. We're taught to share things, to never be an individual, and to always be aware of the other person's needs first.[21]

Consuela's story revealed to me how cross-cultural experiences both complicated her life and resulted in a unique identity. It would be impossible to pry out the influences of her ethnic identity, her reactions to class hierarchies, her experiences as a woman in her extended family and community, or the experiences she had because of her geographic location. As intersectionality stresses, these influences were simultaneous, enmeshed, and mutually reinforcing.

As with every interview I've conducted over many years, I, too, am situated in my own specific categories: those of a white, middle-class, educated, citizen and woman. I represent specific and interacting racial, class, gender, sexual, and geographic locations myself. With each of these locations, there is a power relationship between me and the people I have interviewed, and between me and those "higher" on the social ladder. These categories have affected my concrete interactions with each woman. Chapter 4, on inter-relationships, examines this dynamic more fully. With examples from the lives of Jesusita, Josephine, Helen, Maria Elena, Lupe, and Consuela and the Dreamers, I have shown how each woman is situated, located within a specific historical and cultural context. Their lives reflect these concrete conditions, and the richness of their histories are embedded in wide circles of social circumstances and meaning.

CHAPTER 2

Agency
"God Gave You a Big Mouth"

"Agency" is a term used to express "how humans, in conscious and unconscious ways process their experiences of life and act on them."[1] "Agency" is a
vigorous action people take in order to understand their conditions, improve
their lives, help each other, or fight against the limits put on them by their
historical situation. Another term often used for these actions is "resistance."
People resist the boxes they are trapped in by their life circumstances, often
fighting back against forces that constrict them. The six women introduced
in chapter 1 have acted with agency.

Jesusita Aragon learned midwifery as a vocation. She hand-built her
own midwifery clinic and served thousands of women in her community.
Certainly, she acted on her life conditions in a constructive way. Josephine
Hunter, by leaving domestic service and setting up her own home for foster
children, also acted with agency. Helen Drazenovich Berklich, who raised
her siblings and children and fed many miners in the Mesabi Iron Range,
processed her life experiences and acted on them in a way that allowed her
and her children to survive. Maria Elena Lucas not only fought to survive
her life conditions but wrote poetry in the process. Lupe Castillo grew up to
become a Chicana activist, becoming part of a collective in the political fight
against racism in Tucson, Arizona. Finally, Consuela Tafolla looked at her
life and tried to function as an active member of her family.

The dominant culture's way of looking at agency, however, is usually different from this. It envisions a *private* individual, usually male, taking some
form of forceful action that contributes to the *public* world.[2] Two outstand-
ing examples of that kind of agency are the social reformers César Chávez
and the Rev. Martin Luther King Jr. Both were private citizens who took

action against oppression; however, each was supported by a large group of activists, many females as well as males. But other, more private and internal dimensions of agency are often critical to women's survival. Dominant cultures tend to see subordinate groups as if they have no agency and don't resist.[3] For example, during Mary Robinson's childhood, the white, middle- and upper-class southern culture of segregation paid no attention to Mary, assuming that she didn't have any power and was unaware of actions around her. As Mary recalled in an interview:

> *All those white people we lived around, they didn't know how close I was paying attention. It was like I wasn't a real person, maybe like a shadow, but I watched and learned. A new family moved in around here, and the woman was black, but she looked like she was white. She and her husband got run out of Lowndes County by the Ku Klux Klan because of how light she looked and that she was married to a black man. One day I was up at the store and so was this black woman who looked white and so was Miss Bernice [the wife of the white man for whom Mary's family sharecropped].*
>
> *Miss Bernice went up to the other woman and said, "Hmmm, I don't believe I know you, do I?" The black woman who looked white didn't have a black accent. She said, "I don't think so," and she told Miss Bernice her name and where she lived. So Miss Bernice said, "Well, my name is Bernice Henderson, and when you're down my way, come and see me." So the black woman thanked Miss Bernice and left and walked down the little dirt road toward where she lived.*
>
> *Then Tomas Bass, the owner of the store, said [to Bernice Henderson], "I heard you telling that woman that you'd like for her to come and see you. When did y'all get to where you're entertaining niggers?"*
>
> *I stood there listening. Miss Bernice just went all to pieces. "Why, she ain't no nigger!" she sputtered.*
>
> *"Yes, she is. They just moved in from Lowndes County."*
>
> *Well, she got all upset, but I got tickled. Oh, it was funny. I thought to myself, "That'll teach her."[4]*

Mary kept all these stories to herself until she had grown up. Then she participated in the collective actions of the civil rights movement and the textile union movement, revealing the great error the dominant culture (whites) had made during her childhood: it assumed she had no agency, that she was not a subject in her own right who would act from her own spirit, what Mary would call her soul.[5] The whites thought they could say and do anything in front of her because they considered her to be nearly an object, that she would never make their actions known or undertake some protest against them. As an adult in the 1960s and 1970s, however, Mary took direct action against the dominant white culture she knew so well. She participated in the voter registration program and attacked white power economically through her union organizing. She told me about it in detail, thus creating a document of resistance through the telling of her experiences.

The story of Irene Mack Pyawasit, a Native Menominee woman, and her grandmother illustrates how the dominant (white) culture often does not see the agency in marginalized people. The first time I visited Irene was in an inner-city neighborhood in Milwaukee. Irene's cottage was behind a two-story house where children played. I parked my car, went to her doorstep, and was greeted by a curious sign: "Kev—Open the door with ease, I've let the snake run loose. Gram." Irene met with me three times in the early 1980s before agreeing to be interviewed and, even then, she stayed in charge of how the interviews went. Then in her early sixties, Irene had light brown skin, kept her black and white hair in a bun, and wore heavy silver jewelry. She had a firm chin and an alert face. With a mischievous smile, she spoke with a deep voice. I wrote after this particular interview that "her total presence was of competency, strength, keen awareness, and a shrewd sense of humor."[6]

Thieves had recently robbed Irene's house, and objects collected throughout her lifetime had been taken, including a beloved dog. Also stolen had been boxes of cassette tapes she had dictated in which she had told the stories and history of the Menominee. Months later she still grieved these losses. Irene's husband, Wallace Pyawasit, then also in his early sixties, wore his gray hair to his shoulders. He was a leader of the Big Drum, a Native religion. They were careful not to tell me details of their Native belief system, but I understood its deep importance to them both.

Following four centuries of the "methodical destruction of Indian tribes by the United States government," Irene's people ended up on the Menominee reservation in northern Wisconsin.[7] During Irene's childhood, this was a place of lakes, deep forests, and abundant wildlife. Earlier, the Menominee had lived along the shores of Lake Michigan and westward to the Mississippi; however, the U.S. government gradually seized their lands. The Menominee ended up in ten townships, which composed the reservation. There people suffered from poverty, bad health, and unemployment. The historian Howard Zinn quoted a Native anthropologist who said: "An Indian reservation is the most complete colonial system in the world that I know about."[8] Today many of the Menominee people have moved to Milwaukee but still keep ties to their families on the reservation. When I spoke with Irene, she talked about her closeness to the land and memories of her grandmother, who had raised her.

> My mother died young, and my father was not around, so I was raised by my grandmother. My grandmother was a tough, little old woman, but a good one. She taught me a lot of things, and the first thing she taught me was not to be afraid of the white man. She said, "God gave you a big mouth, and I'm going to teach you how to use it."
>
> She could speak English and understand everything that was said, but when she went outside she spoke our own language. When I was just a little kid I'd act as interpreter when we went to see the agent. She always told me what to say, and I never varied from what she said, because I was more afraid of her than I was of that ugly agent. She was a little toughie, all right. I don't think she ever weighed more than a hundred pounds in her lifetime. I have a picture of her in what she called her Sunday-go-to-meeting-white people dress. Sometimes she wore her hair in braids down her back, and when she went out, she wore a great big bun on the nape of her neck. . . .
>
> Today I'm a sucker for kids and a bug on education. My grandmother believed in education, and she taught me the importance of it. She always said, "Without education you'll get nowhere. You got to be smart as that man out there in the world so that not only can you live side by side, but make sure he don't cheat you or rob you." So I didn't have much choice when it came to going to school; I had to go. I remember one time when I was in the day school on the reservation, several of us kids tried to skip school, and every one of us got a good licking for it. I never tried it again.[9]

Members of the dominant (white) system that Irene Mack Pyawasit interacted with when she was a girl probably barely noticed the old woman with the child, but Irene's grandmother knew that system well. She carefully taught her granddaughter to know its weaknesses and how to resist. Irene told me that the government and religious schools she was sent to attempted to break her through punishment. They tried humiliation, holy water, pouring kerosene on her head, and forced Christian prayer. They required her to scrub the buildings on her knees. They took away recreation and privileges to go to town, but Irene reported to me that nothing broke her. Instead she observed their behavior toward other children. As punishment, school officials wrapped girls up in canvas sheets, put them in a bathtub of cold water, and made them lie there unable to move and soaking in the cold. Irene's explanation for her strength was that her grandmother had taught her well. Both Irene and her grandmother had great agency in the face of their life conditions and resisted oppression.

The agency or resistance of subordinate groups often does not involve a *hero* as such, but a group of committed people.[10] Such a group lived in Stearns, Kentucky, part of Appalachia, a cultural region in the eastern United States that stretches from southern New York state to northern Alabama. At the time of my interviews in the 1980s, the people of Appalachia were stereotyped by the dominant culture as hillbillies. Mine owners had exploited the region as an internal colony of the United States. They used the people as subsistence laborers and expropriated coal.[11] Coal mining in Appalachia had once produced two-thirds of the nation's supply.

But the coal workers had not been passive. They had struggled to unionize the mines between the 1890s and 1940s and again between 1978 and 1999, but the owners gradually automated the mines. Today only 2 percent of the Appalachian workforce makes its living mining coal. Still, at the time of my interviews in the region, many families directly depended on wages from mining. In March 1976 two explosions in the coal mines of eastern Kentucky killed twenty-six coal miners and inspectors, sweeping fear and heartbreak through the area's mountain mining communities. The Blue Diamond Coal Company owned the mines where the explosions occurred. Federal safety officials found that the company had violated federal mine safety laws 855 times in the six years before the explosions. As church bells in the miners' mountain community tolled unceasingly, wives of male miners throughout the region broke down, stunned with sympathy for the dead and their families and filled with the knowledge that the dead could have been their husbands.

Shortly after the explosions, a nonunion contract ran out in the Stearns mine, also owned by the Blue Diamond Coal Company. The Stearns miners, worried about the deaths and the noncompliance with safety regulations in their own mine, voted by a 126 to 57 margin to join the United Mine Workers. They hoped to improve their own safety. After five months of delay and non-negotiation by Blue Diamond, the miners voted to go on strike. This began a three-year-long bitter and often violent struggle between the strikers and the company. The company hired a private armed security group. The strike took a great toll on the community and the people involved. It tore at Stearns and nearby Whitley City, dividing the residents between support for the strikers and support for the strikebreakers and the company. The individuals and communities suffered economic losses, families broke apart over conflicted loyalties, and fear and intimidation became overwhelming. However, the strikers held, and their wives organized an active women's committee to deal with emergency needs. They set up the support systems so necessary to maintain families' hope, courage, and perseverance. Finally, three years later, in late April 1979, the United Mine Workers announced an out-of-court settlement with Blue Diamond. A number of women I interviewed expressed their belief that in the end the national union had let them down.

In 1980, I met with six white women whose husbands had been on strike. I interviewed Irene Vanover and Betty Dixon together. A matronly, somewhat heavy-set white woman with a gray Afro, then in her early sixties, Irene had a gentle but strong appearance. She spoke with a deep, unrushed, melodious voice. She had suffered a stroke in the past and had some slowness in her handwriting but otherwise functioned well. Irene had presided over the women's committee throughout the strike, and her husband, Mahan, headed the picket line. Consequently, for three years they gave leadership to the strikers and their families. Betty Dixon was younger than Irene, short with delicate features and a small mouth. She had a dark complexion, closely cut dark hair, and large brown eyes. She talked slowly, with a gentle but firm voice.

> [Irene Vanover:] My husband's been in the mines thirty-six years, and I worried a lot in those years. And my son, he went to work, and he's worked eight years down there. There were accidents. One man got killed down there. There was a big rock that was going to fall down on them, and the men tried and tried to get the company to fix it. The company said, "Oh, it isn't dangerous. We'll fix it sometime." And one day the rock fell on one of the men and killed him.
>
> My husband has black lung, and it bothers him. If he goes out and just does a bit of work, he's out of breath. They gave him total disability. My father was a coal miner, and he died of black lung, and my husband had two brothers who were coal miners. One of them died with black lung, and the other's just about dead.

The earlier strikes weren't like this one. There wasn't a lot of people mad like the one we just went through. Families didn't tear up the way it hap-pened between me and my sister. My sister's husband worked down in the mines, and she's got five boys that work there too, and they went in scabbing. Now she don't even speak to me. It's just something awful.

[Betty Dixon:] My family was split up like Irene's. There were ten of us children and I was the oldest, and it seemed just that we was all tore apart. Just like the first time I marched with the women. We all got together and started protesting and marching through town. I went over to my mom's after that, and she says, "Aren't you ashamed?"

I said, "No, I'm not ashamed."

She said, "You looked like a bunch of idiots out there marching."

"Well, I felt good. It's my kids' table they're taking the food off of." And I really did feel good about it. It was the first time where a bunch of women got out and protested together. The first thing you know, we got together and formed a women's committee.

[Irene Vanover:] I was the head of the women's committee. I worked re-ally hard because the women came with their problems to me. Then we started getting used clothes sent in, we got some food, we got money, checks. I knew all the women, who was in need and who wasn't, and right away I would go to paying doctor bills and having their teeth fixed and paying their light bills and water bills. If one of the women got sick when she had a baby, I'd get it fixed up with another to take care of the kids. If one had to go to work but couldn't afford a babysitter, we got someone to babysit. One of the women had cancer and had to go to Lexington every day. We had the women vote, and they said, "We're going to give her two hundred dollars." If we hadn't done what we did, the women wouldn't have held out like they did.

I think the strike brought some of the husbands and wives together. We had our rallies down at a big 4-H camp with a huge shelter house, and we'd go in there and cook everything. All the ladies pitched in, and we had a good day. There were some special times.

The worse time was when everybody got beat up. The company took in some scabs, so the men went over on the picket line to stop the scabs from going in. There were only supposed to be six on the picket line, but a lot of men went. As soon as they'd gone, we women got news that the police was coming to beat them up. So we went over to about a mile up the side of where the men were. There was a restraining order so we couldn't go down where the men was.

When the police started going through to get the men, we throwed rocks to try to stop them. The first bunch of police went around us, though. They went right on down to the men, and they began to beat heads and bash and carry on awful. Then a second force of police come, and they stopped with us women and did us the same way. One woman was knocked completely out. Another woman's leg was broke.

[Betty Dixon:] You see, there just weren't no justice. No matter what come up in court, they didn't get no justice. Just whatever the company wanted was what they got. It was real hard 'cause I was always raised up to respect the law. I was always taught that they do the right thing. But now I don't believe that. We all sat and wrote the governor a letter after the troopers had come and beat the men and the women like they did. I wrote in mine, "How do you teach your kids to respect the law after this? After they see this?"

[Irene Vanover:] But I got so close to those other people during the strike. I didn't even know these miners' wives before that. But I come to love them, and it just seemed like one big family. Anything that I had at my house that I thought they needed, they got it. If it was the last mess of bread that I had, I gave it if they took it. It's just amazing how we all stood together, what we all done, what we all learned.[12]

Even though Irene Vanover was the leader, the miners' wives expressed their agency collectively. They learned new skills, they undertook untried techniques, and, despite divisions between families and the town, they learned new ways to love and survive.

The sense of communal agency is seen in the contemporary movement Black Lives Matter. It began as a call to action by three queer women of color, Alicia Garza, Patrisse Cullors, and Opal Tometi, after George Zimmerman was acquitted in Florida for the murder of Trayvon Martin. The movement grew further after police in Ferguson, Missouri, in August 2014 shot Michael Brown, another unarmed young black man. African Americans responded with fury, marching in the streets and chanting "Black Lives Matter." Eight months later, in Baltimore, twenty-five-year-old Freddie Gray died of injuries sustained while being transported in a police vehicle, and the movement exploded. The killings have continued, and a largely young people's crusade has come to life. Women have played a central role, although the leadership is decentralized and organized through social media. Like the testimony of Irene Vanover and Lupe, related elsewhere in this book, Black Lives Matter is primarily communal and expresses its "I will" through commitments using a plural "we" rather than a singular "I."

Lupe Castillo's story also shows how agency can be collective. After growing up in a labor union home, she became a full-time political activist in Tucson, her home community. She told me:

> *I never thought of activism as what I did on the side. Instead, it was, "This is what I do full time. This is what I am committed to."* . . . *My primary interest was the community and organizing in the community and committing myself to that.*
>
> *The Chicano House was a place where those of us involved in what we called the Chicano movement met. These were people who worked around the farm worker movement. We joined in the boycott of the stores here for the United Farm Workers, and we went on a four-day march in Phoenix in support of the farm workers that were being organized by Gustavo Gutierrez. We tried to set up Chicano Studies at the university and worked on educational issues around Tucson Unified School District. We were involved in ending the war in Vietnam and making the El Rio golf course into a community park. Also, at that time I got very interested in immigrant rights and the border. It is exciting to think back about those things and to remember all the energy, the enormous energy of young people. We sat down in sit-ins, protested on picket lines, processed on marches.*
>
> *For a long time, I worked through El Concilio Manzo. Manzo was a multiservice, community-based organization. It had been funded through the War on Poverty. We did activities like trying to help end police brutality in the barrios.*
>
> *In 1976 the United States Attorney's office raided the agency. They stated that Manzo was fraudulent in providing welfare benefits to undocumented people. With that pretext, they entered into the office, removed all our files, and began picking up people from the files that we had. Four women who worked there were indicted for allegedly committing these frauds, but a whole social movement developed around the defense of what had happened at Manzo. At the base, we claimed the right of community workers to*

work with the undocumented. The prosecution was an attempt to frighten community centers away from working with them and to criminalize the presence of these individuals. People were deported because of it.[13]

Lupe almost always talked in terms of *we* instead of herself alone. The movement was a community experience to her, and as such she expressed her agency communally. She was deeply involved with the communal aspects of the movement.

It is important to see agency not only in public terms but also in terms of individual and cultural survival. In the racially segregated Jim Crow South of Mary Robinson's childhood, the fiercely enforced, racially based, castelike hierarchies enforced the rules of relationships between blacks and whites. Whites threatened African Americans on a daily basis and exploited blacks in the sharecropper system, in which African American families lived on a white farmer's land and worked for little or no pay under conditions similar to those the enslaved had endured. The whole family labored for a year, and if the crops made money and the white landowner was honest, the black family got a "share" of the profits, usually one-third to one-half. However, during the year the sharecroppers had to borrow from a white-owned store, and after they paid that bill, they would end the year with little or no profits.

These forms of oppression affected African American women in gender-specific ways. Many white men threatened black women with rape. In addition, black women often had less power than African American men. The women worked in the fields with the entire family but were also expected to maintain a home and a labor-intensive cooking process. They gave birth every few years and generally had to raise their children without medical assistance. Men were often allowed more freedom sexually and could go out to socialize with others on Saturday nights. Mary remembered that her mother's great personal passion, besides her children, was fishing, which was another means of providing for her family. The poor, rural African American women of Mary's childhood expressed their agency and affection in multiple ways according to Mary's stories of the era. They worked at their crafts and gave gifts to each other that came from scraps of their hard lives. In the process, they maintained and defined a culture they shared with other women.

I remember Mama used to quilt with Mama Bertha and her daughters before they moved. [Mama Bertha was a motherlike figure to Mary's orphaned mother. She taught Mary's mother most of what she knew about housework.] Mama always had this squarelike quilting frame that could be lowered from the ceiling so she could work on her quilt. Of course, at first we didn't have no electric lights, so Mama and them quilted during the daytime, usually late afternoon or maybe on the weekends. After we got electric lights, we had just one sixty-watt bulb that hung down out of the ceiling, so at night, when they rolled the quilt up a little ways from the ceiling, you didn't have much light to see by.

They wasn't no fancy quilts they made, but they was beautiful, and people shared quilt pieces. Back then, anytime when Mama or Mama Bertha and them was ready to quilt, they could find somebody who had quilt pieces to give them, maybe a box of quilt pieces that another woman had collected. They was gifts to each other. So the quilts they made had a little bit of all of us in them. Although Mama couldn't read or write nothing but her name, she sewed the prettiest stitch.[14]

Thus, together these women expressed their collective agency through communal activities. Mary recounted another story that demonstrates the cultural vigor and pleasure shared by her mother and their friends.

Mama used cooking to create much of her fun. When she made hominy, folkses came over to eat it with us, then after they ate, the grownups sat up and told stories, what I'd call tales today, about what they used to do. I guess I learned to tell stories by sittin' around listening to them. Well, not exactly sitting and listening, 'cause they always ran the kids out of the room. We'd hear them talking and talking, then came a big old crackling laugh, down to the bottom part of their stomach. I just knowed somebody'd be telling stories I'd want to hear.

Hog killing was a big day 'cause all these people came over again, and the womens cleaned the chitlins, made sausage and talked. And it was a big day of eavesdropping for me. Black womens back then said words like shit or ass, but not the big words that women use now. If a woman'd even thought about saying sonofabitch or motherfucker, she'd be labeled the worst woman in the world. We heard the term that old bastard or I'm gonna kick his ass but not none of those big nasty words that deal with mamas.

The womens worked, then sat around and dipped their snuff and fussed in their own ways about something that was going on. "I heard so-and-so and so-and-so was doin' such and such." Typical gossip, that's what it was.

If we kids came where they could see us, they said, "Get your ass on out of here. Ain't nobody talkin' to you. And you ain't even thinkin' about telling what I'm saying. Now go away." But I always moved toward the door real slow, trying to eavesdrop, and with luck I might hear one last word. If they looked up and saw you sort of hanging around, they'd say, "What you doing? Tryin' to be grown, ain't you? Tryin' to listen to the grown people talk?" During all those times, fixing chitlins, Mama'd look happy.[15]

Mary's story indicates the pleasure derived from community and the spaces for joy that the women created.

Agency that does not succeed as the person had hoped is still agency.[16] Examples of this form of agency come from the parents of Cynthia Dakota (a pseudonym). She was an Native Winnebago woman who lived in the woods around Black River Falls, Wisconsin. She was born in 1927, and I interviewed her in 1982. The Winnebago homeland had originally consisted of much of southern Wisconsin and part of Illinois. Despite a number of forced removals by the government, part of the tribe always tried to stay in Wisconsin. Eventually the government dispersed them into ten different counties, with a number of families settled on the Christian mission grounds near Black River Falls.

When Cynthia was young, the Winnebago of her community worked at seasonal labor. They picked vegetables and fruit for white employers. Cranberries grew in the marshes around Black River Falls, and the Winnebago harvested them. Now the work is done by machines, but in the past men raked the berries into containers, and the women gleaned the berries after the raking process. The children usually helped with the work. Winnebago workers also trapped, grew small gardens, and raked moss found in the area. Women made, sold, and exchanged beadwork and basketry. They depended on the money brought into their households by their work. Despite all their efforts, the population lived at a subsistence level, reflecting the national situation of Native people. Still, complex systems of kinship and its obligations helped to give stability and security to life. Children whose parents were unable to care for them found a home with members of the extended family, and extended family members helped each other meet practical and personal needs.

I first met with Cynthia during a thunderstorm in the early spring of 1982. I smelled the change of seasons. Cynthia was then a gentle, soft-spoken woman in her fifties who had recently become a great-grandmother. Her strong, sturdy build indicated many years of physical labor. She wore glasses and had light brown, deeply wrinkled skin and medium-length hair. She spoke slowly, giving a feeling of peace and serenity even as she talked of hard times. She interspersed her stories with soft laughter, aimed at herself more than others. During Cynthia's childhood, like that of Irene Mack Pyawasit, government officials had forcefully removed Native children from their families and sent them to boarding schools. There white policy makers tried to break the Native children's habits and beliefs and school them in working-class, white ways. Native parents fought this cruel system by whatever means possible, as Cynthia's own parents' struggles reveal. She told me their story.

> *I was born in this Indian settlement, down in a hollow. I didn't come from a big family. There was just four of us children, two boys and two girls. My sister was younger than me. As far back as I can remember, the children went to boarding school. This was a must; they had to have all the children go, all the children that's of age for school. The boarding school people knew the families and wanted all the kids in school. My folks were up north with my grandma, and I was one or two years old the time my mother got so upset. The superintendent went up there to see my parents. My oldest brother was already in boarding school, but the younger was not in school. He was slow, so my mother didn't send him.*

> *The superintendent told my mother that it was a must that the younger brother go to school, that there would be somebody there to help him in his dressing. The superintendent talked and talked, and my mother got more and more upset. Finally, she told the superintendent he could take my brother. But she was so disappointed that when the superintendent was ready to actually take my brother, my mother wrapped me in a blanket, put me in the car with my brother, and said, "As long as you want him, you might as well take her too. Take all I've got!"*

> *The superintendent talked to her, and she calmed down, so she took me back. They just took my brother, but in a couple of weeks the superintendent brought my brother home. My brother was so homesick and lonesome for his parents that the people at the school couldn't comfort him.*

> *A lot of the parents would camp behind the school so they could be near the children. There was a big wooded area there. That way the children would go down to the camp and be with their families, but before night they would have to go back to the school building to sleep.*

I had a sister who was two years younger than me, and we were very close. We played and talked together. Then she went to boarding school too. In midwinter, when she was twelve and away at school, she got sick. She had spinal meningitis and was sick about ten days. We all came to be with her, but they wouldn't let us in the room to see her. So we stood outside her room in sorrow and never got a chance to say goodbye.

When she died, they sealed the casket. Because my dad was an Indian, he didn't believe in being afraid of the body, so when she was being buried, he waited at the graveside until we weren't around, and then he opened the casket and was alone with her. I was real disappointed when we lost her. My oldest brother died too before long, so my parents had much grief, and there was just the two of us left.[17]

Cynthia's parents' desires did not work out the way they wanted them to, but her parents still acted with agency. They cherished their children and struggled against overwhelmingly dominant white power. Finally, when Cynthia's parents lost perhaps their most important battle, Cynthia's father waited till night, turned to his Native religion, and reclaimed his child.

Helen Drazenovich Berklich, the daughter of Yugoslavian immigrants about whom I wrote in chapter 1, also demonstrated repeated attempts to stand up for herself. As a girl, she ran away from her father after her mother's death and her time in the orphanage. She recounted the following memory.

Of course, every time I went to Duluth the kids [her younger siblings] would want me to take them out of the orphanage; they'd cry and beg me, so when I first went to keep house for my father, I took Emil [her oldest brother] out. He was the first.

But things were bad with my father, and I ran away and my father put Emil back in the orphanage. I hitchhiked from Nashwauk at nine o'clock at night to Duluth when I was fourteen. I didn't know where to go, but there was a Polish family that was close friends of my people, so I went there, and they took me in.

I was big, always big and buxom, so I went with the girl in the family, Mary Machowsky, to the Garon Knitting Mills, and we applied for a job knitting stockings. We said we were eighteen. We got the job and made 25 cents a bundle, and there were twenty-four stockings in a bundle. We'd make

$2.50 a day, which was great big money. There were all us young women working there. God, you'd think we were real big genius; we were so proud.

On weekends, Mary's father would get out the fiddle, and they had homebrew and then he'd play and us kids would dance. I can still see and hear him. [Sings.] He'd drink that homebrew, and he'd play. And Mary's mother would make great big loaves of bread. She'd take a brown bag and open it up and grease it and then mold these huge loaves and put them on her range so they would get just beautiful. And Sunday mornings we'd go to Mass and would come from Mass, and she'd have this fresh bread and homemade Polish sausage and boiled milk for breakfast. We were happy, happy, happy. Work was never hard, never.

My father didn't know where I was, but he kept looking and finally he found me. So I went back with him again, and we took Emil out [of the orphanage] again.

When I came back that time, my father was staying at Mrs. Bozich's boardinghouse. Women would run boardinghouses where the mining men lived. So I stayed there also and worked for her for fifteen dollars a month, which was big money. Other girls worked too. She had forty boarders that she'd cook, clean, and wash clothes for. . . .

I'd go to Duluth to visit the kids [her siblings] from time to time. I'd bring them candy and big bags of fruit, but they always cried when I left, and they would beg me to take them out. And I remembered the last words my mother ever said to me, to take care of them.[18]

Again, the times were difficult, but Helen acted with agency, always doing what she could despite the circumstances. In another interview, she described her marriage and her husband's verbal abuse of her. She decided to run away again.

I says, "Emil, I'm going back. I'm leaving. I can't stand him. He's calling me dirty names just 'cause I danced once around with Old Steve, and you know that I'm not like he says."

Then Emil started to cry, and he says, "Please, Helen, don't go, 'cause I'll have to go back to the orphanage." He had to go back to the orphanage three times already. [Crying hard.] So I didn't go. But any love I could have had for Tony was dead. We had our children, but I was always in that sex bit without love, and I hate it to this day.[19]

Helen's agency did not work the way she wanted it to, but she was a forceful actor in her own life story. She ultimately chose to stay in her marriage, a conscious action she undertook in order to care for her siblings. Likewise, Irene Vanover and Betty Dixon, the coal miners' wives who had been so involved in the strike they ultimately lost, were agents in their own lives and acted out with resistance against the system. Mary Robinson, Irene Mack Pyawasit, Lupe Castillo, Helen Drazenovich Berklich, and the parents of Cynthia Dakota all fought against social structures that attempted to suppress their rights and the well-being of those they loved. Finally, Black Lives Matter is a contemporary resistance movement. Agency is the power that enables resistance, the stance that fights oppression by categories of race, ethnicity, class, gender, or sexuality.

CHAPTER 3

Memory Construction
"Since Daddy Made God Die"

Memories are constructed out of real-life experiences, cultural symbols, and interpretations.[1] They are active, living events, taking place at the time of the telling, and told within an explicit context. Memories use storytelling techniques and express the narrator's values. The women I have interviewed over the course of my career as an oral historian have drawn upon language, symbols, and beliefs, as well as on material structures and experiences, to understand the concrete events that they have encountered within their specific cultural, political, and economic systems—that is, their *situated locations.* They then constructed stories out of these materials—interpretations used to explain the conditions under which they lived their lives. Each woman constructed her narrative in the retelling according to the images and means of expression available to her. Then she told them within a specific context.[2]

Quoting the cultural anthropologist Edward M. Bruner, sociologist Norman K. Denzin put it this way: "A life lived is what actually happens. A life experienced consists of the images, feelings, sentiments, desires, thoughts, and meaning known to the person whose life it is. . . . A life as told, a life history, is a narrative, influenced by the cultural conventions of telling, by the audience, and by the social context."[3] The experiences of Maria Elena Lucas, as told to me, serve as an example. Years ago she and I sat in a stopped car at night along the border of Texas and Mexico. Stars dangled above us. My tape recorder ran. Her tiny, tattered home sat back in the darkness. Maria Elena knew my progressive political beliefs and my interest in the progressive process by which she created her poems and diary entries. She began to speak, and I didn't interrupt. She told a story, an oral illustration of her life.

When I was a little girl, and we were working in Portage, Ohio, I remember that they had found workers stealing food from the comisario. These people were stealing because they didn't have food. We didn't have food either, but my father was always against that . . . .

It was raining real hard. I was outside at the water pump getting water when I saw Daddy go into the woods . . . Then he was cursing and saying things, and he was hollering at God. I followed him. I hid behind a tree. . . .

"Then he was crying, and he was cursing God. He was saying, "Dammit, why? If we go and do our work, why do we always have crumbs?" So he just cursed God. He said, "Damn you, God." And he shook his fist at the sky. When he did it, there was lightning and thunder, a centella, lightning that goes around in a circle.

And I went, "Oh, my God!" I didn't know what was happening. I was so frightened, I ran back home before he discovered me because I would be in a lot of trouble.

Every night my father would read part of the Bible to us . . . . it was a very special thing to be all together. That night he came home, and we sat as usual, and I asked him, "Well, are you going to read to us?"

He took the Bible and opened and looked at it. I asked him again, "Are you going to read?"

"No," he said. "God is dead." And he closed the Bible.

I went to my bunk bed. . . . It was real stormy, and I didn't sleep. Finally, the storm went away, then everything was pitch dark.

I kept wondering whether everything was going to be there in the morning, since God was dead, since Daddy had made God die. Because, you see, all the plants and the flowers and vegetation outside represented God. That's the way my father and my grandma and all those thought, that God represented all of Mother Nature—the sun, the sky. My grandmother had taught me that when I had blisters in my hands, all I had to do in the morning before I started work was let the rays of the sunshine touch the palm of my hands and God would heal them. And I kept thinking, "Everything's going to be gone, how awful! Now we've had it. Now what are we going to do?" I was in anguish and so afraid all night.

But in the morning, when I saw the rays of the sunshine and the plants and tomatoes, I rejoiced. I said, "No, God's still here. God just died for my Daddy." And he did, I guess, because Dad never again believed.

And I wrote that into a poem. I was such a small child, but I wrote it because I didn't have any other way of expressing. . . . The poem was something like,

Daddy got mad.
God died.
Daddy caused the crack in the sky.[4]

In the retelling of this memory, Maria Elena has framed the story in the family's struggles to not be cheated out of their meager wages. Then she draws from her female family members' pervasive view of God and her own child's vision of her father's power. Using the only language and symbols she knew as a child, she has constructed a jarring indictment of a cruel social system and created poetry in the process. This story well illustrates the understanding that "effective analyses of personal narratives must take into consideration that *any rendition of the past has to be seen in the context of its motives in the present (i.e. at the time of its telling), its symbolic power and its contextual framing.*"[5] Maria Elena's motive (in the present, the point of "the telling") was to explain to me the cruel, spirit-crushing nature of injustice. The story also symbolizes hope and her sense that God is always there. Finally, the telling of the memory took place within the context of the two of us trying to create a narrative that would explain Maria Elena's life and use it as one example of other migrant workers' lives.

Biblical theorist Anthony Le Donne has explained that "the more significant a memory is, the more interpreted it will be."[6] He seems to be talking about great figures, movements, and shifts of history; however, I believe that statement is also true in individuals' lives. For Maria Elena, the experience with her perception of God's death was highly significant, and she has interpreted it in great detail. Other women I've interviewed remembered important stories in their lives using complex interpretive features. My close friend Mary Robinson, the subject of my book *Moisture of the Earth*, drew on the symbols and meaning systems of the cruel world of her childhood: the segregated, exploitative, sometimes deadly world of white owners and black sharecroppers in the South. She told me the following story the first time I met her in 1980, right after the interview had started. The story stunned me, and Mary was quite aware of my response. In a way, I think it served as a test at the beginning of our relationship. If I hadn't known Mary grew up to be the positive and powerful woman she is, the story she told me would have broken my heart as I thought about black children everywhere.

One Christmas, Shane [Mary's older sister by a year] and me each got a doll, the only one we'd ever have. But when we looked at our dolls, Shane got a white doll and I got a black doll, and neither had no hair. I was little, probably six or seven, and I began to holler. I didn't want no black doll. I wanted a white one like Joy's [a white friend] or at least one like Shane's.

So Mama told me that there was only two left, 'cause Santa Claus didn't have but two. He had a black one and a white one, so he gave me the black one.

I felt so bad, I beat that doll to death. It was a hard rubber doll, little bitty, with no hair, just lines on it. And I took that doll out there behind the smokehouse. We had a big stick, and I beat it and beat it and beat it, 'til I beat off all the legs, the arms off, the head off. And all the time I was beating it, I cried, "I don't want you, you old black doll, you!" I just cried and cried.

The doll was hard, and it took quite a bit of beating to break it apart. Then I went and got me a hoe and I chopped it into pieces, and I buried every one of those pieces in a different hole.

For a long time didn't nobody know what happened. Shane made her doll all kinds of clothes, and I thought her doll was much prettier than mine had been. Finally, one day she was playing with it, and Mama asked me, "Mary Jimmie?"

"Ma'am?"

"Where your doll at?"

I told her, and she said, "Well, I bet you one thing, young lady. I bet you ain't never gonna get you another one!" And I never did.[7]

In this recounted scenario, Mary has both totally absorbed and rebelled against the symbol systems and language that she inherited. As a young girl, she could only act within that system, but it brought death to her six-year-old heart and soul. The story leaves us with an image of a little girl flailing against a symbol of the brutal system of racial, economic, and gender ideas of beauty she was bequeathed. Frisch explains that "memory is living history. . . . Memory is a deeply cultural artifact to reproduce culturally appropriate attitudes and behavior."[8] Similar to the effect that recounting lynching statistics would have, Mary's specific memory as retold to me re-created the terrifying racial world of her childhood, teaching a history that almost is too much for a child to bear.

Storytelling is an important, lifelong undertaking that underlies a person's identity. The psychologist Jefferson A. Singer has explained this: "An individual's ongoing sense of self in contemporary Western society coheres around a narrative structure, which casts the individual as a protagonist in a lifelong journey."[9] We all tell stories, to one degree or another, and in important ways those stories create our sense of self. They are constructions we create to express our personal truths. They explain our own lives to us and to those to whom we tell the stories. For me, the key events I experienced when I lived on a welfare budget as a young mother shaped the way I formed my identity for the rest of my life. I told myself the stories at important times and vowed that I would never forget what it was like to be poor and that I would work to help those still living in such circumstances.

We construct our stories using storytelling techniques circulating in our own cultures. The psychologists Dan P. McAdams and Ann Diamond have written that we use a description of high and low points, thematic lines, and ideological settings when analyzing stories.[10] We can explore Maria Elena's story of lightning using those reference points. She described a desperately low point when she observed her father cursing God, worrying through the night, sure of the world's destruction. Then she told of the high point the next morning when she found the sun, sky, and earth still there, realizing that her father had not in fact caused the death of God. Maria Elena's retelling of her experiences also moves along thematic lines. Over and over in her narratives of her later life, she describes poverty and despair, then the renewed belief that life has meaning and is beautiful. She sets her stories in an ideological framework. She understands the world to be set up so it almost inexplicably tramples the poor. Throughout her life, Maria Elena has struggled to figure out why the structure worked out that way. Certainly not because God wanted it so, she believes.

McAdam and Diamond describe other characteristics they feel personal stories contain in most cultures. They talk about "origin myths, turning points, heroes and villains, and endings."[11] The stories I've been told throughout my career as an oral historian have had these characteristics. However, I really am not comfortable using the term "origin myths" with the women I have interviewed. The term "myth" comes too close to an implication that I didn't believe what they told me, and I believe all the women I interviewed strove with all their hearts to explain their best understanding of what actually happened. Still, almost any story about a birth or the beginning of a problem or a crusade involves interpretations, and in that way the term "origin stories" is accurate.

One such origin story is that told to me by Rose Augustine, a Mexican American community organizer in Tucson, Arizona. Certainly her story is a construction, but it involves real people and a real community. To Rose, the experience provides a narrative sign that she was meant to do special work in her future. Rose grew up in the largely Mexican American community of Tucson, just a few miles southeast of where the activist Lupe Castillo would grow up a few years later. In 1998, when I was doing a series of interviews with women activists in Tucson, Lupe suggested I interview Rose. We met first at a public library, then many times in my home. Rose's origin story follows.

> My grandmother raised me from when I was born, and I'm glad she raised me. I got to see the end of the real Mexican culture here. . . . I did my first organizing when I was a young child. We used to live in this house in front, and there was a little alley in the back and then there was a little house facing the alley. I was playing, and I heard this little girl crying, and I went over and asked what was wrong. She said, "I'm hungry!" And I asked her why didn't she get some food from her mother, and she said, "I can't!"
>
> I said, "Why not?"
>
> She said, "My mother's sick."
>
> "I don't believe you."
>
> "She's sick!"
>
> "Show me!"
>
> So the little girl took me in the house, and her mother was in bed. I thought maybe the lady looked dead. So I got real near, and I said, "What's wrong with you?"
>
> "I'm sick."
>
> "How come you can't feed your baby?"
>
> "I can't get up."
>
> So I took off. My grandma used to wear long skirts, and I started pulling on her dress and said, "Grandma, come over here, I want you to meet this lady."
>
> "What lady?"
>
> "She lives in back."
>
> She said, "I can't just walk into her house."
>
> I said, "Grandma, the baby is hungry, and the lady is sick, and she needs your help."
>
> "I don't know the lady."
>
> "But I want you to meet her!"
>
> So, finally, she said, "Let's see what's going on here."
>
> "Oh, my God," she said when she saw the woman. What they had was scarlet fever, and nobody would get near them.

My grandma said, "I'll be right back."

So my grandma got a tray and put food on the tray, and she took An-nie, the little girl, with her and sat her down at the table and fed her, and then she took the tray over to Ruby, her mother. Then she got some clean sheets and changed Ruby, bathed her, put a clean nightgown on her, and made it a point to feed her three times a day.

Annie was three, and I was five. I continued to play with Annie, and we've been friends ever since.[12]

Rose grew up and got married but did not go past high school with any formal education. She continued to live on the south side of Tucson. When her family and neighbors were sick, she did whatever she could for them. In 1985 a newspaper reporter, Jane Kay, published a weeklong series on water contamination in Rose's part of Tucson. The reporter found that Hughes Missile Systems, now called Raytheon, had dumped its toxic waste in poorly lined ponds not far from where Rose lived. The waste had leaked into the groundwater, and the water was contaminated with trichlorethane (TCE). Appalled, Rose asked how the government could have allowed that to happen. She led a long campaign to have the water cleaned up and to compensate those made ill. The people who had drunk the water and become sick eventually settled for $84.5 million, the largest groundwater contamination settlement in the country. The government declared it a Superfund site and began cleaning it up. Rose continued to organize for other toxic waste cleanups.

The origin story that Rose told about her first organizing actions as a child—when she arranged for a mother and her daughter to be fed—foreshadowed the force with which she would later take on community-organizing actions as an adult. She continues to express a sense of responsibility for the welfare of others. She considers it her fate—to give leadership to her people when they need it—a fate for which she has been trained since childhood.

We can gain insight into these narratives from postmodernism, a philosophical movement that goes beyond modernism, which said that real truth can be discovered. Coauthors Catrina Brown and Tod Augusta-Scott provide an especially clear summary of postmodernism's stands: "There is no one truth, no one universal, discoverable truth that exists outside human existence. . . . Truth is only ever partial, located, and invested. What we take for granted to be true, reasonable, and normative are in fact social constructions that emerge within social and historical contexts and cannot be separated from human meaning-making processes. Knowledge is never innocent, but always culture bound."[13]

An example of how these ideas about truth work comes from my relationship and interviews with my friend Lee Richards (a pseudonym), who is white. I first met Lee in 1975, when we worked on a rape crisis team in Las Vegas, New Mexico. We were only acquaintances until officials in the men's state prison, about two hours from our homes, asked to have several women from the rape crisis program come and speak to men who had been imprisoned for sexual violence. Lee and I volunteered to go. We drove to the prison in the evening a few days later. During the drive, the potential drama of the upcoming experience broke down barriers between us as we each talked about our own sexual assaults. Years before, when I was single, a man had broken into my house while my children were in bed with me and assaulted me sexually. The police did not take the crime seriously because I had fought him off. The next day I got a dog, which gave us a sense of safety.

My disclosure led Lee to tell me that her daughters were incest victims of their father, Lee's ex-husband. This very personal revelation led us to an even deeper discussion of power imbalances between men and women. Lee told me that she felt much guilt about her daughters' rapes, that everywhere she turned the media said that a mother must have known the abuse was happening. Had she colluded in her daughters' victimization? Besides our talk during that drive, the one thing I remember most vividly from the actual visit at the prison was the echoing clang as a series of doors were locked behind us. The experience jarred both of us, and we continued to talk intimately on the trip home.

Several years later, when I was working on my book *Dignity*, I returned to New Mexico (David and I were living in Wisconsin at the time), and I asked Lee if I could interview her. I explained, as I did with the other women I interviewed for the project, that I was especially interested in her experiences as she tried to survive economically. During the actual interviews, however, Lee not only responded to that truth about her survival as a poor woman, but she also told me details about the facts we had disclosed to each other when we had traveled to that state prison years earlier. Consequently, there existed now several different possible truths. One was the truth that I heard based on our previous relationship. But some other interviewer, without our previous experience and relationship, might have heard a different kind of truth. That truth might have included many more details about life on a welfare-type budget and much less about gender dynamics. Each truth about Lee's story would have been partial, a construction located in the relationship between the interviewer (me in this case) and her.

Brown and Augusta-Scott, discussing the insights of postmodernism, write that "what we take for granted to be true, reasonable, and normative are in fact social constructions."[14] The beliefs and observations we consider "normal" are thus products of our general social system. Lee's guilt about her daughters' rapes and her conflict over her belief that she should have known illustrate this idea. The belief held at that time—that almost all mothers were guilty of collusion—was based on some psychologists' suppositions, sexism, and media frenzies. This constructed belief existed within a specific historical time, a time when second-wave feminism brought concerns about incest to the general population and a sexist, media-saturated culture responded with its prejudices. Lee partly blamed herself because she believed in her culture's blame of her. She accepted as normal or true what was actually a social construct. Brown and Augusta-Scott conclude that "knowledge is thus never innocent, but always culture bound."[15] The knowledge that Lee revealed to me and that the two of us later constructed through interviews was bound by the larger culture in which we both lived: my culture, which led me to do oral histories; and Lee's culture, which blamed her for her daughters' rapes. The knowledge was also formed by the intimate culture the two of us had established as we drove to the prison years earlier.

Values are also an important part of memory construction. They can be both a source of identity and a force that encourages resistance. A responsible person chooses his or her moral convictions actively and acts upon them. Almost all the women I have interviewed held deep values, values that helped structure their stories. Lilly Baker, the mountain nurse whose baptism story I repeated in this book's introduction, acted throughout her life and into her senility according to the values she believed she had been given by God. Over and over, this white Appalachian woman from Kentucky, who was losing her memory, told me that her mission was "to visit the sick and the afflicted." I remember the specific morning I described in the introduction. Lilly couldn't remember my name, but as she led me up the hollow in the Appalachian mountainside, she was well aware of her destination. She had taken along a bag of food. We smelled the house before we reached it— a terrible stench of human waste and illness. The green, eight-foot-square house stood on tilted brick stilts. Rotten debris was piled under the base, and a thin, limping gray kitten crawled among some trash.

The elderly woman Lilly had taken me to see leaned against the decaying doorway, holding herself up against the frame. She looked like she was starving. Her skin was almost as white as her hair, and large, orange-brown freckles lay across her nose and under her eyes. She smiled at us, but her eyes looked confused and wary. A wide-eyed, skinny blond boy of about nine watched us just outside the door. Lilly looked at the boy. "It's okay. We've brought food and have just come visiting." The woman in the doorway still seemed confused, so we stood outside her house talking with the boy. He spoke haltingly about a road being built up their hollow, grabbed the kitten, which tried to crawl under the house, then held the animal awkwardly by one leg and smiled and lifted it up to us. The emaciated woman said sideways to us, "You got to watch the kid. He's a little off. He don't get things straight. Hard on cats." She then turned slowly toward him and continued, "It's good to have him though. He's my company boy."

It seemed as if speaking with us made her more at ease, and she sank away from the door, holding onto a walker and easing down into a hard chair in the corner of her shelter. We took it as an invitation and stepped up and inside the door. I looked around and became aware of the room's contents: the old chair she was sitting on, a single bed with soiled blankets, a small firewood heater, and a table with an empty can of peaches. There was no toilet inside the house, and a pan of dirty water sat against the wall. Lilly put the food she'd brought on the table. "There's enough for the boy too," she said. She turned to me and explained, "The folks below take her money and just send up a meal every once in a while."

Suddenly the other old woman spoke. "Mr. Lewis was a corn popper. We popped corn for carnivals. He's gone now. I'm all alone, except for the boy." Then she sat silently, smiling at us and nodding at our questions. Lilly said, "We'll say good-bye and let you eat now." We left the old woman sitting quietly in the corner of the room, beginning to eat, but the boy waved at us from the doorway. As we walked away, the smell of honeysuckle replaced the scent of decay. I later contacted a nun working in public health in the area and told her about the starving woman and child. She assured me that they would try to get them services. If public health did get food to the woman and child, it would be because Lilly, even when losing her own memory, had acted out the basic values of her life.

Jacky Turchick, a petite Jewish woman from Tucson, also constructed stories framed by her values and acted out of her convictions. Jacky's family background illustrates part of Jewish American history. Waves of primarily European Jews emigrated to the United States in the colonial and revolutionary periods. During the 1840s and 1850s, educated German Jews brought ideas about the European Enlightenment. Then, between 1880 and 1914, two million Eastern European, Yiddish-speaking Jews fled conditions in their home villages and the pogroms (violent mob attacks directed against a minority, in this case the Jews) that broke out in the Russian empire. Many Jews were killed, and much Jewish property was destroyed in the attacks.

But there were other reasons why Eastern European Jews emigrated to the United States. The historian Jonathan D. Sarna has described these reasons: "The root causes of the mass migration lay deeper—in over population, oppressive legislation, economic dislocation, forced conscription, wretched poverty, and crushing despair, coupled with tales of wondrous opportunity in America and offers of cut-rate tickets from steamship companies plying the Atlantic."[16] Large numbers of Jews landed and stayed in New York, where they especially engaged in the clothing trade and took leadership roles in union drives, but others entered the United States through other ports. Jacky's mother's father, her grandfather Jack Leader, fled Russia in 1902 when he was told he would be conscripted for a war. He made it to London, where he met Jacky's grandmother. They finally arrived in Galveston, Texas, and were married in Minneapolis. Her grandfather started a bag company, sewing in his home. Jacky was named for him. Her father's father, Morris Schwartz, had come from Luboml, a small village on the Polish-Russian border. The village was destroyed by the Nazis during World War II.

Jacky was born in 1942, and her family was profoundly affected by the European Holocaust, news of which began to leak out in 1941 and 1942. The United States had low quotas for Jewish refugees at that time, and prejudice and bureaucratic restrictions kept it from saving people fleeing for their lives. In reaction to the murder of six million Jews by the Nazis, most leaders of among Eastern European Jews supported Zionism by the end of the war. Zionism saw a homeland for Jews as the only guarantee that the Holocaust would not happen again. As a teenager, Jacky had been deeply influenced by a Zionist youth group, where she argued with others about the nature of a good society.

My husband David and I worked together with Jacky in the Sanctuary movement beginning in 1986, and we remained friends. People in the Sanctuary movement smuggled undocumented war refugees from Central America into the United States, where they tried to get the refugees political asylum or find them a safe place to stay. It was a time when the United States under President Ronald Reagan backed wars in Central America and contributed training to death squads that slaughtered peasants. Jacky, David, and I had met while we were trying to hide some refugees. The Sanctuary movement gradually ended as the United States finally withdrew support for these wars. I continued my oral history work, Jacky continued her activism, and in 2009 I asked if she would be willing to be interviewed for a new book I was working on about border issues. We met in my office and at her home for the interviews. Early in our talks, she told me what can almost be called an origin story. It was about her dad when she lived in Minneapolis, and this story framed her values for the rest of her life.

> I come from a Jewish-identified home. We weren't orthodox, however. My dad was a scientist, and he really believed in God. And he believed that you had to be a righteous person. He tried his best his whole life, and I think he was an amazing human being. When my dad prayed, I could feel his reverence. What I understood was that the experience of life could be sanctified. My mother was really good, too, so what a luck-out for everybody.
>
> I have a memory of something small, compared with some of the big things. . . . One day when I was little, we were driving home from the movies, and all of a sudden, he's stopping the car. He doesn't say anything. He jumps out. We look around, and there's a woman with this huge laundry basket. He runs up to her and says, "Can I help you? That looks heavy." So he went off and took her laundry basket wherever it had to go, then ran back to the car and drove off.
>
> The thing that was so breathtaking and stays with me until this moment is, could I do that? He didn't say, "Oh, look, there's a woman with a big, heavy basket. I bet she could use some help." Or "I think I might help her," and on and on, with him trying to work through the whole thing. But, no, what he did was he just stopped the car, jumped out, and did it. Isn't that an amazing thing? Nobody made a big deal of it. It made a profound impression on me as a child.
>
> I was born in 1942, the year the United States entered World War II. I was a child of the war, and I think that always had a big effect on me. I keep thinking about what our parents went through during this time. Who knew what was going to happen. Everyone's afraid and people are gone, and a whole society is being ripped apart.

The Holocaust was a vivid, real event to me. I read Anne Frank, and people used to say, "You look like Anne Frank."

When I was a teenager, I belonged to this group that was a labor Zionist youth group. It was idealistic, but labor was part of it. Social equity issues were part of what we were about, and it backed Israel. So that was part of my youth, thinking about how to build a just society. Then, at our youth group, a man came and talked to us and asked who would be willing to go south for the voter registration drive. However, I was only sixteen. I couldn't do it. The tragedy of my youth. There was a Woolworths sit-in which I wanted to go to. Another tragedy. It was ten below, and I couldn't breathe [because of asthma] and couldn't go.[17]

Jacky ultimately married, had three baby boys, and moved with her husband to New York, where she worked with a racially integrated day-care center in Harlem. Later the family moved to Iowa, and she and her husband divorced. She met her present husband, Ted, a political activist, and they all moved to Tucson. Several years later Jacky had a baby girl. She and her husband Ted became involved in various political causes, especially concerns about nuclear waste. She slowly became aware of the Sanctuary movement, which was originally based largely in Tucson, and began smuggling people north. Jacky first became active in the movement when it wanted someone to take a refugee from one church to another. Her job was transporting people.

I remember just giving Anna [her baby girl] to Ted and saying, "I'm doing it. And that was it. Once I did that, I kept going to Southside [a church] and eventually, they needed help bringing someone up to Phoenix. So I got in gradually, transporting, which was illegal. . . .

Now I knew I wanted to make myself available [to bring people from Mexico], but it was hard to know who to talk to and what was going on exactly. I guess I thought, "Who am I if I don't do it?" Maybe if I lived in Minneapolis, I could have ignored what was going on in Central America. But being right there, and it being presented right in my face, I couldn't really turn away. I wasn't ignorant. Doing work in Sanctuary was like helping people escape the Holocaust. . . .

I think Kathe [Jacky's friend and coworker, Kathe Padilla] and I must have helped at least several hundred refugees altogether. . . . Every single time I went on what we called a "run" for Sanctuary, I decided I'd never do it again. It was just too much. It was scary. It was tiring. It was hard on my family. Every time I said, "That's it." Then as soon as somebody called and needed our help or I'd hear someone's story, off I'd go again. But I had to decide it every single time.[18]

In Jacky's origin story, we see her equating what was going on in Central America with the Holocaust. Her values compelled her to help people escape. Today Jacky works on neighborhood water projects and toxic cleanups. Her activist values have remained steady throughout her life, serving as a foundation for all the stories she told me.

The women's values also framed their stories, as well as their lives, in less overtly political ways. For example, Helen Drazenovich Berklich, the child of Yugoslavian immigrants that I wrote about in chapter 1, married at sixteen to be able to afford to bring her siblings out of an orphanage. Her husband's lung illness—from his work in the mines—forced Helen to leave her children at home and work long hours in a nightclub and later a restaurant.

> *I was always so afraid that something would happen to me, and my kids would have to go to the orphanage. It was almost an obsession that I might die. It's better for a child to lose ten fathers than to lose a mother. Men are not cut out to take care of little children. It's not in their nature, like it wasn't in my father's.*
>
> *I had another obsession. I was determined that those boys were going to get an education so their wives wouldn't have to go out and work. That was the prime plot behind all those years of work. If they had good jobs, their wives could stay home and take care of their families and not have to be like me. And I did it; I got them all through college, and now they have good jobs as teachers.*[19]

Helen's values, based on her own difficult early childhood experiences, informed her entire life and drove every action. On the last day of our interviews, she explained:

> *Last night the boys and I were reminiscing about all these different things, and later, when I fell asleep, I dreamed. In my dream my husband Joe ran away, and I followed him and found him in somebody's barn. He was drunk and said, "What are you doing here? Are you looking for me?"*

I said, "No, I'm running away." Then he fell down drunk, on the floor,
and I said, "You're drunk, and I'm taking off." And I took off and I ran,
and I got to a strange, old store. I stayed there, and it was quiet and I was
alone. Then my brother Emil came [her oldest brother, the first child she
had taken out of the orphanage when she was newly married and the reason
she could not run away from her first husband]. I looked at Emil and said,
"What are you doing here, Emil?"

"I'm looking for you. You ran away, and everybody at home is worried
about you. You must come back; we all need you, Helen. So I looked around
the quiet store and said good-bye and went back to take care of them all.[20]

Helen's dream was a story within a story, both based on a value system. Maria Elena Lucas and Mary Robinson created narratives that explained some of their deepest suffering as children. Rose Augustine told an origin story that she believed foreshadowed her later activism. My close relationship with Lee Richards illustrates the way certain memories are articulated in relationship to others. Finally, the stories of Lilly Baker, Jacky Turchick, and Helen Drazenovich Berklich underscore how basic life values contribute to the formation of memories. When doing these interviews, I was constantly awed by the deep meaning the women's memories had for them. I discuss that meaning in more detail in chapter 5.

CHAPTER 4

Interrelationships
"The Third Testament"

Memory and relationships are closely intertwined. In their book *Telling Stories*, social theorists Mary Jo Maynes, Jennifer Pierce, and Barbara Laslett site the work of the French sociologist Maurice Halbwachs, saying that he situated "the processes of memory formation and recall into collective contexts, arguing that, analogous to language, memory is formed in and has no meaning outside of social relationships."[1] The coauthors continue, writing that children learn to understand themselves as they acquire skill in constructing self-narratives. This happens within the family when parents sit with children looking at photographs and people tell stories about the family's, and, especially the child's, past. Mary Robinson's beloved mother had no opportunity to situate herself in a relationship with living parents. She had been raised as an orphan. When Mary herself was young, the stories told by and about her mother (as well as other people's actions toward her mother) became an important part of Mary's understanding about the family and herself as a cherished child. She told me the following story.

> *I learned a lot from Daddy, but Mama really taught us how to love. Not a day goes by that I don't think about her. Having children meant so much to Mama. I never remember one time hearing her say, "I wish to God I didn't have me a one of you. Y'all getting on my nerves." I never did. She found peace and love with her children.*
>
> *Mama was my ideal person, but I know she felt real alone when she be growing 'cause she didn't have no sisters or brothers, mom or dad, or aunts or uncles on her father's side, any people that loved her. She'd been kept by her mama's peoples, her old step-aunts but they didn't want her except to*

work. They always told her she was illegitimate, that her mama died when
she was born.

Somehow, Mama felt like she be letting us down. She always talked
about how other kids had grandmas and we didn't have none, like she be
lacking us in a way. Mother's Day was the hardest. I got to the point where
I wouldn't go to church with her 'cause she had to wear the white rose. If you
wore a white flower, that meant your mama was dead, and if you wore a
red one, she was alive. So Mama wore the white rose. It was like we all had
a hole inside 'cause of Mama missing a parent's love.[2]

Mary and I searched for records of her mother's past as part of our interviewing project, going from courthouse to courthouse and meeting with
elderly members of the community. As Mary explained to me, she felt she
and her siblings were especially loved because of her mother's lack of other
relatives, yet the hole she felt inside as a child drove her to eventually find
knowledge of her mother and fill her own life with newfound cousins. One
day, on the way back from a meeting with one of Mary's older relatives by
marriage, Mary told me an origin story, a construction built on details of
stories other people had told. I had been inspecting the garden with the sister of an old woman when a key conversation took place between Mary and
Miss Addie Mae Robinson. Miss Robinson was terminally ill with cancer at
the time, and we barely learned her story before she died.

It hurts me so bad that Mama didn't know it [the story Addie Mae
Robinson told Mary] when she was still alive. . . . It would have meant so
much to her. . . . [Addie Mae Robinson] said she heard it from another
old woman who died before her. The way Addie Mae told me the story, it
probably was 1907. Grandpa Lucius, my great-grandpa, was way out in the
country. He was riding in his white carriage with its white horse, about sun-
set, and passed this woman. She carried a baby in her arms and staggered
down the road. Grandpa Lucius thought the woman was drunk and passed
on by. Then he got to thinking to hisself, "Maybe she's not drunk," and he
turned around and he came back and stopped and picked her up. She be his
own daughter. It was Salena, my grandmama, and the baby was my mama.
Salena done lost so much weight and be so sick that Grandpa Lucius didn't
know her.

According to Addie Mae, Salena didn't have nothing but the clothes she
was wearing and her baby, and she was trying to walk from Tallassee back

to Wetumpka. That's at least twenty miles. Addie Mae said Salena was leaving her husband. They thought maybe he abused her or maybe she got no proper attention when she had the baby. But maybe she just got sick and didn't see no doctor. They figured she knowed she was dying, and she be trying to get this baby to her family, trying to walk all the way. . . . So, anyway, Grandpa Lucius had found Salena walking down the road, and he took her on home, her and the baby. They got a doctor for Salena, but she be so sick, she died anyhow.

Mary told me that Salena's mother had also died. Grandpa Lucius had married another woman, who didn't accept the baby.

> *Then, it was like after Mama's mama and our Great-Grandma Sally died, nobody talked about Mama's mama to her again. My grandma was like this outcast person, and nobody ever told my mama she actually had a daddy, she was not a one-night stand. Now I realize that all those years when Mama be alive, she had all these first cousins right around her, but she growed up thinking she didn't have nobody on her daddy's side, believing that nobody ever really loved her. But that wasn't true. Her dying mama walked twenty miles to give her baby a home, but Mama never knowed it.*[3]

This origin story, built on details of other people's stories, served an important emotional and material role for Mary. Not only was the hole in her heart somewhat filled, but her knowledge of legitimate relatives on her mother's side led her to search out a whole new family. Today she hosts massive family reunions with these relatives.

The most obvious interrelationship when looking at oral histories is that between the storyteller and the analyst, the one who compiles and interprets the story for the outside world. The oral historian Michael Frisch has forcefully stated that we must be acutely aware of the social position of both people in the relationship: "It could be argued that the question of class consciousness is not simply another issue for oral historians to think about," he writes, rather "it is an indispensable tool for exploring the nature of that methodology, precisely because it lies so close to the heart of the interview situation."[4]

Considering this lens, given my white and middle-class status, I certainly have been in a power position with many of the women I have interviewed, even Irene Mack Pyawasit, the Native Menominee woman in Milwaukee, who interviewed me three times before we began our interview. The reasons I had the power in these interviews were so complex and represented so many layers of social privilege, begun so early in our lives, that they were impossible to ignore—nor did I want to. The reasons include my white skin, a higher income, my husband's educated extended family, and the childhood expectation by teachers that I would go to college. The best we, as interviewer and interviewee, could do was to acknowledge the presence of privilege and oppression, vow to present the stories in an effective and respectful manner, share any profits, and work as hard as we could to bring about social change.

I felt these differences in social privilege most acutely with Maria Elena Lucas, for whom life had generally been tenuous. It was simply a crime that as a child I had been educated and Maria Elena had not, largely because of our positions in society. She was so brilliant. Her early deprivations had taken a deep toll on her health, and her life was hazardous on a day-to-day basis. I felt my comparative wealth whenever we were together. I personally could not change our class status, but I could make sure her story was told effectively in a setting that portrayed the multiple oppressions that had led to her life conditions. I needed more education to do that adequately. It was not until I was working on my Ph.D. and studying the mechanisms by which oppressed groups are trapped in their social locations that I was able to write an adequate introduction to Maria Elena's story. Only then did I realize the specific economic incentives for growers to exploit large and desperate families.

Stories can also be told internally, within oneself. We all have conversations with ourselves or others that we carry on inside our minds. Lee Richards, the white woman with whom I visited the men's prison in 1975 and whose daughters had been raped by their father, told me such a tale. Obsessed with wanting her husband dead after learning about his rapes of their daughters, she told herself the same story over and over.

> *I was so angry with Ed [her husband] for interfering the one time I'd had an opportunity to get help for Terri [her middle daughter], and that triggered another episode of wanting to kill Ed, which I thought was dead long ago. After our separation, I'd had that obsession with wanting him dead. It had been so frightening, and after it went away I thought it was*

done. But when Ed interfered with Terri's treatment, I went through about two days and nights of just plotting his murder, down to the last detail, and laying there crying and being so angry I was just out of my mind.[5]

Years later Lee told me that she would lie there in bed during those times, in her imagination shouting out details about why she was torturing her ex-husband for what he had done to her daughters. The relationship between storyteller and listener, as with Lee in this instance, can be between oneself and oneself. This can also be exemplified when a person writes a story poem or song or keeps a journal or diary. Maria Elena did all these things throughout her life. She gave me a big box of her writings while we were collaborating on our book in 1988. They included diaries, notations, skits, poems, and songs, including one titled "Forged under the Sun." One day, as I worked my way through these materials, I came upon a diary entry written during a hard time with the men in her life. On March 16, 1990, Maria Elena had written: "I refuse to believe God is a man or that there is only one God. God is not a man and if she is a man, no wonder!"[6] Throughout her diary entries, Maria Elena wrestled with her outrage over gender discrimination. These various documents gave her a way to tell angry stories to herself and any people who might attempt to read her private writings.

Looking at the relationship between the storyteller and the interviewer (me), it is clear that each storyteller responded to what she believed was my objective for the interviews. For example, such an expectation propelled my interviews with Florence Davis in 2004. I knew Florence because we were both members of a small community of activists. A white woman, born at the beginning of the Depression in 1930, Florence had lived with her family on a small chicken farm in southern New Jersey. Her grandfather was fortunate enough to have a job as a machinist during those hard years. Her parents separated, and her grandparents raised her. In 2004, I was in the process of doing a short series of interviews with political activists in Tucson. I interviewed Florence because of her long life of protest and fighting for human rights. She knew that was what I was interested in and therefore responded to it.

I began the interview asking Florence to describe some of her activism, what her influences had been. In response, she talked about her childhood, especially the importance of her grandfather in shaping her values.

My childhood memories of my grandfather was that he was big. By the time I became an adult, he was stooped over, but he probably was close to six feet tall. And he had snowy white hair and very brown eyes. My earliest memories of him was sitting in his lap when he was telling stories.

His heart and soul were in the labor movement. Something happened when I was an adult and working for the Presbyterian Church. I was sent to Delano, California, to write about the United Farm Workers and César Chávez. He took me to one of their meetings, and they opened with singing in Spanish the union song "Solidarity Forever." When I was about five, my grandfather took me to union meetings along with him, and I heard that song at the meetings, so I was very moved when I heard the farm workers sing it.

My memories of my grandfather's union was of big men talking and singing. It was all men, although I know now that there were women in other unions. About all I remember of those first meetings was them singing songs and us kids having cookies afterward.

My grandfather's goal was to get his workplace into a five-day week. They were also trying to get a pension plan going. The company was encouraging people to retire. They started out with a retirement age at seventy-five, and because times were so hard, people wanted to work until eighty. My grandfather worked until eighty-five.

I think my grandfather'd be proud of my political action. He certainly was for the people. I've always maintained that I came honestly by my protesting behavior. My grandmother was a suffragette when she was in Maine.

So I was involved with many causes. Probably my most dramatic experience happened when I was working for the Presbyterians, and they sent me down to report on a catfish farm in Mayfield, Georgia. This would have been in 1969. It was a totally black community that was investing in this catfish farm, hoping it would give some jobs to their people.

They had a community house, so I figured I'd stay there. As it turned out, I was the only white woman in the house. For all I know, I was the only white woman in the county, and I'd brought my son with me. He was fishing in the pay farm.

But somehow the word got out that there was a white woman at this place, and someone came and told me not to worry, but the Klan was coming. They said there were enough people there to protect us and they had guns, so I didn't need to worry.

We had dinner and nobody from the Klan showed up, and I was talking to a couple of women who worked there at the center. We suddenly heard shots. White people in cars drove around and around and around the building, shooting into the air. The men, the ones who worked in the catfish farm, stood there, holding their shotguns, their .22s. I surely didn't want to see anybody shot, but on the other hand, I was also glad to have the protection. The cars never stopped, but they honked their horns and shouted.

The next day I was to talk to the black schoolteacher. She told me to come after dark. So I was driven by one of the men who worked at the farm, and she had all the curtains drawn, and she obviously didn't want anyone to know there was a white woman in the house.

Afterwards, my driver and I ran from the kitchen door to the car. We got in the car and were driving back to the center. It was probably ten miles along black roads. There was a light behind us, then a siren went off. I thought, "Oh, my God."

The fellow who was driving me said, "It's probably the sheriff, which is okay, but if it isn't, there's a sawed-off shotgun under the seat. Use it." I'd never used a shotgun in my life. And it turned out it was the sheriff, and he was the first black elected sheriff they had, and I was so happy to see him. He just stopped because one of the taillights was off.

Like my relationship with my grandfather, this was a crucial experience in my life. Profound. It was the sort of thing: "You are not playing now. This is serious. This is the real America." And I'd brought my son.[7]

In 2016, Florence became increasingly feeble and eventually quit eating. Her stepdaughter came to care for her, and she went into hospice. On February 27, her daughter called my husband and me. "Mother is dying," she said. "Will you come and sing for her?" David and I went to her home, where others from our community joined us. This small group sang movement songs and told stories for four hours as Florence died a peaceful death. Afterward the other women and I washed her body. A few days later, we scattered her ashes.

The interviews Florence and I had done made us especially close, and I missed her a great deal. She had responded to my interview questions and initial prompts with gripping stories. In that way, her awareness of what I was hoping for in the interviews had shaped her telling of her experiences.

Storytelling is also a community undertaking. Storytelling in which one party simply listens, perhaps with a tape recorder, may be a rare event. For example, Mary Robinson tells stories to her friends and intimates on a daily basis, and they in turn tell stories to her. One of the happiest, funniest afternoons in my life took place when Mary, her ninety-year-old aunt, and I went first to the white cemetery and then to the black cemetery of Mary's childhood home. Starting in the white cemetery with its one tree, Mary processed from grave to grave, acting out characteristics of the person buried there and telling stories of his or her life as I kept my tape recorder going. At first Mary's aunt seemed hesitant because of my presence, but then she, too, began to laugh with Mary, chuckling from deep within her stomach, with the laughter rising to her shoulders and face. Little by little, she began to add details to Mary's stories and impersonations. Mary and her aunt had observed the white culture in great detail, although they had been quiet and unobtrusive when the events initially occurred. Decades later Mary now acted on those observations. In these re-creations, Mary created both a document of resistance and fresh stories to relate to her family and friends.

A discussion between Maria Elena and me about communal storytelling elicited one of the most profound stories that she ever told me. At sixteen, Maria Elena had the first of her seven children, and they followed the crops the way she had as a child. Eventually she worked as a union organizer for the United Farm Workers, under César Chávez, and the Farm Labor Organizing Committee, under Baldimar Valásques. One January afternoon in 1989, Maria Elena and I walked and talked by the Rio Grande in South Texas. I tape-recorded our discussion. Because I am a historian and Maria Elena knew about my deep interest in the labor movement, I asked her how she envisioned telling the history of the farm labor movement to new people she was trying to organize. Even though she had almost no formal schooling, Maria Elena understood much about the historical process. Listening to her tell her stories, I was moved far beyond other, more standard labor histories that I had heard or read.

> *I tell them [the other farm workers] how I think it really started way back in the beginning, that Adam and Eve were the first farm workers. But then I explain how Moses was the first activist who tried to get, how do you say it, who tried to get un descanso para la gente. He was the first bricklayer leader, organizer, and he asked the Pharaoh for a break for the people. And I say, "This was in the First Testament, the Old Testament."*
>
> *Then I explain what I believe about Jesus. I tell them I believe that at*

first Jesus Christ organized all the people in Galilee. He taught them a different way of life. Now this is my own theory, but what I believe is that he thought and he studied and said, "What is wrong? These now have learned a better way of living, but the situation doesn't change. They're still poor. They're still hurting." So he got the idea that el mal, the problem, was coming from over there with the politicians. He thought, I've already organized these people, so now I have to go to Jerusalem and start with the politicians. Then, of course, I tell the people that Jesus went to Jerusalem and fought with the politicians and died for us in the process.

Maria Elena and I sat on a log as she continued the story with a history of Europe and the Americas, the story of the Mexican, then Mexican American people, and brought the history up to the near present. She explained how some Mexican American people in the United States began migrating north for work in the fields.

That led us into nuestro fracaso, our own downfall. Because a lot of the growers and the people said, "Gosh, what a good opportunity for cheap labor." So we go up north with no rights, just shacks, to do hard labor.

After that I go into the story about the black people and all they fought for and President Kennedy. [She reminds people of when they had to go to the back of the bus and other forms of discrimination.] But I tell them that the black people struggled and struggled and one day obtained their civil rights, and to me it seems like they opened a great big gate, and we just walked behind them.

Finally, I say, "Have you ever heard of César Chávez? He is like Moses in the Bible. He took into his hands a whole nation of farm workers across to the land of milk and honey."

I think about how the story will be continued, and it seems to me that we have two testaments that tell the story, the Old Testament and the New Testament, and that what we need is a Third Testament of Life. I want to make sure that women are included this time. Sometimes I start thinking about who's going to keep records and chronicles about what's happening. I wonder if there's a way that records could be saved for future children. I keep thinking about not just my story but the stories of all the women I've known. I hope the next testament will talk about the chemical problems and the pesticides and about how women have been excluded and what it has taken to make any gains.

I probably would have never heard Maria Elena's history of the labor movement and her speculation about a Third Testament if I hadn't asked the
right question within the context of our relationship, my own interests,
and her understanding of our respective situations. Thus I played a role in
the shaping of her response. It seemed like she was formulating the answer
about the history as she spoke, constructing a version of this history from
her own theories as well as religious and union stories she had heard. In
Maria Elena's diary on January 24, 1990, she wrote a dedication for inclusion
in the Third Testament.

> Dedicated to all the dear brothers and sisters who I love so deeply.
> Who've come and gone and who still remain as God's apostles on Earth
> truly and faithfully serving the poor and the oppressed, being their voice.
> For many know not even their own languages and many are just too timid
> to speak and all are powerless. For standing with us in the picket lines,
> for standing by the side of a hospital bed where many times we've prayed
> together for the life of a dear one dying of pesticide poisoning. For standing
> inside a small shack crowded with children, new friends and old friends but
> all brothers and sisters.[8]

She then names sixty-nine people who she would include in the Third
Testament. I believe Maria Elena had worked on this idea for some time.
She tried desperately for many years to find some way of producing a resistance culture that would make a radical difference to the dominant system.
If they could hear the stories, she hoped, they would understand life among
the oppressed and would be compelled to create different conditions. The
diary entry in which she wrote this dedication was a construction that, ultimately, she meant to be read by others. It was a story she created.

Today Maria Elena lives in a tiny cement-block home along the border
in Brownsville, Texas. Her worsening eyesight keeps her from reading, but
she writes daily, chronicling stories about the poorest of the poor. She has,
she feels, a sacred relationship with these people, one that requires her to tell
their stories as they tell their stories to her. I decided to invite Maria Elena
and Mary Robinson to interview me as another way for them to participate
in the oral history project. In doing so, I tried to create a community with
them on a deeper level. Throughout the process of doing their oral histories,
I had repeatedly found myself wanting to share my experiences on a more
intense basis than the interview format allowed. Yet I did not want to in-

terrupt their storytelling process. Ultimately, despite our vast differences, I longed for us to be part of a mutual friendship community, as only reciprocal storytelling allows.

Doing oral histories involves relationships on multiple levels. The interrelationships may be between the storyteller and various listeners and tellers, as with many of Mary's stories. It can be internal, as portions of Lee Richards's and Maria Elena's stories indicate. It can be in relation to a stated request, as when Florence Davis responded to my questions. Perhaps, with oral histories, the most important interrelationship is between the storyteller and the analyst, who must be clear about her own life situation and its relation to that of the narrator. Maria Elena took my breath away when, in reaction to my interests, she told me a version of migrant labor history and expressed her ideas of the Third Testament. I found myself desiring to be part of a larger community of storytellers with Maria Elena and Mary. I wanted to tell my story as part of the process. I describe an episode of that undertaking in the epilogue. According to Maria Elena and Mary, our resulting interactions moved them deeply. It certainly affected my relationship with my own story. The painful parts of my past receded for me, and I felt a lightness where there had been grief.

CHAPTER 5

Meaning

"The Footprints of Our Lives"

A sense of meaning was critically important to many of the women I interviewed. With meaning they struggled through their hard lives; their sense of meaning gave them the strength to resist their oppression. I recall only one woman I've interviewed who struggled to find meaning in her life but was unable to do so, her pain palpable. I interviewed Audrey Jones in 1980, when talking with the wives of coal miners in Kentucky who had fought the Stearns mine. Audrey and her family lived in McCreary County, the location of the Stearns strike and one of the poorest counties in Kentucky. At that time, half the families in the county lived in poverty. Despite the poverty evident in the dilapidated buildings and old cars that lay along the winding roads, it was an area of gentle beauty with green, pine-studded mountains, summer wildflowers, and streams flowing down the hills. This natural beauty was marred by areas of strip mining, where the tan and barren land lay open like a wound, and by the gray, rectangular openings to underground mines, where murky water collected.

Audrey and her husband, Lonnie, had grown up in this region and had never lived anywhere else. Audrey's small childhood home lay back through twisting mountain dirt roads. The homestead had little contact with the outside world but was connected by a path to a small church, a school, and a cemetery, all abandoned. During Audrey's childhood, her family carried water from a spring far from their home and did subsistence farming as her father worked in the mines, but no amount of struggle in her childhood prepared her for the turmoil she would face during and following the strike. Lonnie and two other men had been arrested and convicted of exploding dynamite in a field during the strike. Even though the evidence was circumstantial and no one had been injured, federal authorities sentenced Lonnie to five years in prison. Lonnie experienced great difficulty adjusting to prison. As Audrey told the following story, her eyes were exhausted and her face rigid with tension and pain.

We have three kids, and my littlest is seven. After her daddy left, she started withdrawing and wringing her hands and crying for him when she'd go to bed at night. I figured it was probably 'cause of her nerves, she was awfully close to her daddy. I took her to a doctor from Lexington, and he put her on this ten milligram nerve pill. She didn't get better, and them other two kids is bad too.

And Lonnie's having a hard time 'cause of his nerves too. He's getting worser, instead of getting better. Lonnie's just a country boy, and he's used to having his freedom. I told him to trust in Jesus and live from day to day, but he says, "It's hard to do that in here, knowing that I can't come back to these kids and take care of them."

I feel that we're all being punished, the kids too, for something we knew nothing about. I try so hard to make sense of it all. Lonnie and the other men in prison were framed, that's what I believe, because if you live with someone as long as I have lived with Lonnie, you would know if something like that was going on in your home. He was a gentle man, and he protected our kids. In the middle of the night, when the people against the strike would come shooting by our house, he would get the kids, and he would lay 'em on the bathroom floor and lay over 'em with his self to protect them till the shooting was over or till the State Police or law would come.

Then the law just come and took him. At supper time, the State Police pulled in at my mailbox and told Lonnie to hold up his hands.

I ran out and asked them what they were doing. They was putting him in the backseat, but they wouldn't tell me. It was a few days later that I found out actually what was taking place. The trial was so hard, I sat and cried. Even after it was over, I'd sit and cry, night after night, wondering why it happened, why him. Then they took him to jail, about four hundred miles away.

It does seem unfair. I wonder who really did it, who set it up. I don't know their names, and I don't know their faces, but I know beyond a doubt that they're walking around free, and they're with their family.

I'm getting welfare, but it's not enough to live on, and I try to send Lonnie some money for candy. I asked welfare if I could get a raise, but Lonnie has this truck, and they want me to sell the truck in order to get food stamps. If I sell the truck we won't have no way to get to town, and if Lonnie lives to come home to us, he won't have the truck to use for hauling logs.

I didn't never dream anything like this could happen to us. Now we live by ourselves, down in the country in what you call a bayou, in a wooded area about six and a half miles from a grocery store. People keep bothering us when we're out there by ourselves. Phone calls is mostly what I get. They will be breathing into the phone and asking me if Lonnie's still gone. One night my son answered, and he started crying and hiding behind the door, crunched down. He said, "Mommy, some guy said that he was coming over here to get the rest of us."

There were hard times for both Lonnie and me as we grew but never times like this. But I don't want to move. Sitting down there where I live now, I can see parts of Lonnie, memories of what happened when he was there, and that helps ease my pain. If we moved, it would seem like he was dead. For a little while after they sent all his clothes home, it seemed as if he could be, was, passed over. I'll stay up all night long, wondering, why it happened. You can't explain it to no one, not really. I depend on my friends and that I'm a Christian woman. I try to trust in the Lord that someday we'll all be together again, but I just don't know if I can hang on or not. There's always pain in me, from daylight till dark, with a lot more pain when I sit down and start studying why it happened. I wonder and study and study on it, but nothing comes, he's gone.[1]

After three years in prison, an appeal established that there had not been enough evidence to initially convict Lonnie, and he was released. By then, however, the family had lost all of its possessions, the children suffered from serious problems, and Lonnie finally returned home a changed man, subject to periods of deep anxiety and anger. After that, he moved from place to place, trying to find work in the decreasing number of mines. At times Audrey and the children moved with him; at other times the family was again separated. Audrey's absence of a sense of meaning intensified all this suffering. She was taught to believe in God, but how could God be anything but cruel when he allowed such meaningless suffering?

Storytelling is critical to forming one's sense of meaning. It is by storytelling that we form and structure the meanings in our lives that we connect with events and experiences. Individuals have experiences, then create stories of these experiences to help find meaning in them.[2] I have seen this phenomenon in many of the women I've interviewed. Helen Drazenovich Berklich, the daughter of Yugoslavian immigrants to the Iron Range in Minnesota, experienced her mother's death, then started to tell stories about it to herself—and probably others. In this way she constructed meaning from the stories, and the meaning formed her decisions for the rest of her life. The meaning of her mother's death was so central that when Helen told her stories to me, her mother's last words were the core around which Helen had framed her life.

The oral history theorist Alessandro Portelli has written that recurring "motifs, themes, and patterns of plot and performance" indicate meaning in storytelling.[3] For example, Jesusita Aragon, the midwife from New Mexico whom I interviewed in the late 1970s, repeatedly explained that God was with her during all her trials. The philosopher Paul Ricoeur further explains this idea of one's own meaning making: "The passion inherent in the creating of a text [a story] is not only to make sense of what goes on around the narrator but also to make sense of unconscious passions and sufferings within the narrator. When we tell stories about our lives, the point is to make our lives not only more intelligible, but also more bearable. We can make ourselves heroes of our own story—we cannot, however, actually become the authors of our own lives."[4]

The women thus told stories in an effort to make life more bearable, and, although they could make themselves "heroes" of their own stories, they were not able to control much in their lives. For example, Helen was unable to prevent her mother's death and the children's early experiences in the orphanage. She was unable to prevent the brutality she experienced from her husband, her hard life as a miner's wife, or her husband's death, but she did act within these cruel experiences and became a hero to herself, to her children, and to others as well. The meaning evident in Helen's stories therefore made her life more bearable. Nevertheless, "society can use the individual's need for meaning to its own advantage."[5] This was also true in Helen's life. The economic system of the iron mines was based not only on the men's wage work but also on the women's nonstop, exhausting, nonwage labor. Behind every miner, a woman needed to be working, adding subsistence labor so the man could live on meager wages that didn't pay enough to provide food and shelter for his family. Helen's agency—her resistance against her family's destruction, the meaning she found in her life—helped give the mine owners their profits.

Jesusita similarly organized her lived experiences through stories that she remembered during critical times. These stories have a number of themes that were repeated throughout her long life. She talked about the happiness of being outdoors in nature. Shortly after her mother's death, the family moved to a ranch on the plains of eastern New Mexico. She recalled:

> *For fun I used to race on my horse with my uncle, Isidro Gallegos. He was ten years older than me and the one who teaches me how to ride. I usually win 'cause I'm lighter than him. I love riding fast on Tumbaga with the wind in my hair. . . .*
>
> *I was happy back then on my horse or just climbing on the rocks in the canyon. I was just like a little goat, hopping from rock to rock, singing and whistling and making noise.*
>
> *My grandma says, "Aren't you tired? Don't you get tired making all that noise!"*
>
> *And I say, "No, I don't get tired. I am happy." And I don't get tired today, just my feet sometimes.*[6]

Over and over in our interviews, Jesusita talked about being raised "like a boy or a man." She explained:

> *But I was raised out like a man, like a boy. I don't know why. Maybe because my daddy don't have any other boys, not till I was eighteen. Maybe that's why I was raised out like a boy.*[7]
>
> *Yes, I work outside like a man back then; I was raised out like a boy. Sometimes I think it would be better to be a boy. It's easy to be raised for a boy. You can go and work wherever you want. And for a girl is different. You can go somewhere else and work, but it's different to get along. People are stricter with a girl. Can't try as many things if a girl. But I do many things like a boy.*[8]

Jesusita referred to hard lessons she had learned and the reasons why she helped poor women, especially women without husbands. She never married. After her son Ernesto's birth, she had no clothing for him. A nurse heard about this and brought Jesusita used clothing and other items. Jesusita picks up the story.

> *Next day she came on a truck, and, oh, she gave me a lot of things, so many that I couldn't use for two years. I like her, and I never forget that,*

never. She brings me a blanket, sheets and pillowcases, and underwear for me, nightgowns and aprons, and clothes for Ernesto. I was so happy. And now I give clothes to other ladies when they need them 'cause I remember.[9]

Before long, Jesusita got pregnant again. This time her family kicked her out, a pivotal experience in her life. She told me that her grandmother and father forced her to leave and take an ax so she could hand-build a little house to live in with her children. She took a few animals and farmed on her own. At times, she and her children had little food. She repeatedly said, "If I had my mother, she wouldn't let them put me out like that. She would have helped me, but they didn't care for me, and I didn't have my mother. That's why I was put out. A father is different from a mother. He's different."[10] Despite the many hardships, Jesusita found meaning by forgiving those who had mistreated her, especially her father and grandmother. Forgiveness thus gave her agency in her own life.

After my grandfather died, I ask her [her grandmother], "Who are you going to stay with, Grandma?"

She says, "My sons, not you."

But she didn't last too long with them. No, she went back to me. And I buy a little goat, and I have green chili, and I make tortillas, a good supper. When she came she said, "Oh, it smells good here."

And I told her, "Yes, come in. You can eat with me, too."

And she said, "I won't go back to my sons again. I will stay with you. If you want me to."

And I told her, "Yes, you're welcome." Because I never get mad with nobody. They hurt me, but I can't get mad with nobody."[11]

Other themes or motifs throughout Jesusita's stories carried over into her adulthood and her work as a midwife. She said that she had tried to help other women because she went through hard times herself.

Now I feel sorry for those girls, real sorry for them 'cause I know, I know. When these girls that I take care of are alone, they cry and feel ashamed. I tell them, "Don't be ashamed, I go that way too." But I feel sorry for them, sometimes I cry with them. 'Cause I know, and I feel sorry for that little baby too. Back then they want to hurt me, and they didn't care; they hurt me and that's all.[12]

I know how people can hurt. That's part the reason I don't charge too much [as a midwife]. They ask me the other day, on the clinic, "Why don't you charge one hundred dollars? Everything is going high; why don't you, Jesusita?" Because I don't want to, and I work for my own. I'm my own boss; that's why they can't make me. I want to help the people; they need help.[13]

In another conversation, she described why she thinks people are poor.

I think of why people are so poor, so many poor ladies all along. I think that there's no more rain, that there's not too many jobs, and I think that people don't have their land and that people are unhappy and drink. I think of single mothers who are afraid to ask their parents for money, and I think of ladies whose husbands don't want to work or they're getting drunk all the time, and that's why they don't have money. Some of the men don't care; they don't even come for their ladies [after she delivers their babies].[14]

Over and over in Jesusita's stories, she said, "There is no help but God." Referring to the time when she lived alone with her two small children, she recalled:

Yes, I had my animals, but some times were still hard, real hard. And, you know, they don't care. They don't care if I have something to eat or not. Sometimes I only eat bread with water. I don't have anything else to eat. So I feel so disappointed, and I cry and say, "Why?" I don't know why. Sometimes you make a mistake, you don't know how. I never ask them for help. No. I never ask nobody because I feel like they don't want to help me. I didn't have any help but God, that's all.[15]

Later in life, a grateful mother asked how Jesusita had been able to diagnose a tumor in the woman's daughter. Jesusita answered, "I tell her, 'No, it's God. God do everything for me.' And that's how I feel. God helps me, and when I touch people they feel better 'cause they trust me. You see, I just use my hands and my mind, my hands and my mind and God."[16] Throughout her stories, Jesusita refers to her own hard work. For example, for several summers she and her children went to Colorado as migrant workers. She told me:

The kids work with me on the onions, lettuce, and beets. I used to work in the fields in Trujillo pulling beans and cutting corn, everything, so I was

used to working in the fields and know how. And we pick carrots, tomatoes,
watermelons. To pick them, they were heavy, you can't pick just one or two.
They're too heavy, so you can carry them where the truck can get them. And
cantaloupes, lettuce, and pickles. We pick them all.

We work hard, and the kids help pretty good. They don't complain too
much. Yes, we got tired, but we got to work too. But I never get too tired
when I was young. Never, and nothing hurts me. I didn't get sore nor any-
thing. Oh, sometimes I cut my hands; it's unusual, but I never get too tired.
I don't know why, but never, and that's a good gift. God gave me that.[17]

After she moved her family to Las Vegas, New Mexico, Jesusita continued to work as a midwife and took a job in a parachute factory. Her retelling
of these years also emphasizes the themes of hard work and forgiveness that
gave her meaning in her life.

Yes, we had a good boss in those days, but I worked hard too. I didn't
get much sleep back then, but I didn't get tired. Well, you know, a little
tired, but I never get lazy nor nothing. I'm not lazy now neither, but I am a
little tired. Well, I'm getting old; years make the difference.

I did lots back then. While I was working at the parachute factory I
get ready to build my house [and midwife clinic], the house I live in now.
I was working there, and then when we get off, about 4:00 or 4:30, I come
here and work on my house. When it gets dark I build a fire, so I can see to
work.[18]

. . . I have another one [baby she delivered], and her mother told me,
"Oh, she's just like you. She likes to work, and if she needs wood she don't
bother nobody; she gets the truck and goes and gets some wood." So I feel
proud.[19]

Jesusita was also proud that doctors often turned to her with their questions. Her experiences were thus valued by the dominant medical culture.

The other day I have one [patient]. Oh, she was so sick, so sick she can
hardly stand. She have a pain in her right side. The family calls me 'cause
she can't get up.

I go and examine that girl, and it's a tube baby, and this was the second
baby she loses. She had a miscarriage with her first. She was oh so anxious
to have one okay and is crying and feeling so bad.

*I call the obstetrician right away and tell him I have a girl like this, and
he says, "Tell her to come right over."*
    He operate on her that night, and it was a tube baby like I said.
    Then he calls me and tells me, "Jesusita, how did you know this?"
    *I tell him, "I don't know. I just use my hands, no instruments, and my
hands can tell."*[20]

Jesusita told me again and again that she had to be with her people, that
it was a life requirement for her. When she was young and her father and
stepmother went away to visit other relatives, she did not go with them because she felt she had to be with her grandparents, who might need her.
Now that she was old, she felt more people than ever needed her. When she
was summing up her story, she told me:

*But I would change everything if I could go back again to my ranch.
Sometimes when I go there I don't want to come back. I feel so happy, so
happy and healthy. That wind and sun makes me feel good. I think because
I was raised there. It's when I have those troubles, that's when I feel like
going back to Trujillo, to stay there and cry and rest and be by myself. Back
there where there aren't problems, and I can rest and nobody with me.*
    *I don't blame the old people that don't want to move. They want to stay
where they belong, but I have to stay here and work. 'Cause I have to take
care of people. Yes, I love my ranch, but I love my people. I have to stay here
with my people.*[21]

Jesusita told her stories to me alone, but we often had witnesses that
listened along with me, and I have no reason to think she hadn't told many
of the stories before. Her daughter and granddaughter, often present, nod-
ded like they had heard some of these stories many times. However, Jesusita
said she had never told her stories together over a series of days to anyone
like she had told them to me. The process made her feel like my sister, she
said. I believe Jesusita took the motifs in her life story and used them to give
herself energy and direction in what she did—that is, meaning. Believing
that God had been with her throughout her life helped her believe that God
was with her now and that she would have the strength to face her present
circumstances, whatever they might be. Likewise, remembering stories that
reinforced her great skills as a midwife helped her have confidence when
dealing with nontraditional, Anglo medical workers.

Meaning can come from many places. I have puzzled over the meaning in Lee Richards's life. (Lee is my friend whose daughters had been raped by their father.) There was so much suffering in Lee's story, in both her own life and those of others. Throughout her telling of these experiences, Lee explained that her part in the tragedies (the sexual abuse of her daughters at the hand of their own father, her husband) came from her "natural-born stubbornness." She repeated stories about being stubborn many times in her narrative. A bright, courageous child, Lee herself had been abused by both her parents, partly (she still feels) in reaction to her stubbornness. In this way she has internalized some of the blame for her own abuse. When talking about her childhood as a tomboy and her experience of only playing with boys, Lee recalled, "One time I got tied up on an Indian raid and left there, and I was too stubborn to call for help, so I was there past supper-time and my mother found me and brought me in."[22] As she got older, Lee explained, "Many times I'd be so frustrated because I'd try to do something feminine, and I'd feel foolish while I was doing it, but I'd still be stubborn enough to try to do it, and then I'd get laughed at, and I would get furious."[23]

As an adult, Lee eventually worked with child abusers. Calling upon this sense of stubbornness, she said, "I get very stubborn about not losing the funding for the program and trying to keep the program alive. My stubbornness helped me through a lot of crises in my life. I switch over to stubborn and I can get through practically anything. Sometimes I do myself more harm than good, but it's in more control now than it used to be and with the fund-raising, it is helpful."[24] I believe Lee used her self-identity as a "stubborn person" as a partial explanation for what happened to her and her children. If she hadn't so stubbornly tried to stay in her marriage, the rapes might not have occurred. To Lee, if there was no explanation for suffering, how could she make sense of what happened?

The fact that she had been "born stubborn" therefore took some of the guilt off her shoulders and eventually allowed her to forgive herself. She had been overwhelmed with trying to care for six children born within ten years in an unhappy marriage. She had suffered from deep postpartum depressions. She had been so desperate in these years that when she became pregnant two other times in that ten-year period, she gave herself self-induced abortions. One time she ended up in the hospital with a severe infection. Lee talked to me about the difficulty of caring for the children.

I couldn't do for all of them. I don't hardly ever remember reading to them. I did encourage them to read to each other. And I know a lot of times, when the kids needed a hug or affection, I was too wiped out to give it, even a small gesture. I think back on all the things, the deprivation. When people say, "I'd like another child, but we can't afford one, "I'd say, "Forget that. It isn't the money. You just can't stretch yourself."[25]

The key event, the experience that totally changed her life, of course, was her daughters' rapes by her then husband, Ed. Lee painfully recounted these revelations.

One Sunday, when Terri, my second daughter, was about eight, Terri wanted to talk to me, and she was laying on my bed and we were talking. I was telling her I didn't think she should hang around the old barn with the boys so much. I said that the boys get ideas, and you could get yourself in trouble, and you shouldn't let boys see you or touch you until you get older. And she just said, "Then what Daddy is doing is wrong."

It was like somebody had hit me with an ax. I was just totally stunned when it dawned on me what I was hearing. I remember I was very quiet, and I wanted her to explain, so I didn't want any tone of voice to change. So I took a deep breath and asked her, "What do you mean? What has Daddy been doing?"

Apparently I kept calm enough that she went ahead and explained it all, saying that both she and Jill, my older daughter, had been being sexually assaulted and raped by Ed for some time. Of course, she didn't use those words. After a while I told her I didn't want her to talk about it anymore that day and we'd talk about it tomorrow. And I went in the other room and got the kids to bed and spent the evening with Ed and acted very normal.

The next morning, after Ed went to work and the kids went to school, I went to see my doctor, and he suggested that I talk to Jill before doing anything. The doctor was a really brusque, insulting, noisy kind of man, rough, but he was so sweet to me and put an arm around me and called me honey that he scared me so bad I didn't know if I had lost my mind. So I went and got Jill out of school and asked her what had been happening, and she said, yes, Ed had been sexually using them. . . .

I felt immensely torn up by the whole thing. I kept thinking that if I was any mother at all, I should have known. I should have been able to spot it. Now I realize that I was just so emotionally out of balance by the depression and despair I had been experiencing that I just couldn't see anything. I was just so miserable that I didn't see.[26]

Following Lee's divorce from the offender and her lengthy attempts to help her daughters, she changed her life. She moved to Las Vegas, New Mexico, attended college, and majored in psychology. In this new life, she worked in a women's crisis center and attempted to help others going through somewhat similar hard times. Following our formal interviews, Lee began working with women who had been charged with child abuse. She had learned to forgive herself for "being a bad mother," which she equated with her depression when her children were young, and for not knowing what had been happening to her daughters.

> Sometime back then, I finally forgave myself for being a bad mother. I realized I had been going through so many things when the kids were young that I was as good of a mother as I could be at the time. I looked back and saw Lee [herself] struggling with all those things, how she was. She was pretty pathetic but was really trying, and I could forgive. . . . But I just came to grips with all that guilt and could feel sympathy for the woman I had been.[27]

Lee had been on welfare for a period of time and lived in the projects for low-income people. There she tried informally to help other people in her housing complex. She recounted some of these experiences, which gave her a sense of meaning in her life.

> When I would talk with other people who lived in the projects, I taught them as much about their rights as possible because they need to know how to protect themselves. It's hard when you live in this twilight world of not owning anything and knowing that your whole existence is so transient. It depends on whether there is funding; it depends on whether the procedures have changed. The government is such an anonymous, huge thing that you feel like they're breathing down your neck all the time. The people on welfare and in the projects feel like if they don't say hello delightedly to an authority figure when they see one, they are going to get stepped on. The people don't band together for petitions or anything because they are afraid that if they put their name on a petition and it doesn't work right, then they'll really be in bad trouble.[28]

Reflecting on the meaning of her story, Lee said:

All in all, I think I've had a damned interesting life. And a satisfactory life. I don't think I'd trade with anybody. A lot of it seemed pretty rugged, and it takes pretty rugged living to get through my head. Being born naturally stubborn, you have to get hit by a pretty good sized two-by-four to have it seep in.

A lot of what I've talked about is very sad, and a lot of it is terrible, but I've always had people, like the kids when I grew up and the different men I've known and women friends. There have been so many good, unselfish people that were understanding and helpful. Otherwise I would have never made it. I think that is what is really important, and I think that is what I understood about working with the Crisis Center and with the child abuse program and why it mattered so much to be there to help when I could. Through callousness and lack of foresight, I got myself into some terrible messes, but there was always somebody there when I couldn't swim anymore, and that person took ahold of me. That's the good part.[29]

Lee and I came together many times for interviews and friendship, despite the distance that separated us. Her personality was so accepting that I felt she was someone I could "rest" on. I believe these kinds of relationships gave her a sense of meaning. I feel relatively sure, given our friendship, that Lee had never told her stories to anyone else in such a complete manner. The telling seemed to give her peace and a feeling of coherence. It helped her make sense of her world, thus making it easier to bear some of the difficult parts. In this way, storytelling gave her the courage necessary to fight to change the harsh lives of her child abuse clients. Two years after my husband and I moved to Tucson, Lee died of liver failure. Her daughter called to tell me. "You know how much she mattered to me," I said. "Yes," her daughter answered. "Mama loved you." Over the years, I have grieved for Lee, and she still remains a vivid part of my history.

I turn again to Mary Robinson and the complex and multilayered meanings she reflected in her stories. I can only pick out a few examples from our book, *Moisture of the Earth*, but I should mention that when Mary talks about God, she is talking about meaning. One's ultimate worth, she believes, comes from being allied with the greatest moral force in the universe. Other motifs work their way through her narrative. One of the main connecting links that has twined throughout her life is her love for her family, especially her mother, whom she called her "ideal person." Mary loves the land on which her sharecropping family lived. This love was accompanied by the painful knowledge that her family did not own the land, which was ultimately taken away by whites. Still, Mary claimed the land on a moral basis.

> We was a happy family, and I wouldn't change my childhood for nothing. Sometimes when I'm up there at the land where I was raised, even though I know the soil that's there has been turned over and that somebody else's footprints is being put on it now, I realize that the footprints of our lives is still embedded in that soil. There's things that we will carry to our graves that the place left on us: the scar on my sister Shane's knee, the scar on my ankle. My older brother Tom took his sawed-off finger to his grave: he lost part of it cutting wood, right there, on this piece of soil.
>
> When we was kids we loved to watch whirlwinds moving across the earth, leaving a clean path, and, today, it's like there came a whirlwind across the home we loved. That's what it feels like to me; when the rich whites came in, they took the land poor blacks had worked all their lives. It was like they took a whirlwind across the earth and sheared off the land. But even a whirlwind couldn't erase what was underneath that soil. That was still a part of us.[30]

> I go back and I look at the land now, the sixty-three acres, all the hills and trees we climbed. The new owners just swooped our past off the earth; they tore down our house and wiped up our poor little childhood and threw it away.
>
> We don't understand God's creation. We get out there and take a bulldozer and bulldoze down the earth, just like they did the location of our childhood. But see, in my mind, when I look at the place, I see the little hill that used to come down to our house from Mr. Paul's, and when I look at it I see me and Shane [Mary's sister] walking up to get water with old high heels on, then the dogs chasing us back down the hill. I see the little creek running back there. And I remember when me and Mama used to go into the woods, and every year when the azaleas bloom in front of my house today, I think about the wild azaleas back among the trees and how we'd go out and break them off and put them in a big old fruit jar on the table.[31]

Mary's love of the land, her deep connection to it, gave her a sense of meaning, as expressed through these stories. She also used stories to express her feelings about her mother, who died at fifty-seven from cancer.

Mama wasn't always hugging us and saying, "I love you." We've never been really affectionate, but she loved us so much and wanted us to love each other. She knew what it was not to have nobody, no brother, no sister, mother, or father, that's why she loved so many different people. I can say this with a pure heart. Mama didn't leave this world with no enemies but a lot of love. In her fifty-seven years she loved more than lots of people who live longer than one hundred.[32]

Mary loved her home community, and the two of us drew complex maps of the families and landmarks of her childhood. Together we worked hard preparing documents that would record what had been a vibrant, sustaining neighborhood. Despite what we were able to re-create, however, Mary expressed a sense of loss.

I just sit up sometimes and think about all the things that we lost—a whole community taking care of its kids, loving them, disciplining them, that's a big cost for change. Me and Shane and other kids growed up together, and we carved our initials in our chinaberry tree. Then the other kids vanished, we got bigger, and the whirlwind come and it all disappeared.[33]

Through her storytelling, Mary considers herself a guardian of the memories. She takes extended family members to the old locations and points out what is left on the landscape. She organizes elaborate family and neighborhood reunions, and she is keeping files that document these early years. "God gives us a young mind [as a child] so everything is fresh and new," she says. "And it stays with us when we get older, more than the day to day."[34] Throughout her life, Mary has worked to figure out how the dominant culture had oppressed the people she loved. Eventually she took this knowledge and resisted and through her resistance found direction and purpose. She found meaning through the knowledge that she was a person who could comprehend what was happening and fight back.

When I was little, I always wondered why the black man was the really smart one, yet he and his family always ended up with nothing. I watched REAL close as a kid, trying to figure it out. Mr. Paul [the white man the family worked for] couldn't do nothin'. Nothing! He was just as lost as a bitsy bug. Mr. Paul and his brothers right around him was just fortunate enough to have inherited this land that we lived on.[35]

The whites that worked in textile mills was poor by white Wetumpka standards, but they was well off by black. In fact, Miss Bernice's brother and sister-in-law worked at the textile mill I worked at later. We kids used to go up to their house on Saturdays and work for them and hear them talking. They was making a fairly decent living, enough that you could tell they was accomplishing something.

The subject came up one time while we was there that there was not any blacks working in their cotton mill, just a few working outside as janitors. I listened real careful, and it really started to dawn on me how much injustice there was. Because we was out there, we was the ones that was making the cotton for them to send through these plants. We had the hardest part, and we wasn't getting anything for it. I didn't become totally aware at that moment, 'cause I was young, but it started me thinking even more.[36]

When Mary was twelve and at a white woman's house, she learned about Rosa Parks from the TV. The white woman was Mary's friend, the one white community member who treated Mary's family with respect. Soon the black community was discussing the early civil rights movement, and Mary began to envision a different life. With this awakening, she worked to improve her life and the lives of those around her. Mary also observed her older sister Shane's struggle with sexual assaults by white men. Shane left the South as soon as she was of age. Mary, bereft after her sister's departure, pondered all these realities, analyzing the situations of her loved ones. As she got older, she combined her childhood observations with her adult understandings of the oppressive systems that had determined the lives of the poor black laborers.

After being recruited by civil rights workers in 1966, Mary went to work in a textile plant in an attempt to integrate it. There she observed and experienced firsthand the racial, gender, and class system that held the laborers in tight bondage. When union recruiters came to the plant, Mary responded with great enthusiasm. Through them, she learned the history of the workings of the textile industry and fought fiercely for the union. Today Mary finds meaning in the fight for human rights and telling stories from that early time of resistance.

I used to hear people say that God brought them here on earth with a purpose, that God knowed what your life was gonna be like before you was conceived in your mama's womb, but a lot of people go through life without

*ever finding out what they were here for. But I know what I'm here for. I
done figured that out. I was put on earth for the underdog, for the people
that can't fight for themselves. I just raise all kind of hell and cause all kinds
of problems. Taking advantage of vulnerable people, it's uncalled for.*[37]

Mary has used storytelling throughout her life as she struggles to find
spiritual meaning in the face of the intense racism she and her community
have experienced. One story expresses the horror of racial violence and the
inability of the African American community of Mary's childhood to stop it.
The narratives surrounding these traditional African American stories and
convictions were whispered by community storytellers.

> *I remember Mama crying one day when I was pretty little. I couldn't
> understand what she was crying about. Later on, she told us about it. Five
> white men lynched this black guy, hung him up and burned him alive. . . .
> I know that the lynching and the burning really happened. Daddy told us
> about it first, then the good white lady, Miss Abby, told me about it. She
> should know. She told me it was her father-in-law, James Boyd, who said he
> struck the match. . . .*
>
> *We heard the lynching took place in the little town of Eclectic, and all
> the older people knowed about it when it happened. The last time that I
> talked to somebody from that time, that person said that the tree on which
> they hung the man had lost every piece of bark and every little bitty limb,
> and it stands there, stark naked. No grass, nothing grows around it.*
>
> *Also, when it happened, some old black person foresaw the future.
> "'Cause of its guilt," he said, "Eclectic'll never grow." And he was right.
> No business, nothing, comes in there. The town's just like it was when it
> happened. One time they had two traffic lights, but they turned one off. No
> need. Cotton gins in Eclectic caught fire and burned up all the time with no
> explanation. The cotton backed up in the cotton houses 'cause of the fires. It
> was like Eclectic was being punished.*
>
> *African Americans had great faith back then, and when someone com-
> mitted a crime that evil, blacks said, "Just give God time, he'll fix it. He'll
> fix it. We don't know how, but it'll balance out."*[38]

This story reflects Mary's intense faith, as both a child and an adult, that
when people cannot force justice and the injustice is so horrible, God and
nature itself will record history and bring reckoning. God will take the peo-

ple's place. That long-held belief, Mary remembered, came from her mother and her own African American community. In another example, Mary tells a story emphasizing her belief in God's will.

> *There wasn't nothing that none of the blacks could do 'cause the sheriff was the worst of all when it came to violence. Even the sight of the sheriff's car coming down the road, its tall old antenna swaying from side to side, be putting fear in us childrens. 'Cause we knowed the stories, the things that he did to African American people.*
>
> *And African American adults couldn't vote. You didn't have no way of getting nobody out of office when that person be doing all the low-down stuff. All people could do was believe and trust in God. Old folkses would say, "You don't have to do nothing, just give God time. God'll balance it out. Don't worry, God don't like ugly. Those low-down sapsuckers'll pay a price.*[39]

> *Old black people talked a lot about James Boyd's death. [James Boyd was the lyncher who was said to have lit the match.] They said, "See, give God time. Give God time. God'll fix things, and then it'll be done." And it happened. Each of the low-down men that lynched the black guy got sick and dragged on years and years, waiting to die, to be released from his suffering. Some went five or six years waiting, some went for ten, and death wouldn't come. Like James Boyd, they begged to die. Living was terrible for them.*
>
> *Yeah, after James Boyd killed hisself in 1959, the old ones said, "That's the last of those low-down sapsuckers that burned that guy."*[40]

> *Old Sheriff Holley went to the Elmore County Hospital, and one thing that black people did back then, if they knowed some white man had been really, really bad to the people that worked on his place or if he had acted low-down in some other way, black people would watch real close and spread the news about what they saw. The blacks around there was curious to see how bad Lester Holley suffered, so those that worked in the hospital kept a constant watch over him, then they reported out to other black folks, who told others.*
>
> *Sometimes Holley begged, begged people to find some of those he'd wronged so he could plead for their forgiveness, and sometimes he yelled, "Get 'em back, get 'em back. Don't let 'em get me." It was like all the peoples*

*that he had hurt or killed came back to torment him. Holley laid there and
begged to die. He asked God, "Why? Why aren't you taking me? I'm ready
to go." By and by, people came to the conclusion that God was making him
suffer while he was still alive for all the things that he did on this earth to
hurt people. Then, finally, he died.*

*Maybe it was just fate or maybe it was God's will, but those lowdowns
died horrible, horrible deaths. I think death should be the ultimate, peaceful
sacrifice, and they died bad, real bad.*[41]

Mary's stories relate her belief that God will provide justice in concrete
ways, but they also point to her memory of the tremendous power of African American storytellers who were unable to fight back in overt ways. Instead, she explains, they take the form of people's judgment. These righteous
ideas (that God will administer retribution for great sins) were important
to Mary's upbringing. They reflected community standards and framed the
starkly moral background of the rural women who migrated to Montgomery, Alabama, and formed the backbone of the Montgomery bus boycott in
1955. There women with histories like Mary's mother took their experiences
(in this case, the humiliation and suffering that accompanied Montgomery's bus system), connected it to their deep feelings of morality, and linked
the personal to the larger social forces. Thus they struggled politically with
whites over the meaning of these experiences. The black women of Montgomery joined together over issues of sacrifice and oppression, forming a
united force that gave the civil rights movement its first energy. In this case,
as in feminist theory, the personal was political.[42]

Mary's storytelling expressed her own periods of doubt. One such story
recalls an event that took place after the tragic bombing of the Sixteenth
Street Baptist Church in Birmingham, Alabama, in 1963.

*Way before this I had already questioned where was God, and that
night I felt like I could damn God right then and there. We always had
grown up with the understanding that you trust and believe in God. Then
here was four little girls that went to church that morning, to worship him,
and some son of a bitch goes in there, plants a bomb, and just blows them to
smithereens.*

*I felt like if God was this superpower, why didn't he stop it? They say
everything is did for a reason, and I could find no reason in that. No reason
why four little girls that got up that Sunday morning, that had trusted and*

believed in their parents, who'd said, "You get ready, you go to Sunday
school, you praise God and thank him for the things you got," should get
blown up. Some no-good, low-down bastard plants a bomb in a sanctuary
and just blows them away. I started wondering then, thinking, "Maybe God
is a white god." That hurt me so bad.[43]

Mary struggled with these questions throughout her adulthood. She told me, "I wonder why evil happens. . . . And I think when I get impatient, trying to understand evil, it may be that just over that next hill are the answers that we always looked for. I know that one day everything will be made known. He will show why he had to let it happen."[44] Despite the doubts, however, Mary repeatedly affirms in her stories that God is good. Reflecting on the famous march from Selma in 1965, she said, "And God is good. God is good. He took all that anger that was inside peoples and turned it into something that was beautiful and joyous."[45] She seemed to work things out through her stories. The doubt would sometimes move toward clarity. She said:

I used to get frustrated when I couldn't get things better. I'd get just re-
ally, really frustrated, but I don't do that no more. Slowly it came to me: Let
God do it, let him. He's the only one that can do it anyway, although he uses
me as the person to do it. And when the time is really right, he will let me
make it happen.[46]

In her older adulthood, Mary had a vision. As she recounted it to me, she saw a city in the sky with beautiful buildings with many windows. Every window was a room, and Mary believed the rooms were for God's people. Thus she resolved her long struggle for an understanding of God's justice. We must struggle to change things here and now, she came to believe, but ultimately our fate is in the hands of a righteous and merciful God.

I can feel God's emotions. I'll be sitting in the church, listening, and I
will touch my face with my hands, and there'll be tears that I couldn't even
feel come out. I can sense his joy. I can feel when he's happy or sad, and
when I see little childrens, God makes me just reach out and touch them.[47]

All the women quoted here have used storytelling as an attempt to find and articulate meaning in their lives. Audrey Jones struggled to express her fear that her family's suffering made no sense. Helen Drazenovich Berklich found meaning in rescuing her family, but her efforts were used by the dominant culture to prop up mining profits. Jesusita Aragon found meaning in serving people, especially the women she treated. She expressed, however, a belief that there was no help, really, except that from God. In her fight to find meaning and make sense of her family's suffering, Lee Richards internalized some blame. Finally, Mary Robinson and her community used storytelling as a way to express multilayered meaning, claiming that there is justice—if not on the part of humans then from nature itself and God.

CHAPTER 6

Knowledge from Below
"We Left Our Berries to Rot"

Many of the women I have interviewed throughout my career as an oral historian have drawn upon "knowledges from below"—a concept developed by the French philosopher Michel Foucault. Such "unqualified or even disqualified knowledges" come from the subordinate groups, the ones on the bottom of the social hierarchy.[1] They are narratives the dominant group does not want to hear. Mary Robinson's insightful, careful narration about the injustices of her childhood exemplifies such knowledge. We might also call such stories from below counterstories or counternarratives because they counter the dominant systems of meaning. They are stories told by and about those from whom the mainstream rarely hears. Their stories provide tools we can use to analyze conditions that are considered "normal" in a society. With these tools, the oppressed segments can confront power.

The working-class women I have interviewed as an oral historian have given poignant testimony to knowledge from below. They have told striking stories that contradict established (i.e., dominant) methods of viewing the world. Drawing from feminist theory, the professor of philosophy Shari Stone-Mediatore has written that the stories told by oppressed people offer critical understandings of the beliefs and structures of those who possess power. As such, the stories give us insights that might transform those institutions and help create a more just world.[2] To analyze counterstories, stories from the bottom, we first must acknowledge that power tends to make itself seem natural, normal, and beyond question. This is often true even in the lives of the women I have interviewed, even when they have been able to fight back to a degree. Lee Richards, whom I interviewed in the mid-1970s, encountered one such situation in which male supremacy was considered natural. A white woman, she was ambivalent about her own behavior when she was threatened with the power of male violence as a young woman.

I worked as a cashier in a movie theater back when I was a girl, and once when I was fifteen or sixteen, a soldier offered to walk me home. It was a full moon and beautiful, and it must have been a romantic movie because I was out of my head. I suggested we walk down by the river in the moonlight, which he took to be two or three other things.

We sat down in the grass by the river, and suddenly I was flat on my back in the grass and couldn't move. I had never thought of our walk that way, and I was so astonished that I didn't have any power. I was helpless, and that threw me for a minute. His shoulder was across my face, and I told him, "Let me go or I'll bite you." He either ignored me or didn't hear me, and I bit clear through to the bone. I'm surprised he didn't beat me to a pulp. I guess the shock of it protected me. Even then I was ridiculously stubborn. I wouldn't run. I got up and straightened my clothes and I marched straight home. I wasn't about to run.

The next night at the theater this soldier was walking around the box office looking at me from all angles; you know how those glassed-in cages are. He kept hanging around and watching me until he finally made me nervous. I asked him, "What's wrong with you? Do you want to go to the show or not?"

He said, "Is your name Lee?"

"Yes, it is."

"You're the one that wounded one of my boys."

"What are you talking about?"

He said, "You bit Private so-and-so." I was so embarrassed I could have died. This man was the medic and had treated the guy I bit.

I said, "Well, I warned him that I was going to bite him, and he didn't let me go, so I bit him." I got very defensive about that.

Then the guy that I bit came in two or three nights later. It was after the box office had closed, and I was in the lobby just standing there by the curtains watching the show. He was mad and said, "Come here."

"Why?"

"I want to show you something." And he unfastened his shirt and pulled it back, and it nearly made me throw up. The bite was just black and blue and green and yellow and just horrible with all these teeth marks. It was really bad.

I told him, "I'm really sorry, but I told you I was going to if you didn't let me go," and he just walked off. I really felt sick, pale and weak, because it was hideous. But it was just done in panic because I had never been helpless before and that was the only way out.[3]

Lee took partial blame for the incident and was so shaken by her behavior that she felt sick. That she was at least somewhat at fault appeared to be beyond question, so she accepted the dominant culture's explanation for what had happened. Sexual assault in certain situations seemed natural and normal, even though she had fought back.

Darlene Leache, a thirty-one-year-old mountain woman from northern Tennessee, told a story about the interaction between the power of a specific man and a culture's belief that such power was natural and not to be questioned. I interviewed her in 1980. Darlene had been raised in a loving but impoverished home. She met her husband-to-be when she was fifteen and thought being with him would take some financial pressure off her birth family. She told me about her marriage.

We were married by a justice of the peace. . . . I was so scared when I was standing up there in front of the justice of the peace, I wanted to run. I wanted to run back out and not get married. But I thought that if I got out from home things would be easier for Mom and for us. And I thought, "Oh, I can't run away, he's spent all that money for blood tests and the license. I can't do that." But if I knew then what I know now, I would have run.[4]

Within months, Darlene became pregnant, and her husband drank and beat her. The beatings got worse as she gave birth to six children in rapid succession.

I knew how bad things were with [her husband] Virgil, but I didn't think I could get out of it, not when the babies kept coming. And I thought the husband had to agree with it for you to take birth control pills. I tried an IUD, but it went wrong. So I had six children, and I lost one when I was pregnant.
. . . I got to where I felt like I was absolutely nothing. I didn't want to face people or talk with them because I was so ashamed. . . . I didn't think I had any brains at all and that I was completely alone in the world. . . .

My sister came to the house one time when he was drinking, and he had just beat me to where I couldn't move. I couldn't walk, and she took me to the hospital and took care of me. She would help me by just talking to me and being there with me. She would take care of me, but she wouldn't interfere. She never wanted to get involved in it. . . .

But I still felt so alone sometimes. I thought, "Why not just go on and do something to finish it, to get out of the way." Because sometimes I felt like I was standing in the way of people. I'd often think on my way to work, "Well, why not just drive over something and hit a big tree. . . .

And my great-grandmother, she would help me because she was really religious. She believed in God. And I would run to her when problems got real bad. She'd pray for me, and it wouldn't be long till I got what seemed like new strength. My great-grandma lived according to strict religious beliefs. . . . Still, she didn't believe in divorce, and I was raised not believing in it either.

But even she said, "Darlene, sit down. You need to divorce him. You can have a better life."

"But, Grandma, the Bible says no divorce." . . . It didn't seem right according to what I'd been taught, and I went on and on.[5]

Darlene's entrenched belief in male power was initiated then enforced by the dominant systems of religion and social organization. Eventually she went to a mental health clinic, and the people there helped her get a divorce. After that, Virgil quit drinking and begged her to take him back. She said that her religion told her she should accept him, and she remarried him. Virgil became so physically sick from his years of heavy drinking that he was unable to beat her. In addition, Darlene lived near her mom and dad, who tried to control Virgil's violence. Her life eventually improved. Some nuns in the area helped local women set up what they called the Mountain Women's Exchange, a coordinating group with the goal of improving lives by developing social programs and forming a power base for political action.

From this group, Darlene learned the term "battered woman," which gave her a language for what she had experienced and allowed her to think of herself in a strikingly different way. Instead of believing herself defective, Darlene saw herself as a victim who was now becoming empowered. I interviewed her after she had this insight, and it probably helped her describe her past in different terms from those she would have used if she had never found a description of herself as an empowered victim. In Darlene's words, the purpose of the Mountain Women's Exchange was to help women to not

> *be pushed back into the corner like some kind of animal that's afraid to move or a little mouse that is afraid to stick its head out from under.*
>
> *I guess that's how I saw myself and other women, too, like little mice. We look out to see what's going on, but then we want to crawl back in; we are afraid to come out. But we shouldn't be. Because the world was made for the women as well as the men. We have a place here too.*[6]

Darlene's consciousness was raised, to use a second-wave feminist term. The Mountain Women's Exchange also trained her in bookkeeping, and she kept books for the organization: "It seems that there's things that people are born to do. Like the Lord has a calling for each one of us, and bookkeeping feels that way for me."[7] She still described her life in religious terms and believed marriage was a natural state in which the man is in the dominant position unless he forfeits that position by extremely immoral behavior. She reflected this belief in her reasoning about her daughter, who was fifteen and wanting to get married, just as Darlene herself had done.

> *I don't want her to marry, not this young, but her boyfriend is consider-ate and doesn't drink and has a good job. He's a real thoughtful person. For Mother's Day, he brought me six red roses, the first roses I've ever received in my life. She's been going out with this boy for three years and has been wanting to get married for over a year. I wonder, "Will I be making a mis-take by letting her marry, or will I be making one by not letting her?" ... So I don't know which way to turn.*[8]

Darlene's story reminds us of the complex ways people respond to restrictive structural conditions in society. In many ways her daughter may be about to repeat aspects of Darlene's life, but perhaps that daughter will see how her mother has grown and will become more empowered. She may also embrace that model.

Certainly, young women often act with agency or resistance, as Lee and Dar-lene eventually did. Lauren J. Germain, writing in *Campus Sexual Assault:*

College Women Respond, states that statistics estimate that one-fifth to one-fourth of women experience sexual assault during their college career. In 2011, in an anonymous eastern university, Germain did an extensive study of the ways in which twenty-six assaulted college women acted with agency in terms of their victimization. She explained that they organized events for the community, spoke at or presented in awareness-raising events, researched gender violence, served in organizations aimed at supporting other students, taught self-defense classes, and worked one-on-one with peers who had experienced sexual violence.[9]

Knowledge from below and counterstories like Darlene's interweave complexly with dominant forms of power. Another example comes from Sarah Jones, whom I interviewed in 1979. Sarah was seventy-two years old and at that time lived in a public low-income senior citizens' apartment complex in an African American neighborhood in Milwaukee, Wisconsin. A frail-appearing woman, she had dark brown skin and large, dark weary eyes. She wore her hair twisted up in a rubber band. When we talked, she muttered and laughed to herself. She had a tendency to repeat herself and wandered around her apartment during the interviews.

Sarah was not popular with the other residents of the apartment complex. Before urban renewal demolished poor communities, supposedly to create "better" cities, Sarah had lived in a couple of roach- and rat-infested rooms. Illiterate, she had worked as a dishwasher for the YMCA for years. When she moved to the senior citizens' apartment, Sarah inadvertently brought the roaches with her, and her room frequently needed to be fumigated. One time she started a small fire on the ninth floor because she'd never cooked on an electric or gas stove. She also spit tobacco in the elevator and drank and swore in the lobby. Sarah was fierce. By her own account, she had survived in a household of twenty-one children by being the "cussedest one in the family." Over and over, she told me that she was mean. The only person she had ever loved was her youngest brother, and he had died of a stroke.

Sarah came from a cruel and dangerous land, the Mississippi Delta. The nearly treeless countryside grew cotton as the major crop. When she was young, African Americans outnumbered whites, but the social structure was built on the old plantation system. In these years most blacks worked for whites as sharecroppers or day laborers. Like other croppers, Sarah's parents had no capital, and they lived on a form of credit that basically indentured them. Like Mary Robinson's family in Alabama, Sarah's brothers and sisters worked with their parents from sunup to sundown all year, and each year they found themselves more deeply in debt.

Sarah had grown up in a culture with absolute segregation and no voting rights for blacks. Whites lynched African Americans to terrify the black community. The dominant white social structure considered such violence normal, and the justice system supported such extrajudicial control of African Americans. Sarah claimed that the cemeteries were full of hanged people. When we spoke, she traced her terrible fear of the dead to her own mother's horror upon seeing a lynch victim. Like Josephine Hunter, another African American woman I interviewed in 1979, Sarah had fled to the North as part of the Great Migration. She first lived in Indiana, then moved to Wisconsin. No matter what she suffered in the North, Sarah told me, she never regretted leaving Mississippi.

> *There was twenty-one kids, twelve girls and nine boys, in the family. Me and my brother who died here; he was the baby boy, and I was the baby girl.*
>
> *I was the cussedest one in the family. Sure were. And I ain't played with nobody; don't do nothing with nobody. Still don't. When you see me, you see my daddy. Look like him and got his ways, too. Hatefulness. He'd have nothing to do with you, just like I didn't.*[10]

> *I start working in the cotton fields when I was nine. See, every people put you in the fields, down there. You don't run up and down the street, up and down the highway. Yes, sir, when you get nine years old, you got to hoe and pick.*[11]

> *My mother took care of all the kids. Raised them all. And they all just as crazy about my mother as I am. All them. They didn't treat me special 'cause I'm the youngest girl. I didn't give them a chance. 'Cause I's mean. I'd fight them. I didn't like nobody. They treat the baby boy better than me. They just loved him to death. I were mean and always have been. I got funny ways.*[12]

> *Most of all, when I was little, I was scared of the cemetery. . . . Been scared of dead folks all my days.*
>
> *Nobody scared but me, and I always been scared of them. I ain't never*

been to a burial. You're dead and you're done, done with me and I done with you. . . .

But my mother ain't scared of no dead folks. My mother bathe them, put the clothes on them, everything else. But they won't get buried if I have to bury them. I was born scared like that, I guess.

My mother said she made me scared. She say that when she was car- rying me, she went to see a dead man, and his eyes and mouth be open and awful. He'd got hung, and she got scared of him, and it made me like I am. . . . People were hung down there and everything else. And I know they're hung 'cause I seen them. Tongue out real long, eyes real big and popping. Them son of a bitches [whites] awful down there [in Mississippi]. They don't like blacks. I seen them walk right up and yell at me. . . . Black folks don't do nothing in Mississippi and get away with it.[13]

The housing authorities eventually evicted Sarah from her apartment in Milwaukee, and she lived on the streets. No one knows what happened to her. She lived her whole life with keen knowledge from below. Sarah's knowledge serves as a counterstory, a narrative in direct contrast to that told by the whites of her childhood. However much they understood their situa- tion, Sarah and her family could not fight the power dynamics of her child- hood directly. Whites continued to lynch "uppity" African Americans. Sarah never adapted to a type of behavior in which she would be the well-behaved and cheerful African American from Mississippi. She hated the dominant system and was vehement about how it had negatively affected her life. Her opinions, compared to those of whites, indicate that "the circulation and preservation of politicized identities are always matters of contest."[14] Sys- tems of power can never take it for granted that subordinated people do not critique established ways. Documents like Sarah's oral history are a valuable contribution to societal knowledge.

As the Black Lives Matter movement has demonstrated, those in power cannot assume the complacency of subordinated people; they are telling their counterstories, sometimes vehemently. African American groups have worked to expose and challenge institutional violence in all its forms, in- cluding organizing to oppose violence against women, the undocumented, and the lesbian, gay, bisexual, transgender, and queer (LGBTQ) community, while young whites are organizing in support of Black Lives Matter and other movements. While the lynchings that Sarah Jones experienced have ceased, institutional racial violence still exists in this country. Showing Up for Racial Justice (SURJ) is an egalitarian and collectively led national network of groups and individuals working to recognize and counteract white privilege and the way it interfaces with dominant social structures.

Mary Tsukamoto, a second-generation Japanese American woman whom I interviewed in 1979, revealed a profound knowledge from below through her powerful counterstory. Her narrative allows readers to critique the dominant social system. At the time of our interview, Mary was a petite, sixty-six-year-old woman disabled by rheumatoid arthritis. She spoke quietly but with conviction. Her Japanese parents had emigrated to the United States early in the twentieth century, when Japanese were not allowed to become citizens or own land. They worked as farm laborers, cooks, housemaids, and in laundries, trying to survive. Mary remembers whites calling her and her siblings "dirty." The children attended segregated schools and worked with their parents in the fields surrounding Florin, California, near Sacramento. The Japanese laborers cultivated strawberries between grape plants on land owned by others. Eventually the family acquired land when Mary's older sister, a citizen, became an adult.

Mary grew to become a leader in her Japanese American community. She and her husband joined the Florin Japanese American Citizens' League and worked to improve conditions for the large Japanese American community there. On December 7, 1941, they learned of the Japanese attack on Pearl Harbor. In the days that followed, the U.S. government arrested thousands of Japanese immigrants living in the United States. Mary recounted those early days before the family's internment.

> *There were people who wanted us out of the way for economic reasons and found the war was a good opportunity to do what they had been wanting to do for the last fifty years. They were upset because of our farming success. But many of the farms would never have produced as much if it hadn't been for the Isseis [first-generation immigrants]. They were willing to work hard, and where other people would never have thought of farming, the Japanese reclaimed the lands and changed them into productive estates. But, with the war, many were anxious to get our land and our flowers, fruit, vegetables, and fishing industry. . . . There were powerful people crying for our evacuation.*[15]

On February 19, 1942, President Franklin Roosevelt signed Executive Order 9066, which called for Japanese Americans to be taken from their homes and livelihoods and imprisoned in isolated camps, surrounded by barbed wire and guarded by soldiers. That order initiated one of the greatest moral struggles of Mary's life. The government asked members of the Japanese American Citizens' League, as community leaders, to help them prepare the Japanese Americans in the community for their evacuation. Mary decided to cooperate with the government so she could cushion some of the suffering—a decision that gave her self-doubts when she was older. In the frantic days before the evacuation, Mary rushed around trying to prepare the people medically, financially, and legally.

> *The last day was on May 29. Strawberries were red in the fields; in the peak of our season we left our berries to rot! [Cries hard] And many farmers depended on that crop to pay back debts they had borrowed in the stores and shipping companies, because each year they had to borrow in advance to make it. That was the kind of life we were living; they were just poor farmers. And so they didn't get to harvest their strawberries and their grapes that year and they had debts they left, and the stores and the businesses had great losses they could never claim. . . .*
>
> *Families were split up at the moment of departure, and there was such anguish . . . people were running around trying to come and tell me that it was my fault that families were split up. That I had betrayed them by helping with the evacuation. We were tearing at each other; when you get frightened, you do that. The ugliest part of us came out, and we were surprised that we were doing that to each other. We had been friends. [Cries]*[16]

Mary's daughter was five at the time of the evacuation and cried for a whole week. Mary suffered from arthritis, and government doctors bent her arm into a cast. She never was able to move her arm again. The family traveled by train to the internment camp. Women birthed babies on the train, and the sick died onboard. They finally arrived in Jerome, Arkansas. The counternarrative continues:

> *We were surrounded by barbed-wire fences and military guards, and people were confused about how to deal with all of it. Some family members turned against each other, and the government blundered in so many ways. . . . Many people lost their farms or stores or homes . . . the evacuation*

destroyed so many. Many people were broken; they were never the same. They just mentally lost their minds, and some committed suicide and some never came back. Many of them got sick when they were young. They were old before they should have been. [Cries again][17]

Years later, when the government allowed the Japanese immigrants and Japanese Americans to return home, one-third of the Japanese American community's property in Florin had been burned. Nobody ever revealed how the fires had started. Their imprisonment and the subsequent fires destroyed the once vibrant Japanese American community. At the time I interviewed Mary, she and other survivors of the internment had asked the U.S. government for financial regress. The government commission that was set up to hear their stories gave each person five minutes in which to describe his or her experience. Some people still were unable to confront the government. Talking about the experience, Mary declared:

> *If the Constitution is going to be interpreted the way it was with the evacuation, another group might be mistreated. Because America did do a wrong. And it was a terrible wrong. [Cries hard] If our story is not heard by Americans . . . then many other people could be treated in the same way, and America is going to continue in this sordid history. We don't want that to happen in this country.*[18]

Adding to Mary's pain, young people in her community were challenging the manner in which Mary and others of her generation had cooperated with the government. She remembered:

> *Other young Japanese Americans are saying, "How come you took so long? Why did you let it happen? . . . Now many of our third generation are turning against those of us who were interred and saying, "How come? Why didn't you have the courage to oppose and speak up? . . . You're crazy to have done that. You were U.S. citizens!" It's true. Those of us who were second generation were citizens, but we didn't feel as though we had many rights as citizens. We were treated so badly that we always felt we were still visiting as guests. And I still sort of sense that, even today. . . .*
> *For all those years, I felt as though we needed to be at our party-best behavior. "It is poor etiquette," my father used to say, "to hurt other people. So don't shame the family. Don't rock the boat." That was the way we were*

raised. . . . With that training, it made me feel ashamed to think we were
suing the government, and I felt ashamed to think we would dare to say,
"You were wrong and you need to be sued." At first, I just couldn't do that;
it was just like pointing my finger at my father for making a mistake. . . .

So seeking redress is a very difficult thing for me to do because I'm
breaking through a cultural background that is different and that taught me
to be meek. But I'm finally learning that as an American I needed to speak
out.[19]

On August 10, 1988, nine years after the redress hearings, President Ronald Reagan signed the Civil Liberties Act of 1988 into law. This law acknowledged the fundamental injustice of what had been done to Mary and 110,000 others. The act apologized for the grave violation of the constitutional right to due process and made restitution of twenty thousand dollars to each surviving person who had been imprisoned. Most of the older internees were dead, however, and the results of their lifetimes of labor had been lost. Mary Tsukamoto had direct knowledge from below. She expressed a counterstory directly in conflict with mainstream, dominant visions of the civil liberties and basic justice in the United States.

Women's studies professor Alyssa Garcia has defined "counter-storytelling," attributing the origin of her definition to civil rights professor Richard Delgado. Garcia states, "Counter-storytelling is utilized as a tool of resistance, empowerment, and self-representation, a mode of 'talking back' to power. It allows for an individual from an oppressed group to identify and contexualize his/her experiences with others, relieving a sense of isolation and internalized failure." Garcia goes on to say that for people of color (and, I would say, also for poor whites and LGBTQ people), counterstories can powerfully disrupt the thinking of the dominant culture. The status quo may be difficult to maintain for both the dominant and the oppressed segments of society when faced with such powerful testimony. Garcia asks us to unpack the silences that surround counterstories. In the process, many of us deal with the "shame, guilt, and exclusionary forces that can induce silence."[20]

Maria Elena Lucas, who labored in the fields and later became an organizer with the United Farm Workers, wrote a poem about these silences. She and I worked for years on her story in our book *Forged under the Sun*. Her poem speaks to these erasures from social discourse.

Listen to my silence.
It is soundless and empty.
It is vast and deeply profound.
Oh God, my silence is so loud,
that it wakes my nights
and it makes me break down
without sleep.
Listen to my silence,
It moves like the presence
of grief around me
and denies me the right
to speak.[21]

Certainly, many of the women I've interviewed have expressed counter-stories as described by Garcia. Mary Tsukamoto's story of the imprisonment of the Japanese Americans during World War II offers a counterstory to patriotic accounts of that war, but before she forcefully broadcast the story of all the suffering that went on in her retelling of the period to me, she maintained a long period of silence.

> *I shudder to think that in the years after we returned from the evacuation, I was asked to give speeches on it, and, at first, I didn't realize all of the terrible suffering connected with it, and mainly I spoke of the fact that it was not all tears. After a while I learned the details of one of the camps we weren't in and learned of the terrible turmoil and pain and suffering those people went through. I am ashamed to think that in my talks I did not assume my complete responsibility for the whole experience, not just for me, but for the whole Japanese American people.*[22]

After Mary realized the oppressive reality of the internment camps, she broke her silence in powerful ways. She gave public talks about the experience, she testified about it to the U.S. government, and she became the director of the Jan Ken Po Gakka, a private cultural heritage school for fourth-generation Japanese American children. There she taught about the immigrant experience—and the wrongful imprisonment of the children's ancestors. When Mary broke her silence, she articulated a powerful counterstory of knowledge from below.

Josephine Hunter, the African American woman I interviewed in 1979 whose mother had died when she was very young, also tells a counterstory involving a period of silence. In her narrative Josephine claims the full humanhood of any potential child she may bear, resisting any racist names that would diminish the child's dignity. She asserts this against the oppression of her long-term employer. Born in 1907, Josephine struggled simply to stay alive in the neglectful world of her childhood. She married at sixteen, and her husband died shortly after her daughter was born. She went to work as a maid for white employers, her only option. Eventually she moved from Memphis, Tennessee, to Milwaukee, Wisconsin, with a white family. The family exploited her, but she continued to work hard for them. Josephine met and married Fred, a factory worker. They both lived with Josephine's employers. When Josephine became ill, her female employer responded to the illness by saying, "Oh, oh, we're gonna have a little pickaninny running around here."[23] Her use of the term "pickaninny" hurt Josephine profoundly, and it turned out she had a tumor instead of a pregnancy.

> So I had my operation and recovered, but the word she'd [Josephine's white employer] used stayed with me. I worked two years longer for her after she said that. During those two years I never mistreated her children, her mother, or her father or anybody that come up. I just went on as if nothing had happened, but during that time Fred and I bought a house together. . . . It was two weeks to Christmas when we got it together.
>
> I worked on Miz Feinstein's Christmas dinner, and she gave me a blanket. She thought I would be using it upstairs. I thanked her, and she said, "You don't have to come so early tomorrow. You cooked Christmas dinner and everything, so why not come around eleven or twelve o'clock?"
>
> I said, "Miz Feinstein, I will not be here tomorrow at eleven o'clock or any other day."
>
> "Oh, you're starting some more of your foolishness."
>
> "No, I'm not. I have my own place now. I'm gonna stay in my own home."
>
> "Well, what you doing that for? You're always doing something silly. You got a home here."
>
> "Miz Feinstein, I got a husband. . . . That's one of the reasons."
>
> "What's the second reason?"
>
> "Do you remember when I was so sick, and you carried me to the doctor, and before you carried me, you said that I was going to have a little pickaninny?"

"Well, I didn't mean anything by it."

"You said it. You know that's what's said in the South about a Negro child. He is called a pickaninny. You know I come from there, and you know it's resented."

"Well, why didn't you say something about it before?"

"I had to wait until the opportunity presented itself. And today, it has presented itself."

"What am I going to do? I don't have any help?"

I said, "That's not my problem" and walked out. I walked out.[24]

In their own home, Josephine and Fred took in grandchildren and foster children. In a way, the care of these children helped Josephine deal with her own parentless childhood. She also worked as a nurses' aid and for Social Services, but she never went back to the exploitative arrangement she had with her longtime employer. Eventually she told the story to me to be included in a book about poor white women and women of color (ultimately published as *Dignity*). This telling represents a form of counterstorytelling that seemed to help her heal. All the women involved in the research for that book told me stories to be used for publication. It was a way to break their silence in one form or another. Alyssa Garcia uses the term "rupturing the silences"—an appropriate naming of the force by means of which these women took action.[25]

In today's culture, undocumented immigrants often fill positions at the bottom of the social hierarchy, such as janitorial and landscape work, farm labor, child care, and in-home service for the elderly. These workers can provide crucial evidence of class stratification and coercion in the United States. In 1982, Lucia Carmona, a nursery worker in Onarga, Illinois, told me her harrowing experience entering the United States and traveling north. Lucia and I talked in her blue and white trailer in a Mexican neighborhood in the small rural town. She was a tall, handsome woman with light brown skin, even white teeth, and short, shiny black hair. When she smiled, her face was warm and gracious, and she spoke in a deep, mature, gentle voice. I spent the night with Lucia, sleeping in a tiny separate bedroom in the small trailer. Above my bed hung a photocopy of the Virgin of Guadalupe that read "Maria Legions." Throughout that evening and during the next day, my friend Maria Elena Lucas translated for us. Lucia's counternarrative follows.

Diego, my husband, came first [to Illinois]. We had five children in Mexico and were very poor. Life was hard, there wasn't food, and for our children we were afraid. Then I left the children with relatives and came to the United States to be with Diego. I also came to work and send home money to feed the kids. It hurt very much to leave my kids. There's so much pain in breaking the family. To say goodbye to the children in Mexico pains a mother so deep, but we have to do it.

I traveled with about twenty others, including my younger brother. We crossed the Rio Grande in an inflatable raft, and we were picked up by the people who were transporting us. They took us to San Juan, Texas. We were already hungry and tired, and we thought we were going to get a taco, some food, but they didn't give us food, nothing, nothing. We got there about midnight, and they did not let us eat food or drink water for twenty-four hours because we were going to be locked in a crate. They didn't want us to have to use a restroom.

Then they took us out of the city in a car, to a far place, far away in the dark of the night. We stopped on a very dark road, and then a truck came. They yelled, "Get in! Get in!" And we climbed in the crate real fast because anyone that's left behind stays. Then they locked the crate. This was about twenty people, and they made a hole in the vegetables and locked us in and then covered us with potatoes, everybody together.

We were terrified in the dark, all crushed together. We could hardly breathe. Then we heard them yell, "The Immigration! Stay quiet!" We saw lights flashing around as Immigration checked us. We had to stay there piled on top of each other, without no noise or nothing, for about forty minutes. There were elderly ladies that were crying in the quiet because they were on top of each other, and they couldn't stand it anymore.

From San Juan, Texas, to Chicago we maintained that position, without drinking water, without going to the restroom, without eating any food. In that vegetable truck, suffocating because we couldn't breathe. I passed out many times. Also, it was in the middle of a snowstorm in the winter, and we only had summer clothes. There was ice on top and underneath. And those with feet in the ice, their shoes got stuck and they couldn't move their feet. Their shoes came apart from them trying to move. There was ice, wind, and snow.

We tried to signal the people up in the cab of the truck, to try to get their attention. But they'd say, "Be quiet, we can't do nothing!" We were so cold. They should have tried to do something to get us warm, maybe blankets.

There was one lady who was very old, very drained, and she was coming to join her family. I thought she was going to die in the crate. But she lived. We had a young boy, traveling without his parents. The whole trip lasted for six to seven days, with almost no food, but we were in the truck with vegetables, in the crate for two days.

We finally got to Chicago, where they took us out and gave us food. Not only people did they bring, but they brought lots of marijuana too. When they finally got me out, I felt like I was suffocating. I thought I was dying. It was a nightmare, and I have nightmares about it all the time.

When we came in a van to Onarga from Chicago, we saw all the ice and snow. There were trailers turned over and cars stuck along the road. I was very skinny and sick for about fifteen days, with dehydration and a cold. And my brother, who came with me, for about a month, he had his feet black from the cold. After that the feet started to peel.

So we came from our land, risking our lives. And sometimes people even lose what they have in Mexico because you have to mortgage everything so you can come. I worry about my kids, and I shake and have to take pills to keep me calm.[26]

Lucia's counterstory points out the hypocrisy of an economic system that is built upon the labor of immigrants like Lucia but makes them suffer so deeply even to have that possibility. Stigmatized by race and class, they serve the dominant system by filling whatever positions are too difficult or degrading to be undertaken by citizens. When they speak out, their narratives contradict the vision of the United States as a just and compassionate nation.

The next morning, after Lucia recounted her experience crossing the border, we drank coffee together. Lucia's friend Juanita and her little daughter joined us. She was a short, meek woman in her early forties with a soft body. When she smiled, I saw that she had few teeth. Her hair was straight and without luster. She moved with difficulty. Juanita's tiny two-year-old, Cecilia, stumbled over to me where I sat on a kitchen chair. She looked at me with her brown-black eyes. The remains of a braid with a ribbon tied around it captured her hair on one side of her head. The rest was tangled around her head. She was small, I thought about six months or so younger than she actually was. Her legs were bowed, her feet turned in, and I was told she had seizures. Cecilia stumbled around the kitchen and fell when her feet got tangled. She kept returning to me, where she played a silent game. She repeatedly placed a bit of nothing carefully in my hand, then had me hand it back to her. At one point, she carried a nude doll over to me and thoughtfully poked her fingers in the doll's eyes. Cecilia's face still haunts me, and I tried to get help for her mother and her through various churches.

Of course, people still come to the United States from Mexico and Central America to try to find work. The process has changed, however, since Teresa made her harrowing trip north across the Rio Grande. In 1992, U.S. Border Patrol agents made 565,000 arrests, and the Clinton administration felt pressured to do something. The Hold the Line project in Texas and the Operation Gatekeeper program in San Diego, which the administration created, funneled people trying to come north to work into the mountains and deserts of Arizona. Immigration enforcers at that time felt that few people would try to cross the desert because it was so deadly. But desperate people, especially those from southern Mexico and Central America, where they had little comprehension of the dangers involved, do try to hike through the desert.[27] There they die at the rate of about two hundred a year. About six thousand people perished between 1994 and 2011. This morning, as I write these words at my home in Tucson, news has come that the Border Patrol found five more bodies in the desert. The undocumented women's narratives are poignant examples of knowledge from below and can serve as counterstories against the dominant narrative if those of us with a social voice would just listen to them and let them contribute to democratic debates.

None of the stories told by these women is neutral, and I believe there is no such thing as an unbiased story.[28] All stories, even those written by historians writing "standard" histories, are not neutral. The historians have a specific viewpoint, and in the choice of their words, they, too, express a bias. Professor of Philosophy Shari Stone-Mediatore does an excellent job of presenting a description of the bombing of Nagasaki during World War II and exposing the military standpoint of the writing. For example, the word "casualties" is substituted for "people killed by the bomb" and "targets" stands for "cities."[29] The social activist and historian Howard Zinn further explains, "By the time I began teaching and writing, I had no illusions about 'objectivity,' if that meant avoiding a point of view. I knew that a historian (or a journalist, or anyone telling a story) was forced to choose, out of an infinite number of facts, what to present, what to omit. And that decision inevitably would reflect, whether consciously or not, the interests of the historian."[30]

Because these women come from specific "situated locations" with specific moral implications, their stories present an exact point of view with precise political implications. An example is the story of Daisy Cubias, an immigrant from El Salvador.[31] She came to the United States before the class conflict in El Salvador broke out in a civil war. The United States funded and supported the military-led government of El Salvador, which tried to suppress the (FMLN), a coalition of left-wing militias. The government of El Salvador, with the backing of the United States, launched a reign of terror against civilians. The resulting war broke out during the 1970s and lasted until the early 1990s. About seventy-five thousand people, including members of Daisy's family, died.

I met with Daisy at her apartment in Milwaukee in 1981. She was an animated, alert, and attractive woman of thirty-seven with brown skin and a sculpted face. Her black, slightly curled hair curved into her cheeks, and her brown eyes reflected her intense intelligence. While we talked, she showed me photos of her family in El Salvador, those who were now dead or struggling to survive in a state of siege.

When I was a little girl in El Salvador, I was brought up by my grandparents. My grandfather was not rich but not real bad poor. We have a house, and we have land. They are good to me, and there was nothing at my home but peace, quiet, and love.

Now there is death, nothing but death, death all over. All the people and places I know so well. We had a big tree, and under the tree it is so big that we have parties and fiestas. But my girlfriend writes in a letter about a teacher I know, his brother is my friend. The teacher is standing in a bus stop by the tree, and some people come and just shoot him. The guys just come over and blow his brains out! His brains are all over the tree, and they cut off and hide his legs.

I say, "Really? Is this the same country I grow up in? Is it the same spot I was standing in?" Because it was so beautiful. It was all so beautiful. And I think about the children there who don't know yet what life is all about. These children are not getting a chance to grow slow. They are forced to grow up in a minute, in a second, in a split second, with a machine gun. And I think about my brother and sister who are gone and the four little ones left behind and my grandmother and my mother. Who knows if they will make it.

I was the first granddaughter, so my grandparents really raised me as a daughter. I remember that my grandfather was tall, very tall. He was 100 percent Indian and was dark. My grandmother is Spanish, she's white. There were many children in my grandparents' family. And the son was so lazy he didn't want to do anything, so my grandfather raised me almost as a boy.

He says, "You want to ride a horse, go ahead and do it. You want to go to school, go ahead and do it."

In Spanish community, womens are taught to cook better, dress better, clean house because they are going to marry, and they must make the husband happy. My grandfather never mentioned marriage to me. He always say, "You have to learn to read and write. Look, read this poem. Read this book. It is good for you. You learn something."

We had no riches, but we were happy. We were the first people to have a radio, and we have dances and parties. . . . My grandfather sent me to school with my youngest aunt. She was four years older than me, and we grow up together. We went to school and finish the sixth grade, which was fantastic. My aunt and me and my uncle are the first ones in the family, generation after generation, who went to sixth grade.

My grandfather educated me, and from him I learn the positive thinking. He was this kind of man. He was self-educated and he bought newspapers and that's how come I know about other countries. He said, "Whatever thing you want, you go and get it. You don't kill. You don't steal. You don't cheat. You work hard to get it, and you will get it because you came here to be happy and to help your fellow men. Work hard and someday you are going to help your family and God."

My mother had remarried and had three more children, two girls and a boy. My brother was very sick when he was a child because they didn't have no money to get him care. But my mother had much faith and she prayed a lot, and he become well, with herbs and things the Indians use. Then later on, when he was fourteen, he got polio, but they could take him to the doctor, and, again he become healthy. I remember him, and I remember my littlest sister with her dark braids and big eyes.

Daisy worked her way through high school in El Salvador, then she had the opportunity to come to the United States to work. Her family did not want her to go, but she felt that with her earnings she could put her younger siblings through school. She traveled to the United States in December 1965. She didn't know anyone, and it was snowing as the plane landed. She had never seen snow. She came to New York and started babysitting for a woman and going to school at the same time. She married, had a son, and divorced. Finally, she met a man from Mexico who said his employer was looking for someone to do community organizing in the Anti-crime Unit, working with Spanish-speaking populations. Daisy took the job; she loved her work, going from house to house. At the time I interviewed her, she worked full time, went to school full time, and organized about the killings in El Salvador. The news from El Salvador got worse and worse.

> *I had put my brother and younger sister through school, so he got a degree in science and my sister was in secretarial science. And when you go to school, you open up to a new system because only the rich people can afford to go to school. So when he got a B.A., he saw a different kind of life for people, and he say, "How come they can eat better than us?" Then he become involved with the people and say, "Wait a minute. We have to organize. We have to get help for all the people." So he become a leader of the poor people.*
>
> *But the government don't want to see leaders of the poor people because then it will change, and they don't want to change the power. The power is theirs, and they don't want somebody else to have any.*
>
> *The next thing we know, my sister-in-law is taken by the military, then my brother is killed. He die so young. Later we find out how he died. I was driving when I hear, and I have to stop the car. The way they kill my brother was they torture him first, and then they took his head off. They cut off his head! It's like a signature the military did it, because it is very seldom that the revolutionary front do that. So his three little children were left alone with my mother.*
>
> *And my littlest sister too. She had married a teacher, and together they would ask the people, "How come your kid don't go to school? Send him to school." Then most of the people in my little village, they went to school. Then, when you read a book you become knowledgeable about injustices. How come the United States give five million dollars to El Salvador? What have they done with the money? Because you get news; you read the paper; you start asking questions. Then they call you a communist or that you want to be a socialist.*
>
> *After my brother was killed, my sister and brother-in-law decided to come to the United States with my mother and their little boy and my brother's three children. But they have trouble with the birth certificates, so they decide to go to the big city to get copies. They left their three-year-old boy with my mother and the other children and took his pickup truck to drive to San Vicente. The troops stop the truck and ask for IDs. My sister*

and brother-in-law said, "Here they are." But the troops didn't believe them when they saw they were coming from San Lorenzo, and they thought they were leftists and shot them. Then the troops took the pickup truck. The family knew what happened when they didn't come home. So my poor, sad mother is alone with the four little kids in the middle of a war!

In every revolution, there are going to be martyrs. I don't cry. I just work to try to stop it. And I pray to God that they don't kill anymore. If I didn't have my child, I'd go there myself and fight for equality and freedom and peace.

My biggest fight now is with the United States INS, Immigration and Naturalization Services. If my brother and sister were alive, they are considered my blood relatives, but the children are not considered that way, even though they do not have parents. They tell me I cannot bring them here.

So now I'm getting in contact with representatives and senators to help me, but it has to be a private bill, and it take so long that we don't know what we going to do. Some people advise us to bring them in illegally because it's very hard to get a private bill approved. So right now we are working on people to get support from churches, senators, others. We are talking about people who are being kidnapped. We are talking about children who don't have nobody in the world. Why can't the United States understand? People with full bellies are unwilling to fight for something they don't believe in. But if you are hungry, and your children are starving, and you can see them dying, you'll try action. They are desperate![32]

Through Daisy's efforts, her surviving family members eventually made it to the United States and safety. "Someday you are going to help your family and God," her grandfather had predicted. Daisy now cares for her family and was part of the resistance to the war, which played a part in its eventual end.

These women's experiences illuminate a specific social position, a situated place in the social and culture locations in society. The experiences of those in Black Lives Matter, the Dreamers, and the women fighting sexual assault on campus also represent a situated position. Their knowledge from below shows how the women act with agency and resistance, creating counterstories that provide insight into the historical moment. They thus inspire with their courage and call for justice.

CHAPTER 7

Activism and Social Movements
"A Brown Statue of Liberty"

From years of collecting oral histories, I have extensive transcripts of fifteen progressive activist women with working-class backgrounds. By "activist" I mean a woman who in some way has taken action against what she perceives as oppression, someone who has resisted what she considers illegitimate authority. Most of the activist women I have interviewed have been involved with a particular movement. For example, the Menominee woman Irene Mack Pyawasit talked extensively of her involvement in Indian affairs, a movement known today as the struggle of Native or indigenous peoples. Irene Vanover was a leader in the labor union movement by way of her work in the Kentucky coal mines. Probably the best known of these social movements for change is the civil rights movement, of which textile worker and union organizer Mary Robinson was a part.

Lupe Castillo, whom I spoke with in 2004, sees herself as part of the Chicano movement. A progressive border activist, she defines it this way.

> To me, a movement's an experience of a group of people, a community, who share a vision about what things should be like. The group believes that together we seek to accomplish it. One such movement was to end the war, to make a better world with that war [in Vietnam]. A movement works outside of the established forms such as the government. I believe social movements are what really propel changes—rather than established institutions initiating change. The significant changes, the leaps that occur, come from social movements.[1]

The people of BlackLivesMatter and the Dreamers consider themselves to be part of such a movement. The activists whose stories I've collected here have organized other people, protested, marched, struck, signed petitions, written letters, and initiated lawsuits. They have run for office, taught or written about all sorts of conditions and "knowledge from below," and smuggled people whose lives were in great danger. As part of their organizing, they tried to document collective histories or collective memories to be shared with the members of their groups. By the terms "collective histories" and "collective memories," I mean the stories of a group from the group's perspective, such as interviews with those suffering from toxic waste or maps of significant locations and family trees of a specific community of sharecroppers. Each of the activist women interviewed developed as a child or young woman a sense that the world as it existed was unfair. They talked about their pain at finding out the extent of the injustice in their worlds. For example, Maria Elena Lucas said:

> *Sometimes if we were working close to the patrona's [farmwife's] house, like maybe a hundred feet away, we could hear the patrona humming or singing as she was doing her dishes in her beautiful sink. You could tell her body, her mind was at ease. Then you could turn around, and one of the sisters would be crying. And you'd wonder, why does it have to be like this?*

> *Why does the farmwife sing?*
> *Why does my mother cry?*
> *The farmwife has a roof*
> *and my poor mother*
> *shall never have one.*[2]

Maria Elena's life story, as documented in our book *Forged under the Sun*, expressed her pain and her attempt to fight the conditions that had so hurt her and her family.

Rose Augustine, who I first interviewed in 1988, was the Mexican American from Tucson who at five "organized" an intervention with her grandmother when she found a little girl crying because she hadn't been fed. When Rose was a child, health authorities in Tucson sent her to live in a "preventorium," a camp away from her family with strict rules intended to prevent children from getting tuberculosis. Young Rose defied the government and ran away. She married as a teenager and stayed in the same Mexican American area of Tucson where she had grown up. She birthed three children, all of whom had illnesses of some type. She noticed cancer and birth defects all around her but didn't find a reason for it until a series of articles was published in a newspaper. She recounted her moment of awakening.

I always lived on the south side [of Tucson], the part of town that was Mexican American, but in '85, a newspaper reporter did a whole week's series on the water contamination in the south side. It had been Hughes Missile Systems, now Raytheon, that dumped their toxic water there. They knew it was contaminated with trichloroethylene, TCE, but they did so anyway. TCE causes gene mutations. They'd been dumping it for many years, but it wasn't until 1981 that ten wells were shut down for contamination. Still, we didn't know that we had drank from those wells.

One day my friend Marie called me and said, "Rose, go pick up the newspaper. Read the story about contamination and call me. Read it carefully."

I was washing that day, and I was busy at home, so she called me three times before I finally went to the store and bought the paper and said, "Oh, my God. Now I know what happened to us." So I started buying the paper every day. I started reading about all these sick people I knew.

Then Marie called me and said, "Rose, we're having a meeting to discuss the newspaper articles and see what we're going to do about it."

I went and was elected to be a leader at one of the following meetings, and I didn't ask for it. I wasn't out to make a name for myself. It's just that my children were all sick, and I was just angry and I wanted to fight back. How can this be allowed when we trusted our government?

The more I found out, the more I felt like I'd fallen in a whirlpool, and it just kept pulling me down, and I couldn't get out again. The more I worked, the more I found out about how the industry and government betrayed us Mexicans. I feel an innocence lost, and it's so sad because I still wish I had that innocence. We were so naive. It's a rude awakening to find out the government knew, and they did not protect you. People of color are considered expendable, and they really don't care what happens to us. When you find out something like this, it's like being raped; you can't go back.

We had a meeting on the south side, and we expected maybe forty people to show up and nine thousand came. I was overwhelmed.[3]

The innocence you lose is like a story that someone told me once. Apparently, the ancient Greeks used to do a lot of mining, and people lived in the mines, and for entertainment they'd have puppet shows. They were called "shadow puppets." And the people would sit in the evenings, and they'd have

these puppet shows with lamps or candles or whatever they had, and they'd
see the shadows on the wall. But there was one guy who decided he was go-
ing to go out of the tunnel, out of the mine, and he saw the daylight, he saw
real light, and he could never go back and live in the shadow world again.
    That's what it's like. I've seen the testimony. I've heard the stories. I
know what the real world's like. I can never go back.[4]

This lack of innocence, her moment of realization about the depth of
her environmental oppression, still hurts Rose today. All the women I've
interviewed faced turning points in their lives when they became politicized.
Another important turning point for Rose occurred when she was called to
a regional conference to represent Tucson's south side residents at a meeting
in New Mexico. It was there that Rose realized the toxic dumping on communities of color was so widespread.

    Our group was invited to the Southwest Organizing Project, and they
    sent us tickets on the airline to go to New Mexico. I was prepared to tell
    them this whole story about Tucson, and I just sat there with my mouth
    wide open. Because as each table went by, and everybody was telling their
    story, this same thing with toxic dumping was happening in other parts of
    the country. And it was all communities of color. My story was everybody's
    story. I was dumbfounded. I wasn't alone. There were about thirty commu-
    nity representatives.
    We had African Americans, we had Asians, we had Mexican commu-
    nities. Native Americans. I just couldn't believe that our government does
    not protect people of color, the Native Americans especially. This is so evil.
    Our cause was called "environmental justice," and we formed the Southwest
    Network for Environmental and Economic Justice.[5]

Mary Robinson described similar turning points in her story as she realized
she lived in an unfair world. As a young woman she went to work in a textile
factory in order to integrate the then all-white workforce. There she saw all
sorts of injustices toward both black and white workers. Becoming increasingly outraged, she recalled:

    I never will forget the night, about 9:30, when I started into the plant
    as usual, and this little old short, bewildered-looking fellah with curly hair
    stood there in the near dark. And he held all these leaflets in his hand and

talked to several peoples. I was nosy, I always been, and I peeked over sev-
eral shoulders, and they was leaflets—fliers for a union. I still didn't know
too much about unions, except they was supposed to help, so it was like,
"Oh, okay," then, "Yeah!"[6]

From then on, Mary was galvanized to organize for the union. She went on
to praise the union movement for making a "woman out of her."

Maria Elena Lucas, as an adult, worked with her common-law husband
in the nursery fields of Onarga, Illinois. She especially loved the undocumented farm laborers whose lives they shared. As in all her work, she used
religious language in talking about her radicalization.

> *It was not until my early years in Onarga, when I started going through*
> *all those terrible things together with the other migrant people, that I knew*
> *that God was calling me in some very special way. When we went through*
> *the wintertime and hunger and discrimination and everything altogether, I*
> *began to see people not like I would see my kids, my children, but different,*
> *and to see myself, not just like their friend, but I began to see myself like*
> *God was telling me something. I don't even know how to describe it. I began*
> *to see it like my obligation, my duty, like I was their sister, but more than*
> *their sister, like I had to do something on behalf of God.*
>
> *And I began to see people not just like my friends or my sister; I saw*
> *people like a suffering Christ. It seemed like Jesus, like the passion, like*
> *when he had been crucified. It was like I was seeing the crucifixion of God*
> *or Christ through their sufferings.*
>
> *It wasn't just like this group of people who were having problems with*
> *the grower and we're going to fight; it was more a sacred thing. I don't know*
> *why I developed that feeling, but I remember exactly when it started. We*
> *were working out there together in the fields in the snow, and I was looking*
> *at the women and the men, and, somehow, I began to change. It was just*
> *like God was there; it was God I was seeing, and something was terribly*
> *wrong. I was [so] very moved that I had to do something about it. I still*
> *feel that way. If I see something wrong, I say, "This is not what God wants.*
> *This is not the way it has to be." I get into a lot of trouble for feeling that*
> *way, but, oh God, I loved those people in Onarga.*
>
> *It was like there was something holy between us. Sometimes we'd be*
> *out in the fields working on a beautiful day, and I'd look up and the sun is*
> *working, the bees are flying, some children are crying, others are laughing.*

*I'd be with Gloria Chiquita and Comadre Lencha and Lucia, and people'd
be picking tomatoes and putting them on their shoulders. I'd stop and look
at them and say, "Don't you feel something? Don't you think it's just so
beautiful, like God is here?" And sometimes Gloria Chiquita would look up,
too, and say, "Ah, yes, Maria Elena, it's beautiful."*[7]

This feeling led Maria Elena into activism and eventually into the farm
worker movement.

Florence Davis, whom I interviewed at the beginning of my search for activist women in Tucson, was the white woman who was raised on a chicken
farm during the Depression. Her grandfather had been a union man. As
an adult, she traveled to a catfish farm on a writing assignment for a church
magazine and was threatened by the Ku Klux Klan. The experience brought
home to her how real racism is in the United States. She shared with me
another time when her consciousness was raised.

*I went to Lincoln University when I was older, and my son was in school
full time. It was an African American school, and I was one of the few whites.
A young classmate of mine was one of my son's favorite babysitters. He was
one of the few people who could see a kid in a wheelchair and understand this
was an ordinary eight-year-old that loved to play cops and robbers.*

*I didn't know it at the time, but I realized later that Peter was gay. We
kept in touch for a long time, and it was a letter from Peter that really got
me dealing with the issue of homosexuality. Peter was the son of a black
Baptist minister who kicked him out when Peter told his parents about
being gay. Peter had written me that when he was living in Manhattan, he
had been walking down St. Patrick's Street and had gone into the cathedral
because he was feeling so down. He kneeled there and tried to pray. Then he
thought that according to his father, God wouldn't listen to him either, so he
just sat there and cried in the empty church.*

I was editing Trends, *a Presbyterian magazine, about 1972 or '73. I
thought, our mandate is to bring to the readers in the pew the voices of
people they wouldn't otherwise hear. They won't hear of struggles like that of
Peter either unless we deal with it. So we did an issue on "Homosexuality:
Neither Sin nor Sickness." I was told I wouldn't be asked to stay on when
the magazine moved to New York, but I believe gay rights are as important
as racial rights.*[8]

This moment awakened Florence. For the rest of her long life, she cam-paigned for the rights for gays, lesbians, bisexuals, and those with transgen-der identifications. She was an inspiration to the Tucson community and gave intellectual and movement leadership to those who know her.

The experiences of Pat Manning, a white woman born in 1954, demonstrate that consciousness raising and radicalization are a process. I first interviewed her in 2009, when I was sixty-seven. I had known Pat for years because we were both members of a worship group made up of progressive activists. She met me at the front door of her small adobe house in South Tucson. Fuchsia bougainvillea glowed against the fence. Her long hair fell in waves down her back. Extraordinarily loving and gentle, Pat has been a peace and border ac-tivist since her high school days. But even before she undertook her political commitments, while living at home with her parents, she developed a sense of injustice around sex roles. Her mother was sick during much of Pat's childhood, and as the oldest girl, Pat played the stereotypical woman's role, doing the housework, cooking, and laundry. She saw her father mistreat her mother, and she was given different rules than her brothers. In her words:

> *The boys didn't have to do anything, and I had to help my mom. I was making their beds and cleaning up their rooms. Even as a teenager, I asked myself, "Why don't my brothers have to clean up?" My older brother had consciousness. Michael got it, and he'd say, "I'll clean up my space. You don't need to worry. I'll make my bed."*
>
> *But my younger brother did the opposite. He saw that as a way to have power over me, and he'd purposely mess things up, and I had to be the one to clean it. When I was probably thirteen and we were living in El Paso, my mother was put in the hospital during one of her many, many, many hospitalizations for asthma. So I was in charge of keeping the house clean, doing the cooking.*
>
> *Steven, my little brother, decided that was the time to act out. He saw that I was cleaning the house, and I had to have it clean before my father got home because my father'd literally inspect. He'd see what was dusted, if things were swept and washed. That was how you did it in the military. He thought he was doing it the way it should be done.*
>
> *Steven went in and started tossing things around the house and messing everything up just to make me angry, and he made me furious. Then he ran into his room and locked the door. I was yelling, "Steven, come out here and*

clean up! Dad's coming home, and you know it and you did this. It's not fair that I have to pick it up!" He wouldn't come out, so I lost it. I went and got a hammer, and I beat the doorknob off the door. I beat it until the door opened. I opened the door and stood there and said, "Get out there and clean it up."

Suddenly, I'm looking at myself holding the hammer. I felt horror. What else was I going to do with the hammer? So I quickly went and put it away.

There was no way to undo what I'd done to the door. Steve got what I'd been trying to say, and he straightened up his stuff, but fear made him understand he should do it. I scared the dickens out of him, but it scared me worse. So when my dad came home, I had to fess up to what I'd done, and he was mad at Steven. So Steven got punished that time, and my punishment was to have to work so many extra hours to pay for the new doorknob. . . .

So I think my earliest sense of injustice had to do with power abused, authority misused, not getting your fair share, not getting your just due as a woman. All of those things made me particularly sensitive to women's place in the world and to people without power and how they get treated by those with power and those in authority.

Then, when I was a teenager, and we were living in Florida, I worked in the migrant camps as part of the CYO, the Catholic Youth Organization. I read to the kids while their parents worked. That became the vehicle of consciousness raising for me. Activist nuns and laypeople from a Catholic worker background thought up the project. They thought that by being there with the migrant workers, we would hear and see the issues and develop empathy for the people. That's exactly what happened.[9]

Pat went to college and continued her involvement with migrant workers; she later entered training for organizing with the United Farm Workers. She helped a successful campaign lobby and organized for a system that changed hiring from crew bosses to hiring halls. After college she worked at the Farm Worker's Health Clinic in Apopka, Florida. Eventually, Pat decided that if she wanted to make a real social change in the world she had to learn more about how political systems functioned. She wanted to know how to protect people against abusive systems. She decided to go to graduate school to get a grounding in political theory and Latin American politics. She observed refugees from the wars in Central America and joined the Sanctuary movement, the campaign that arose when church workers started criticizing the U.S. government and smuggling Central American refugees into the United States.

> *My desire to become a border activist came from this empathy with the plight of people coming north. Their stories raised my consciousness. I transported undocumented refugees and helped as a liaison. It was through relationships and this empathy for the plight of the people coming through that was my entry into wanting to be a border activist. Just hearing the stories was enough of a consciousness raiser for me to realize the seriousness of it....*
> *I was told about a Witness for Peace meeting and went to it. Witness for Peace represented the values and orientation that I really appreciated. It involved working respectfully in Nicaragua, trying to interrupt the war there....*
> *Witness for Peace turned my life around.... I was just blown away by the whole experience. I fell in love with the people in Nicaragua. I fell in love with the country.*[10]

The activists' stories reveal a truth: that involvement in a movement or a cause gave them the tools to organize against injustice. I met Ana Maria Vasquez in the early 2000s at a fund-raiser. An artist from Colombia who lives at times in Tucson and at times in Magdalena, Mexico, she uses remarkable techniques in her organizing. A small woman whose eyes shine with conviction, she is married and has three young children. From Tucson and Magdalena, Ana Maria organizes for progressive causes: women's development, ecological concerns, indigenous rights, and issues of the U.S.-Mexico border. She sells her detailed and emotionally powerful paintings to help support those causes. She often goes back to Colombia to participate in grassroots community programs there. Her paintings serve as consciousness-raising tools, telling complex stories about the movements in which she participates.

> *I was born in 1965 in the highlands of Colombia.... I guess you could say I was an activist child. I think it is something you're born with. I always saw all this injustice. There were all these poor people and people who had a lot, and it seemed like this is not how it should be. I remember there were a lot of street kids in the slums where I lived. I realized that these children were like me, but they were alone. They had no family, no father or mother,*

nothing. I don't think it was ever natural to me. I had an aunt who started a school for the street kids.

My grandmother told us stories when we were young, and she read the chocolate cup [a cup with the remains of cocoa]. I think a lot of the way I draw has to do with that. She would always see images in the chocolate. It was like this is going to happen to you. She would look at a chocolate cup and see the future. My mom does now also. They truly see the things. I don't know how it happens. So sometimes when I paint, I see things like that. Many times I do something, and then people say, "Ohhh, remember you drew such a thing, and it came to be."

After I finished school, I went back to the community in southern Colombia where the women were doing the weavings. That's when I started to work with women's groups, trying to set them up and get them started. This community suffered a massacre in 2004. Thirteen women and a lot of children were cut up in pieces. It was because coal companies wanted to take all their land. The women I worked with needed some looms. So I thought maybe I could sell some paintings and get the looms. A guy did buy the paintings, and we did get the looms, so it was good. I painted a painting of a lady with her little baby in a hammock because they make beautiful hammocks. I represented the women who died and the people who came to them in solidarity. The women from Witness for Peace were there [Witness for Peace was the program in which Pat Manning participated]. I made a poster for publicity. Every year I made one.

Now I make prints with recycled paper made by a women's cooperative that I work with in Panama. Then I sell them. Most people don't have much money, but they can afford the prints. This is a way to make money for the projects I work with.

I'm painting a Border Christ now, and I did a Lady of No Borders. She's the Virgin of Guadalupe, and she is breaking down the border wall. In breaking the wall, she lets the water come in. She gets the animals, the jaguars, and the birds to cross again. And this break is coming about by the people who do the border work. So many people are being the Virgin of Guadalupe breaking the wall. There is also a connection between the dry land and the people who come from the rain forest. . . .

Another painting is of a man in Magdalena. He's crying because he remembers when the river was full of water and they used to swim. He worries what's going to be a life for the little ones if there is no water. There are people fleeing and there is a deer dancer, and the deer are dead. The people

*are running away in fear, maybe tiring of the pollution and the dry rivers
and trying to cross the border and look for the money. The money is full of
blood, and this is not good. There is a deer dancer that jumps in the heart of
the baby. And it shows that maybe tomorrow again the border will become
a park, and the wall will be torn down. The water will come back and the
trees will be planted again, and life again will be good.*

*I did one painting I didn't finish when we had an encounter in Magda-
lena. It was the encounter of all the indigenous people of the Americas. The
Zapatistas came, so we had Commandante Marcos breaking the ribbons.
I think all the people coming from all the continents will open the wall. It's
going to happen eventually. So I'd like to paint all kinds of images of the
wall falling.*

*I think the paintings are good because you can tell so many stories and
you can communicate. I think that the brain communicates faster with a
visual element. I always write things around the paintings I work on.*

*I think about what would make a good or just world. I think it
would be a world where people could live life the size of humans, not
with the material excess that means others might not be able to make it.
But to make life as simple as possible. Small communities with a very
small government. Then people can know each other. I don't think the
nation system will work because the people do not know each other.
They do not care for each other, and it is money that is running everything. Everything is based on if you can raise enough money, not that
you raise enough solidarity.*

*How do you measure things that cannot be measured on a money scale?
You should be measuring on a human scale. If you could do this, then you
can be thinking about the planet too. What the planet needs for the animals,
the plants, and the humans. For all. I hope that it eventually will come to
that, but I think we have a long struggle to grow inside as much as possible
so we can understand.*[11]

Ana Maria's art is extraordinary. Using detailed symbols and metaphors,
her work describes the circumstances of her people, telling their stories and
interpreting their lives. The women whose stories I've collected—Lupe,
Rose, Mary Robinson, Maria Elena, Florence, Pat, and Ana Maria—are
living examples that individuals and groups can serve as agents of change.
Mary Robinson learned tools for her resistance in the labor movement. She
told me about traditional protest actions.

In 1979 we also went up to Washington, D.C., to this BIG labor rally, with people from all over the United States. And we had a ball. We took several buses from here, and the buses had microphones on them. So I went from bus to bus, leading people in singing labor songs, telling stories. I'd get one bus all laughing and militant, then I'd go to the next.

The rally was at the Labor Department. It tried to pressure Congress to give disability for workers with lung disease. I'll never forget it. It was so many coal miners with black lung and so many people that worked in the mills and had brown lung. I felt awed to see all those people wheeled in wheelchairs because they was cut or maimed or sick. I remember an old woman on oxygen whose face was as wrinkled as a dry field. Every year she worked etched itself in her face. She was used up, like nobody was there. She just gasped. A man came who lost both his legs. Some of the sick workers wore big brown buttons that said "Cotton Dust Kills" and little yellow buttons that said "And it's Killing Me." Thousands and thousands of people had brown lung, byssinosis, at that time. We sang labor songs. . . .

I looked up while we was singing, and all the workers in the Labor Department stood at the window watching us while we pushed peoples up there in wheelchairs. And we had told the sick people to bring all they empty medicine bottles and put them up there on the porch. It be like a truckload of medicine that people had to take to survive from diseases they got working in these industries. We dumped the empty medicine bottles on the labor steps. It be just heart wrenching.

Then they called the police on us. . . . The next thing we knowed, they took about forty people who was right in front down to jail!

But it was worth it because Congress passed a bill that said that brown lung was a disabling disease, and now anybody diagnosed with brown lung can get disability. We was dead and determined to make change for the people in ALL the textile plants, and we did.[12]

Mary was strengthened and inspired by her experience in the protest. It made clear that her struggle was part of something larger. It was a victory that gave her energy; she would continue her organizing with exuberance and joy.

For my book *Dignity: Lower Income Women Tell of Their Lives and Struggles,* Irene Mack Pyawasit talked about the tools she had used for organizing throughout her social activism.

Along with being in show business [a circus], I've been involved in tribal politics since the early thirties. Because of that I did a lot of research about problems for Indians. I was the first woman in our tribe to ever represent them in Washington as an official delegate. I am a registered lobbyist for the federal House and the Senate. Since then the doors have opened, and other women are in there now.

The senators and congressmen paid attention to me. I don't know whether it was tolerance or shock. But, after a while, it got to be respect because I had always done my homework before I went into those offices. And I learned that many ways to a congressman or senator's heart is by observation. When I would walk in the door of their office, I would look around and would try to find something there that would tell me what his hobby or his personal delight was. It might only be a pine cone or rocks displayed. I would comment on those items so that he would raise his eyebrows and open his ears, and we would have a common ground to stand on.

It was always quite a shock to them when they found a woman was there instead of all males. During the time I was there I never allowed the men to even carry my briefcase. I carried my own weight, and when we got through in the evening, we used to go to my room where I'd type up and get material organized for the next day's meeting. . . .

They had a little chapel there, for all denominations, and every once in a while I'd go in and just sit there and relax and pray. If a bill came up that we were really interested in or something very serious, I'd stop in there and ask for help from the Creator. I'd ask the Creator to guide my feet and especially put the right words in my mouth. I'd also ask that I wouldn't flip my lid or blow my stack. I'd ask him to help me keep my temper and help me be a pacifist instead of a militant so we'd be more successful.[13]

Irene's experience of being the sole female in an often male-dominated environment highlights her courage and commitment to the causes she believes in. The activists I've interviewed reacted in a variety of ways to their participation or leadership in various social movements as women. Maria Elena Lucas eloquently spoke about the overt sexism she experienced as a farm labor organizer. In the summer of 1985 she and three other women and their children from Onarga, Illinois, traveled to the fields of Ohio to organize for FLOC (the Farm Labor Organizing Committee) under the leadership of Baldemar Velásquez. She recounted that experience.

It was a very hard summer, very hard for all of us. It was a terrible year in many ways. There were a lot of threats to the organizers and to the workers if they signed up for our union, and we were very harassed by the growers, and Baldemar—or Balde, as we called him—was under a lot of pressure. But we'd finally begun real union organizing where we could try to have a union and bargain for contracts.

Many things happened when we did this. For one thing, people who were against us tried to blackmail the women organizers. One time I had to stop at a camp and tell the people there, "I've come with your membership cards." The men were playing dice and cards when I got there. The guys that had become members were very respectful, but another guy said, "Oh, you're an organizer for FLOC." And right away, I noticed the expression on the rest of the men's faces, like they were trying to communicate a message, but I couldn't understand. Then the guy says, "I'm going to be in another town with a whole bunch of farm workers, and I bet they'd all sign their cards if you meet me there."

So I took the direction, and when I was in that place, I started to look for him. Finally, I found him in his apartment, and it turned out that he really didn't have any influence over anybody, he was just trying to get me alone.

He tried to get me to drink with him, but I told him, "Wait, I'm not wasting my time with you. What I'm doing is very serious and means a lot to me. You've got the wrong person. Don't ever do this again!" And I got out of there, but I was afraid because he could have hurt me.

Later we found out that the crew leaders were using men to try to entice the women organizers. One time a crew leader asked me to come to talk to him in a camp on a certain day. So when I arrived, the crew leader comes out of his house with a bottle of tequila and says, "Come on, how about a drink?"

It was a very hot day, but I said, "No, I'm not here to take drinks. I'm sorry, but I came to talk to you." I'd been very happy when I heard he wanted to talk to me. I'd thought, "My gosh, maybe I've convinced that guy," but, instead he pulled me into the house and practically began to stick the bottle down my throat. I kept saying, "No, wait a minute. I don't drink, and I'm not here to take a drink. I'm not even thirsty. I came here because you said you wanted to talk."

Then it turns out there's a guy in there with a tape recorder and a cam-

era, waiting for me so he could take pictures of me drinking with the crew leader in order to make the union look bad. I got very mad. "I'm leaving!" I yelled and got out of there. . . .[14]

> But there were other issues for us women that summer, with our own leaders who we really looked up to. Balde and his assistant were very dictatorial. I couldn't understand what was happening and why, but they were very into discipline. We women weren't supposed to talk together at night. We weren't supposed to say absolutely nothing to each other about what happened to us during our day while we were out organizing. I began to think that maybe they really didn't really trust us women, and as the weeks went by, we began to whisper together at night. . . .
>
> FLOC made it like everything had to be a test of courage, we had to be real tough people and take whatever came. . . . I was OK by myself, but I was real worried about the younger women. . . . It seemed so strange to talk all the time about the need to discipline. We were all adults. We were all working for something good.[15]

These were painful experiences for Maria Elena. The sexism of the leaders she had so admired was devastating. She wondered if she, too, without the constraints on her as a woman, could have been a labor leader.

I met with Kat Rodriguez in 2008, a forceful, young Tejana (a Mexican American woman from Texas). Majoring in sculpture in college, she had campaigned for farmworker rights in Florida through the Coalition for Immokalee Workers. At one point, the coalition organized a 233-mile march through Florida to raise awareness among the general public about the struggle of farmworkers.

> I ended up making a big farmworker puppet and banners for them [the marchers] because of my art background. Then I made his huge statue that was thirteen feet tall that was going to lead the march.
>
> It was a Statue of Liberty holding a bucket of tomatoes instead of a book, and I made her dark like me. I went and matched the paint to my skin color, so she has black hair and my skin color and a wide nose and cheeks. And I made her on a pedestal that said, "I, too, am America," from the Langston Hughes poem.[16]

While on the march, Kat fell in love for the first time, with an undocumented immigrant farmworker. Although the relationship did not work
out, it raised her consciousness about farmworker and immigrant causes,
and Kat became devoted to the farmworker and Chicano movements. She
eventually moved to Tucson, where she deepened her commitment to the
movement and joined the staff of the Coalición de Derechos Humanos, a
human rights organization that criticizes U.S. border policy, supports immigrant rights, and follows up on border deaths. She talked about problems
for women in the Chicano movement, including the mainstream's fear of
"angry brown women."

> *I think it's also difficult to be a woman in the movement because there
> aren't men lining up to date women in the movement. Some Chicano men
> in the movement have no idea what to do with us because there's a lot of
> sexism in our culture. It's like you want your brown sister by your side in
> the fight but not in the morning. And people in general are scared of power-
> ful women of color. There is this fear of an angry brown person and an
> extra fear of angry brown women.*
>
> *I try to take care of myself by having a little balance, stealing a day off or
> going on a road trip with friends. If you don't, you just get consumed. The
> movement is greedy and it's jealous and it's consuming and will take every-
> thing you give it if you don't claim something for yourself. So I take time for
> my friends. And I live for the sunsets in Arizona.*[17]

Kat, honest and forthright, knew the causes and costs of the movement.
She has continued to provide leadership to the progressive community in
Tucson, especially emphasizing the rights of immigrants.

Lupe Castillo, another activist I interviewed in 2008, also talked about
women's involvement in the Chicano movement and her desires as a leader.
She critiqued the movement but also saw value in community building and
benefits in being inclusive.

> *I've been in movements for a long time. Certainly, when I was younger,
> there were leaders I looked up to. Obviously César Chávez with the farm-
> workers and Bert Corona for immigrant rights. Here in Tucson, there were
> people in the community who were older and who'd been struggling for a
> long time. I remember them being involved in the urban renewal struggle,*

the model cities, and the war on poverty. Also, I remember union people. Later, when we were organizing a political party call La Raza, we had a model like Rudy Garcia, who'd been an organizer for the copper union.

There were also a lot of women. Most were based in their community and really working hard to make Tucson Unified School District better. They also came out to the boycott marches and the marches we had for the golf course. [They were trying to make a golf course in the middle of a very poor Chicano neighborhood into a public park.] There were always a lot of women, but they were not seen as being in leadership. But they were there and helping us make decisions and supporting us or pushing us. Plus cooking a lot of food.

I remember Mrs. Rodriguez, who is long deceased. There was a private golf course, El Rio, right in the middle of very poor Chicano families who didn't have a park. The Chicano House began to take out petitions requesting to meet with the city to have the golf course turned into a park. It was a very long and very involved struggle. We had a long strike. People were arrested; there were sit-ins, marches. It was one of the most intense periods of activism for all of us on the west side.

And Mrs. Rodriguez was always there, encouraging us to even be more radical. Like the day I'll never forget. She just picked up the Mexican flag and said, "Let's go in the golf course," and she led us in, and we marched behind her. There were many, sadly unrecognized, women who were active.

Ultimately we got part of the parking lot at the golf course and established the El Rio Neighborhood Center. We also got the park, not far away.

I wasn't interested in being a leader. That was a choice of mine. I didn't find it as inspiring, as energizing as being someone who was thinking things out, sitting down, discussing, giving form to things, then making them happen. My interest was to be part of a movement.

I'm not saying I wasn't a leader. If I've had to assert leadership, I've done it, but leadership to me is the face of the social movement, the one who gives an expression of vision and who inspires. I think the strongest leaders are those who build a community around them in which the leadership's shared. It debilitates a movement not to be inclusive.[18]

Maria Elena, Kat, and Lupe used what we might call intersectional analysis when they interpreted what had happened to them. They saw the systems of oppression as enmeshed and mutually reinforcing.

All the activist women I have interviewed wanted to promote a collective history or memory of their people's struggle for a better world. Such histories or memories tell the stories of specific groups of people from that group's viewpoint. For example, Raquel Rubio-Goldsmith collected stories of undocumented immigrants along the U.S.-Mexico border. The women activists consciously undertook such activities as recording people's stories, writing records, teaching about people who had often been excluded from the history of the dominant culture, and smuggling documents in an attempt to save lives and change U.S. policy. Throughout their efforts, these women worked so that the voices from below—those blighted by various racial, class, gender, and national oppressions—would not be silenced. Another example is Rose Augustine, the Mexican American community organizer I interviewed beginning in 1988, who videotaped victims telling of their experiences of the toxic dumping of TCE before they died.

Ana Maria Vasquez's paintings illustrate a striking case in point of an activist's attempt to create a collective memory. One specific painting especially speaks to me because of my location in Tucson, so close to the border. It shows a Mexican man holding an infant whose face is patient and hopeful. The man's hat represents abundance: a woman feeds a child by a flowing river, a person dives into the water, trees grow, a bird flies, and horses run free. A tree grows up the man's neck and stretches its branches out into the man's hat. A tear flows down his face and becomes a resurrected river from which deer drink and above which birds fly. The man's hand, caressing the child, has a Yaqui deer dancer in it. A saguaro cactus with a great horned owl sits at his elbow. To the man's right is Mexico, represented by workers in a field, mesquite trees, a little creek, and a cornfield that becomes an ear of corn, a procession, and a dance.

To the left, however, is the impoverished and polluted Mexican city of Nogales, where the U.S.-owned factories spew out chemicals. There we also see the wall. We then reach the Sonoran desert, where undocumented immigrants try to cross on foot. We see footprints of immigrants, small groups of people hiking through the desert, a dead body, a trail of blood, Border Patrol, and discarded and empty water bottles. The Yaqui deer dancer watches it all in sorrow. Finally, uphill and to the north is Tucson, the destination of the immigrants, with its relatively rich neighborhoods in the foothills and their expensive homes. Above it all, the sun turns through its cycle and keeps watch. Ana Maria's painting tells the story of U.S. exploitation of Mexico, the sadness of sacred images in the deer dancer, the wall, the path that un-documented immigrants follow through the desert heading north, their of-ten agonizing deaths, and the relative wealth of the U.S. cities.

Similarly, Maria Elena Lucas hopes to create a collective memory through her Third Testament, a document in which she can tell the stories of poor, undocumented Mexicans and people along the U.S.-Mexico border. As written in her own diary in 1990:

> *Dear God,*
> *Here I is, at the town of Padilla Tamaulipas, Mexico. Pablo and I are*
> *with José Hernández in his red van. . . . [They get out of the van, then she*
> *continues.] There is a little boy, dark skin, cold, dirty, covered with a sleeve-*
> *less raggedy cotton jacket. I go into this narrow 2 × 8 opening; he's laying*
> *on the bare floor, filthy, ugly-smelling floor. I woke him up; he said he's from*
> *Monterrey. He's sick, has no home. I give him a dollar, not enough, that's all*
> *I had.*[19]

Maria Elena hopes that her Third Testament will somehow affect justice debates and bring about policy changes in this area.

As part of her lifetime of activism, Irene Mack Pyawasit also tried to col-lect knowledge for her people. She prepared boxes of cassette tapes telling the stories and legends of the Menominee only to have them stolen during a burglary. She talked to me about telling those stories, emphasizing how important the audience is to the success of storytelling.

> *I've been doing a little bit of writing, as I think about it, trying to recall*
> *the stories. I give them to my son up north so he and his wife can take care*
> *of them. They are the stories I recall, the creation stories, the legends, the*
> *myths as white society calls them. Some might be just humorous stories, and*
> *humorous stories told in our language are really funny.*
>
> *But if you try to translate them into English, they're the driest damn*
> *things. There is no way to describe the meaning in English because with the*
> *gestures, the tone of voice, and the words we use, we just don't know how*
> *to put them in the right sequence in English. But when the old folks get*
> *together and start telling stories, they have all of us rocking with laughter.*
>
> *It means a lot to me that I can carry down what I learned from my*
> *grandmother to my grandchildren and my great-grandchildren.*[20]

Union activist Mary Robinson so deeply desired to create a collective memory that she and I walked the approximately one and a half square miles of rural Elmore County, Alabama, north of Montgomery, and made complicated white and black kinship charts of the people who had lived there. We mapped all the locations of her childhood, including now destroyed creeks, woods, cotton fields, sharecropper cabins, and white owners' homes. Mary also drew the setting of the two black churches, Good Hope and New Style. The African American residents had given their neighborhoods the names of these two churches. The community had not been recorded on any official road maps and thus had been erased by the dominate white establishment. After we finished creating the map, Mary and I went to the county archives, where we traced the official records of the neighborhood. Often all we found was an "X" where some illiterate sharecropper had attempted to make his or her mark.

This desire on the part of an activist to teach about and record collective history was directly expressed to me by Raquel Rubio-Goldsmith. Raquel, a graceful Chicana in her late sixties, and I met in Tucson shortly after Maria Elena and I had published *Forged under the Sun* in 1993. Raquel taught the book in her university classes. I started to interview her in 2008 as part of Josefina Castillo's and my collection of interviews of U.S.-Mexico border activists. Raquel came from a working-class home in Douglas, Arizona. Douglas was a mining town with a large Mexican American population and segregated schools.

> *The school segregation experience taught me about injustice early, and there was always a lot of talk about injustice in my home. "No, that's not right. That shouldn't be that way."* . . .
>
> *When I was about thirteen or fourteen, my best friend . . . became seriously ill. I would go and pray for her every day that summer. I was convinced that she was going to be all right. I thought she was very sick, but it was not like she was going to die. And then she did. And I just became so angry with God.*
>
> *But we had a wonderful Irish parish priest, Father McGovern, who kept an eye on our family and knew us all. I remember going to him and telling him, "I can't come to Communion because I'm angry with God, and I don't love him because he really betrayed me."*
>
> *The priest looked right at me and said, "Your feelings have nothing to do with that. If everybody that got angry with God stopped taking Commu-*

nion, nobody would be there. *This is when you need God more than ever. Feelings are not what makes a difference with God. Love is something you do. You have to do the right thing no matter what you feel.*"[21]

Raquel took seriously the priest's injunction that love requires action, including political action. She finished her segregated school and graduated at fifteen. She was sent by her family to live with an aunt in Mexico, where she attended college at the university in Mexico City. There powerful women surrounded her. Eventually Raquel studied philosophy and went to law school. She was interested in Marxist ideas and helped set up support groups for such things as the railroad unions, which were going on strike. The strikes served as a consciousness-raising experience for her and she participated in demonstrations. She married, had two sons, lived in Yucatán for a time, then Washington, D.C. The family moved to Tucson, where Raquel continued her activism and helped set up a community college that taught Women's Studies and Chicano history. She represented the refugees that were fleeing to the United States during the wars in Central America, and their stories affected her profoundly. Today, as part of her lifetime of organizing, she collects stories of undocumented immigrants. She told me why this work is so important.

It's important that the stories of the ones who suffered get told. I still teach Mexicana and Chicana history, and in my courses, I really try to break down the kind of great woman or great man type of history, which so many students come in with. I try to teach about why a particular moment of change occurs, where it comes from, and the what the stories are. I teach that there are always counterstories at the same time. Counterstories are stories that go against the dominant voices in history. Counterstories are like that of the young woman from El Salvador [with whom she worked in the Sanctuary movement] or the undocumented immigrants that are coming now. I am really concerned about the voices that never make it into what we call history.

In the course, we ask the question why, and I talk about the silence of women and where we can find the stories of these silenced women, whether it's in the records of the Inquisition or whether it's in court records. . . .

Also, we should give some energy to deciding what deserves to be remembered. All aspects of human activity are important, but I am concerned with the collective memory of our struggle for a better world.[22]

Pat Manning, the peace and border activist from Tucson, worked in the war zone in Nicaragua for four years. A white woman, she helped victims of the conflict rebuild infrastructure, she documented abuse, and she went under cover to smuggle information into Guatemala about how the United States was fighting against the government in Nicaragua. This was an attempt to safeguard documents of collective memory.

I also went to Guatemala under cover. My cover story was that I was an anthropology graduate student studying some of the traditional cultures of the highlands. I would be focusing on textiles or something. Since I didn't have much money, I would stay wherever I could, and the good nuns would take me into the parish school where they taught elementary education. I was, in fact, bringing in documents from the Guatemalan Church in Exile, the IGE or Iglesia Guatemalteca En Exilio, to Nicaragua to be fact-checked by networks there through the Quiché bishop, Don Julio Carera. So I would show up with the paperwork and give them to him, and he would give them to the right people, who would check them and get them back to me. Then I would smuggle them back to IGE in Managua.

I remember that particular trip to Quiché. That was one of the times I was most scared because I was carrying those documents that named names of people and villages and how many people had been killed in each one and the dates. So it was documentary evidence of the Guatemalan government's campaign of terror against the indigenous Maya and the systematic destruction of their communities.

I carried the documents in my backpack. I did a lot of embroidery for gifts, and I set up fairly thick cardboard in the back of my backpack. I cut slits on the top of the cardboard, and I wrapped embroidery threads of different colors around the slits. Then I would pull out the threads from all these different skeins when I needed them. I used that as the false back to my backpack. I put papers behind it. In front of it I had a change of clothes and academic-looking books in English.

If someone unzipped my backpack and looked in, that person would not see the papers. Obviously, it would be easy to pull out the cardboard and look behind, but if someone just looked casually, the person wouldn't notice.

I had a couple of close calls. The worst one was when I was in the capital and going to another appointment with people that worked for a labor union. It was one of the groups threatened by the military because of organizing. I'd vary my routines anyway, but on the way I noticed that this guy followed me. No matter which side of the street I was on, he was there. He had a shorter haircut, looked really buff, physically strong, and I thought, I don't know what his intentions are. I don't know if they are sexual. I don't know if they're political. Why is he following me?

So I sat in a café and had a latte and read the newspaper, and he still followed me. I went quickly back to the guesthouse where I was staying, packed up, checked out, and apologized for leaving earlier than planned. I caught a taxi. I never took taxis because I'd walk or take a bus. It was a lot of money for me on my salary, but I took a taxi and went to the main transportation hub area where all the buses for the different parts of the countryside gathered. The person following me would think I was going out.

I walked around and jumped into another cab and checked into another hotel in the same zone. I had to be in zone one in the capital where I could meet with people. Then I just walked around. I called my friends at the labor union from a pay phone and said, "I've been followed. I don't know what it means. I'm canceling my appointment for today. I'll check in later." I told them where I was staying in case anything happened. Then I didn't notice the guy following me anymore, but I was scared.

Another time was also threatening. I was on a rural bus in Quiché, and the men in charge were hassling a guy who was drunk who also rode the bus. He didn't have any money to pay, and they were going to throw him off. I was in the middle of this physically, and there was nowhere else to go. The men in charge started bringing me into it. It was, "What are you doing?" because all this was happening in front of the gringa. "Cancha," I think, is the Guatemalan term for a fair-skinned, fair-haired person. I didn't like being brought into the middle of it at all. I wanted to get off, and they didn't want to let me off.

I didn't know anybody there. If it got out of hand, not only was my person at stake but all the information I carried was too. I thought, how else can I resolve this? I've got all these papers with me. So I paid the drunk guy's fare, and that defused it. I said, "Let him alone. He's having a hard day, and I've got things to do." After some teasing, they left him and me alone.

I felt a tremendous responsibility not to do anything that would further endanger the survivors or their support networks assisting them—especially those in Guatemala, but also those in exile. On the trip itself, I felt like I needed God to be with me the whole time. Sitting around the bonfire outside at night was reassuring, waiting for people to come back with edited

documents. Certainly, I understood the presence of the sacred as they did
everything they could to get the word out about what was really going on
in Guatemala. They also undertook efforts to assure the survival of their
cultures and people. It was pretty much a war of annihilation against the
indigenous people and culture.[23]

Pat's sense of responsibility about the facts of U.S. government policies
toward Guatemala and her concerns about the fate of Central Americans
inspired her to risk her life. In the process, she tells a riveting story of courageous attempts to preserve collective memory. Today Pat works helping
undocumented prisoners in the U.S. detention centers.

The activists who tell their stories talk about the turning points in their
lives when they perceived conditions as unjust. They talk about the training and support they received from social movements. They describe both
well-known and individualistic forms of protest activity. Sometimes using
symbols and metaphors, they express their beliefs and observations. Finally,
they attempt to preserve collective histories and memories through creative
and courageous undertakings.

CHAPTER 8

Activism and Spirituality
"Like a Conversion"

Only Lupe Castillo, of the activist women I have interviewed, was nonspiritual, although she told me she respected the fact that she worked in a deeply religious community. The other activists found that their spirituality helped them in their various undertakings. A number of the women critiqued the political and economic system they lived in according to a religious vision of what a good or just society should be. For example, border activist Bernie Mueller, an elderly Tucson woman I interviewed in 2004, was appalled to find agents from the country she loved murdering thousands of Central Americans.

Maria Elena Lucas, the farmworker poet from Texas, and Ana Maria Vasquez, the Colombian artist, each used Christian and indigenous spiritual symbols in their work. Because of their profound experiences in suffering communities, they were able to build on these symbols and propel them toward new meanings. In the process, Maria Elena and Ana Maria took old methods of resistance, such as political poetry and art, and reimagined them. To not deal with their religious visions and actions would be to silence them.[1] But religion also had the power to bind some of the women I've interviewed to oppression. Sometimes this was caused by an outside force, as in Irene Mack Pyawasit's situation as a Menominee child in a mission boarding school. As she told me:

> When I was in boarding school, they tried to break me down, but I never did break. My grandmother taught me too well. She told me, "I'm going to teach you not to be afraid," and she did a pretty good job of it.
>
> I was in a day school at the reservation for a while, and then the government had a habit of picking up kids and deciding who was going to the

mission boarding schools and who was going to the government boarding schools. Parents really didn't have too much choice. First, I was sent to a mission school, and my grandmother didn't like it. She felt the devil about it. . . .

My grandmother knew they were going to whitewash us [the Menominee children]. She knew the methods they employ, and she knew that we were going to have to learn to speak nothing but English because they were not going to let us speak our own language, and they would try to take our religion away. She said, "You have to keep our religion inside of us, in your heart."[2]

Irene kept her beliefs but suffered greatly under the dominant religious structures of the boarding school system. Nevertheless, she was able to maintain her personal integrity by standing up to their humiliations and punishments. Other women underwent such severe religious constrictions of their spirits that in their memories they had oppressed themselves. Referring to her time in an orphanage, for example, Helen Drazenovich Berklich, the daughter of Yugoslavian immigrants in northern Minnesota, said:

And I want you to know. I felt the fires of hell burning many a time. We were taught not to do things, not to lie. Don't tell stories, don't steal, don't do this or that. We were taught that hell was the punishment for sins.

We never got the same food as the nuns and the priests got. Once I was working in the kitchen and was in the walk-in cooler, and there was the most beautiful slice of beef, a whole platter of beef sitting there. And I ate a great big piece. I don't think I even chewed it. I just swallowed it down. You know what day that was? Friday. [Catholics at that time were not allowed to eat meat on Friday.] And that night we had holy hour. Now don't say that you can't culture people and train them. I could feel that fire of hell. I cried. I was upset. Sister Julianna got me when we got outside, and she said, "Helen, what is your problem?"

I said, "Sister, I ate meat today, and I'm gonna go to hell!"

And she said, "Oh, don't worry about that. God'll forgive you. You don't know how glad I was to hear that.

Later we made our First Communion in there, and we had to go to confession. That's like going to hell, too. Everything was a sin. Holy cats, everything, which was going too far. And we prayed, we prayed all the time. All the time. If there was a fire, if the grass wouldn't grow, if someone was bad, for any little thing, we prayed. Maybe that was good, too; maybe that's what made us good, strong, and honest people. But, still, it was hard.

We did a lot of penance. Usually Sister would take away our syrup for our oatmeal, or we'd have to kneel on two pieces of wood in the middle of a floor for an hour and say five rosaries to so many Hail Marys or Our Fathers. We didn't really deserve to be punished that way.[3]

This form of oppression inflicted on oneself is possibly even more destructive than external forms of oppression.

Lilly Baker and Audrey Jones—both of whom I interviewed in 1980—drew from the religious traditions of Appalachia. Understanding that background is key to understanding how these women defined their lives, values, and priorities for themselves. Their sense of independence and distrust of religious hierarchies was rooted in the Protestant evangelical tendencies of the region's pioneers. The ecstatic behaviors of the small, unaffiliated congregations in rural areas were first manifested in revivals. The historian John Alexander Williams has written about the characteristics of rural Appalachian congregations, stating that the faith was founded on inner convictions derived from their pietistic roots—beliefs that stressed personal religious experience and Bible study. The worshipers in these mountainous congregations take part in sacramental rituals, such as foot washing, the Lord's Supper, and adult baptism by immersion. Ministers chant when they preach, and the congregation calls back to them. They hold camp meetings, sacramental meetings, and revivals. The churches are egalitarian within the congregations but patriarchal. "Religion became one of the identifying marks of Appalachian culture," Williams explains, "but a religion that dwelt on the inevitability of sin also preached a gospel of salvation."[4]

In 1980, I attended one of these mountain churches with Lilly, who was seventy-six at the time. It met in the evening, a long drive up mountain roads. The congregation warmly welcomed me as Lilly's guest. Above the altar hung a sequined painting describing the characteristics of a preacher. It included the phrase "a husband to one wife," which I took to mean that the preacher would have to live up to sexual moral codes. Plainly dressed men and women sang songs together and played instruments; children wandered back and forth in the aisle, then the preacher broke into his chantlike preaching. Congregation members responded to him, becoming increasingly alive to the spirit. The preacher directed much of his preaching to me, calling on me to give up sin and commit myself to Jesus. Lilly looked at me from time to time, her eyes shining. Suddenly the congregation began speaking in tongues—something I'd never experienced before. When the service was over, Lilly said to me, "He's my favorite preacher because he preaches against sin." Traditional Appalachian religion provided Lilly with a belief system that encouraged individual conversion and mission. Her religion kept her faithful to what she believed was her God-given task: to care for the "sick and afflicted" throughout her long life.

Audrey Jones, whose husband Lonnie had been falsely imprisoned in Kentucky, struggled with her similar religious heritage. She and Lonnie had been good people in Audrey's estimation. They had not committed sins. Why, then, had something so terrible happened to them? Audrey never found her answer throughout our long acquaintance, but she depended on the religion of her childhood. It gave her social contacts and provided her with the only symbols for meaning she was able to discover in her setting. The farmworker and poet Maria Elena Lucas also absorbed psychological constrictions from her religion. She talked about a time in her adulthood when she felt guilt about living with her partner Pablo without being married.

> *I felt terrible guilt and pain about our being together. I'd been married in the church, and now I was living with another man. I tried to get lost so the family wouldn't know. But my shame came to me in my dreams.*
>
> *I walked into a house. I think it was my mother's. I saw the Virgin of San Juan in a picture. I stood in amazement because her eyes were burned.*
>
> *"Mother, what's wrong with the Virgin? Why are her eyes burned?"*
>
> *The Virgin keeps looking at me very sad, she can hardly look at me, and she says, "My daughter, your mother burned them as a promise, so that you would return to your house, and because of you I am suffering, and you are living in sin and I am punished for that. You should leave him and not live with him until you are married by the church."*[5]

Maria Elena felt oppressed by religion during much of her preorganizing life. When she finally came in contact with people from the farmworker movement, they helped her to build on her internal rebellion. In this way, Maria Elena was able to create for herself an alternative, liberated spiritual conception. Many of the activist women I've interviewed felt supported by their religion or their spiritual understandings in their lives of protest and the building of new communities. Jacky Turchick, a Jewish woman living in Tucson whom I interviewed between 2005 and 2010, remembers a dream during her childhood in which she answered a call of God. She recalled:

> *Sometime . . . in the '40s, I dreamed a picture of the earth, and it felt as if God was calling me in my sleep. In Judaism, when you hear a story where God calls, you say, "Here I am." I guess because I am shy, I said, "Who?" and then said, "Here I am."*
>
> *The earth looked like a jewel in my dream and was so beautiful. When I woke up, I thought, "The earth is a jewel." The message seemed to be, "It's God's planet." My dad was a scientist so I'm sure he must have brought the earth up so my brain could have the connection. To my child self, it was a religious experience. It's a whole area that I struggle with because I don't know how to understand it, exactly.*[6]

Later in her life, when confronted by the moral problem of smuggling war refugees from Central America north to safety, Jacky in effect answered God's call: "Here I am." She gave her baby to her husband to care for, and she volunteered for the dangerous task. In the process, Jacky risked her life. Rose Augustine, a Mexican American community organizer in Tucson whom I first interviewed in 1988, expressed how she depended on God in her activism:

> *When I think what happened to me, I was in training from a very young age. Maybe God gave me that certain stubbornness. Every time I've testified before Congress or given testimony elsewhere, I've always prayed to God to give me the strength, to put the words in my mouth, because what I am going to say is going to affect thousands or millions of lives. That's a big load on your back. Sometimes I've been speechless, but also words have come out of my mouth that I am surprised about.*
>
> *I know God is with me, and I have personally felt the hand of God, his love. My mother was dying, and I was all alone with her, and it was tough. They had told me my mother had a few hours to live, and I was trying to figure out what I could do, how can I please her.*
>
> *I felt so alone. And basically, when we go out as activists, we're alone. You have so many people against you, those that are so powerful. In the airport, you're alone. You're traveling, you're alone.*
>
> *And that time when my mother was dying, I just held her in my arms,*

and when she took her last breath, I felt like something in her just exploded. It shook us both because I was holding her tight. And love just washed over both of us. It was a tremendous feeling. I've never experienced that before, and I don't know if I will ever experience that again.

Afterward, I kept thinking, "What was the message here?" And I think God was trying to tell me, "You're not alone. No matter what you do, how hard it is. I am with you." And when that happened with my mom, I felt very much at peace. I felt that she left me with the knowledge that I'm not alone. God was trying to tell me that.[7]

Maria Elena, like Rose, talked to me about depending on God during her public speaking.

When we first started doing the Teatro Campesino and I started doing public speaking, I just had to depend on God. I kept saying, "I don't have the vocabulary. I don't have what it takes to talk to people." But I prayed and prayed, and I knew I had to do it because nobody else was going to, and I knew that God would help me. . . . My writing and my religion and my politics are all part of the same thing, they all go together. Many of my feelings come from my care and loving for Mother Earth. And I think my creativity comes from so much suffering also, so much oppression, which is where my desire to organize comes from also. Going through so much hell sensitizes you. And I think my creativity comes from God. I can be creative 'cause God was creative first.[8]

Rose and Maria Elena both claim that the sacred not only helps them in their political work but is the very basis of that undertaking. Modeling her creativity on God, Maria Elena believes that her love for Mother Earth and the planet's suffering inspires her work. Both women feel religion is at their core and without it they would be altered beyond recognition.

Irene Mack Pyawasit, an indigenous Menominee living in Milwaukee, talked to me about how she had fought for her spiritual beliefs throughout her life. These beliefs, no matter where Irene was in her existence, stayed with her.

There are a lot of people I know through politics, and I've also been with a lot of people because of my religion. My present husband, Wallace, is a leader in the Indian religion we have, the Big Drum. We travel an awful lot, and we visit prisons, too, because of the Indian inmates who are there. We conduct services for them, and then we have visitation with them. They give us three or four hours instead of half an hour or forty-five minutes to be with the prisoners. It means a lot to the prisoners, and they look forward to it. We get a great deal of response from them.

We don't talk much about our religion, and the reason is that in the translation it gets distorted. Sometimes the meaning is lost. It's really hard to speak about it in depth, to explain it so that if it's written on a piece of paper people could understand it. When there's the written word. People immediately begin to imagine things other than what is down there because they don't have that in-depth perception; they have illusion. Very rarely do we invite outsiders into our services, because unless we have known them a long time, we know they aren't going to understand.

My children and grandchildren already have knowledge of it. My grandchild, just six years old, knows what it's all about. He knows that when it's time for the Big Drum services, it's time for silence and careful listening and praying and singing, and, for the men and boys, it means dancing, but not the type of dancing that you see out in these fun powwows. It's a different type altogether. These are prayer dances.[9]

Irene guarded her narrative during our interviews, carefully steering around her sacred beliefs. I was careful not to inquire about subjects she chose not to mention. Nevertheless, the recitation of other stories made it clear how deeply she cherished her spiritual convictions and how much she wanted to share them with other Menominee people.

Lupe Castillo, whom I interviewed in 2009 as part of my U.S.-Mexico border project, talked about liberation theology, a religious belief system that greatly influenced the Central American war refugees with whom she worked. Although Lupe was not a Christian herself, she was respectful of the ideology.

I really appreciated the liberation theology that often was part of their lives. Liberation theology centers on Jesus, not as a do-gooder, but as an organizer for social change. As the theologians of liberation would say, Jesus was a revolutionary, someone who is bringing radical change to a society. It aims for a society that implements the teachings of Jesus in real, concrete ways. The theology of liberation attempts to not only liberate a community but to free people's minds and hearts so they can liberate themselves from the

*colonial constrictions that have been tying them down. It frees your heart
and your mind to understand why you are living the way you are and that
it's OK to change it. That is what Jesus would have done.*

*The transformation of the Central Americans' lives often began in base
communities. A base community would be a small affinity group of people
coming together—maybe to share a problem of not having water. First you
communicate to each other and analyze why there is not water. Then you
take action to get it.*[10]

Lupe deeply appreciated the depth of influence liberation theology would
have in the lives of the people to whom she was so dedicated. She analyzed
it carefully, recognizing aspects of it she felt had the potential to induce profound change. Liberation theology influenced other women I've interviewed
over the years, including Raquel Rubio-Goldsmith, Pat Manning, and Kat
Rodriguez. This theology also touched the people who had an impact on
Maria Elena, so it also indirectly shaped her beliefs.

Born in 1925, Bernie Mueller, a white woman and mother of eight who became a nurse, grew up surrounded by her family's Catholicism. These spiritual beliefs framed Bernie's life. When activists exposed her to the Central
American cause, she experienced her response as a conversion.

*As an adult, my consciousness raising began on what I think was July
4, 1980 [when Bernie was living in Tucson with her husband and children].
They found Salvadorans dead or close to death in the desert in Organ
Pipe National Monument. It was in all the papers. We wondered why the
Salvadorans were coming here. There had always been Mexicans coming,
but the people from El Salvador had to cross Guatemala, all of Mexico to
get here. Why? Gradually, I learned about the U.S.-backed wars in Central
America.*

*Finding out about Central America was like a conversion for me. It
still affects me. Last night I went to a kindergarten graduation, and they
pledged allegiance and sang "God Bless America." We all went through
that learning. My country, right or wrong. Throughout school, you learn
to be good patriotic citizens without knowing what our country had done.
In history, you learn something about the Indians, they couldn't keep that
quiet, but you don't know anything about having Marines in Nicaragua. I
always wonder what was Teddy Roosevelt doing in Cuba. The same thing*

with the Philippines. You don't learn that, but finding out about the murder
in Central America converted me.

The way I got involved in the Sanctuary movement [in which North
Americans smuggled Central American refugees to shelter] was going to
South Side Presbyterian Church. They had a meeting one time in July in
the old sanctuary, and it was pretty full. They passed around papers to fill
out if we were interested in contributing. I said we had empty bedrooms and
that I could take in people. And I knew that would be okay with Charles
[Bernie's husband].[11]

Bernie housed countless undocumented Central Americans and helped
transport them across the U.S.-Mexico border. She always took her paints
and easel with her when traveling near Mexico. If the Border Patrol stopped
her, she could say that she was going to paint in the countryside. She organized medical supplies to be taken to Central America and painted murals
on the buses. She traveled to Nicaragua and stayed in a war zone with Witness for Peace, Pat Manning's organization. She fed the hungry and nursed
people through injuries and illnesses. For Bernie, this conversion inspired a
life of activism that was framed by a deep faith that she celebrated in weekly
masses with other people involved in the Sanctuary movement. Bernie died
on October 10, 2005, not long after a final protest of migrants' deaths in the
Arizona desert. The community came together for her funeral and printed
an eight-page booklet remembering her long and productive life.

Another aspect of activism and spirituality for many of the women I've
interviewed is the sacredness of the everyday facets of their lives. Peace and
border activist Pat Manning recalled:

There was blending, syncretism, in Latin America where I was. It had
the heavy Mayan influence. They were descendants of Aztecs and other
cultures where many things were represented as deities. I didn't see it as
pantheism as much as they were tapping into things that we all need to
be reminded of—the sacredness of many aspects of life and sometimes the
contradictory nature of things. You needed sometimes the violence of death
in the whirlwinds to come and scour things clean every bit as much as you
needed the comforting and the nurturing aspects of life. It deepened me as I
saw the face of the divine represented in many different ways.

It made me feel awe that I was part of anything so grand. I felt graced
somehow by the sense that I was part of everything else. I really respected

that in the cultures that I worked with in Latin America, which got me
even more interested in learning more about the indigenous cultures of this
country. The time in Nicaragua was definitive for me, in reinforcing and
clarifying how I thought people of faith should act in the world.[12]

Later in her life Pat remembered:

The border itself is symbolic to me today. It's not just contested political
space, but it's also a sacred ground for many peoples and traditions that are
being abused. It's become a theater of violence for both personal gains and
political ends . . .
I think of the border as a wound. It's a body, a sacred setting, a living
setting. It's a sacred cosmology as is the rest of the world. What's differ-
ent is that because it's politically divided, it becomes the setting where we
see the worst of human failings lived out as well as the best humanitarian
impulses.[13]

Pat's wisdom, respect for members of different cultures, and sense that life is
blessed inspire me. She continues to work to heal the rupture that is manifest
along the U.S.-Mexico border and in much U.S. policy toward weaker nations.

The artist Ana Maria Vasquez, an organizer for various progressive
causes, drew the sacredness of the land and the actions of the poorest people.
In her painting of a Mexican man holding a baby, a Yaqui deer dancer dances
in his heart. The deer dancer is a prominent tribal symbol for the indigenous
Yaqui people of southern Arizona. It represents a merger of Yaqui traditions
with Catholic beliefs and remains a central feature of the spiritual lives of
today's Yaqui people. In the bottom corner of Ana Maria's painting, the deer
dancer kneels at the bodies of two deer. Blood from the deer streams north,
accompanying migrants, ending in wealth and a dollar sign in the United
States. Ana Maria's painting and the world it represents are steeped in spiritual meaning that accompanies the most marginal of people through their
deepest trials. Her artwork is thus a form of activism.

The poet Maria Elena wrote a song that expressed the moment-by-
moment sacredness she experienced in farm labor. Written in 1987, the song
"Forged under the Sun" is told from the perspective of a tomato picker.

A moan is heard in the fields
From the fatigue of a farmworker

A deep and longing sigh
of the grace of God to the harvest picker poet.

I'm a creature forged under the sun
with love and pain
My humble smile and my color
are evidence of the Creator.

Our Father, my farmworker Christ
baptized in my fountain with sweat
Here is a bite of my rice
It's the Eucharist I eat in the fields.

From my body lives the sinner,
Oh oh oh what pain
And my blood they drink in your honor
Oh, forgive them, my Lord

The sun sets and the Angelus begins to cry,
For it's time to quit working
She calls unto me in the voice of darkness
God Our Father wants to rest now.

When I get out of this row
I'm going to change
I'm going to run, I'm going to cry
And from now on, I'm going to fight
With anger I'm going to fight
For Justice, for Peace, for Dignity.[14]

Maria Elena explained the song:

> My song, "Forjada bajo el sol," means "Forged under the Sun." There's a
> moan in the fields from a person that's very tired and is working. It's coming
> out of a tomato picker, a cucumber picker, whatever. I can look out over the
> fields and actually see the person and see what goes on and feel the same
> anguish.
>   It's late in the evening, and, all of a sudden, the person takes a deep

breath, a sigh really. And the poem talks about how beautiful everybody is, all brown, because they've been forged under the sun, and especially the kids have their wonderful smiles. Then, we farm workers, we share our food and say, "Here is a bite of my rice." This is the Eucharist that we have in the fields.

Then a little later it says, "Cae el sol y llora el angelus." This is referring to a belief we have that at a certain time of the day, all the people, like the birds and the trees, go to sleep, that everybody should quit working and go to rest because the poem says that the sun goes down and the angel of light begins to cry and says, "It's time to quit working." But sometimes the growers keep farm workers working out there until it is so dark they can't see. Our God wants to rest and can't quit working unless we do too. Of course, I also have my stories of the beautiful dark angel of the night, the one with wings of the black eagle. See, I try to bring what really happens and poetry and how things should change altogether.[15]

Maria Elena sees a world enmeshed in spirituality despite obvious hardship. The most basic conditions of life are therefore sacred.

These activist women have struggled with a question: if God is good, why is there so much suffering? Mary Robinson's doubts about God's goodness—especially when four Sunday school girls were murdered in Birmingham in 1963—were explored in chapter 7. She had a vision of a city in the sky with a room for all of God's people. She spoke further about that vision: "I think about the city in the sky. I know that the vulnerable, the illiterate, belong in that city. They ain't going to be throwed out of there. Nope, no doubt about it. All the wrong that was did here is going to be made right up there. And that's where Mama is."[16] She still has doubts, however. "I know the world's in God's hands, but when I get to heaven I have so many questions to ask God. Why does he allow such suffering? Why earthquakes? Why rape and murder? Why do politicians sometimes do such evil? Yes, I have lots of questions."

Raquel Rubio-Goldsmith talked to me about her own crisis of faith when facing all the suffering of the Central American war refugees. They had great difficulty getting asylum in the United States, and Raquel questions a God that doesn't help them.

I've felt a real distancing from God in the last few years. I can't seem to find a way to get close again. I don't really know why. Sometimes I think it's

*because I see so much suffering and it really angers me. But that's been true
other times, and I've been able to maintain a conversation with God.*

*A real change in my understanding of belief came when I started
working with the Central American refugees, although I didn't do nearly
the work that many other people did. My husband was very active in
Sanctuary. But by taking asylum applications and hearing people's stories,
I learned of stories like that of the young woman from El Salvador [whose
family was murdered], the most terrible uprooting, and the loss of family,
home, and everything.*

*Of all the cases, that was the one that impacted me the most in terms of
spirituality. I had a really hard time knowing where to turn. All that hor-
rendous violence was taking place, and so many people were trying to help
the victims of that violence, and it seemed there were closed doors everywhere. It was really, really hard for me to keep faith.*

*But it was seeing the faith in the people who were suffering that helped
me. Their faith was just unflappable. So those of us who weren't even suffering had to take faith from those who were. . . .*

*I was so gone. I suddenly realized I was really a lost soul, although I had
always worked for justice and tried to do the right thing and make ethical
decisions, but I had not really ever developed such a faith [cries]. . . .*

*My friends had said to me, "You might get real angry, but God did not
create this mess. We are the ones who did it. We need the strength from
God to respond to it. We are the ones that have to fix it up if it is going to be
fixed. It took me a long time to really, really believe that. Still, how to fix it
becomes so problematic.*

*It seems like I've been losing my faith in the last few years because I
just get so exasperated. We have been working on these immigration issues
for years and years. When I started doing this immigration work, I can
remember saying, "If we don't fix it now, the day is going to come when it's
going to be so much worse." And it's gone way beyond anything I imagined,
how badly migrants are treated.*

*Still, I try to remember it's like Father McGovern said, "You do good
things because you have to do them. Maybe we can't have the faith all the
time, but that doesn't mean you can't do what you are supposed to do." But
I miss the faith.*[17]

Raquel seems to work out the dilemma by accepting her lack of faith
while there is such injustice in the world. In a way, the crisis of faith further

motivates her activism. Pat Manning found her own response to the question of why there is so much suffering in the world in Nicaragua's culture. As she explained it:

> *Nicaragua's culture had a lot of celebration built around Mary [the mother of Jesus]. It's not the idol of Mary, but it was like the Nicaraguan people were doing the same thing I was doing in terms of religion. It was, "Let's celebrate goodness in a broken and tragic and sad world where we don't learn, where we keep hurting one another. Where we keep resorting to violence to try to impose our vision on things."*[18]

So Pat sees great suffering but chooses, as do the Nicaraguan people, to respond to creatively good symbols and put her energy into building a better world. Later she continued:

> *It was a constant heartache that the U.S. government was attacking Nicaragua. I'd respond with anger, but I learned a lot from the Nicaraguans there about how to channel that anger and to not replicate their mistakes by becoming as hateful as the Contras were. It was an immense conversion process for me around forgiveness, healing, inclusion. We denounced what the Contras were doing and worked furiously against it, but we tried not to hate the people and tried to separate out the people from the politicians and the agendas. I'd work on that rather than simply demonizing the U.S., the way our country was demonizing Nicaragua.*[19]

Pat continues that effort not to hate, to not look at the opposing side as completely irredeemable. She constantly nudges her activist partners away from a tendency to paint the opposition in extreme terms.

Maria Elena also wrestled in a profound way with another question: if God is good, why is there so much suffering? In the winter of 1988, I visited her in Brownsville, Texas, along the Texas-Mexico border. It was cold, nearly freezing at night. At that time, violence in the U.S.-backed wars in Central America had intensified, and waves of refugees were flooding into the United States. Suddenly U.S. immigration policy had changed. Now the Border Patrol detained those fleeing violence in their home countries at the port of entry, no longer allowing them to apply for refugee status and then disperse throughout the United States. Within days, the Border Patrol in Maria Elena's town had trapped thousands of homeless refugees outside the immigration headquarters.

Distraught by the suffering she had witnessed, Maria Elena picked me up at the airport and drove me out to where the refugees were camped. My tape recorder ran between us in the front seat. Countless Central Americans were spread out in front of us. They crowded into a mesquite grove, clustered in long lines in front of the immigration building, and waited by a fast-food stand. Toilet paper and some cardboard littered the ground. A group of children wearing light sweaters and jackets rushed up to our car, stretching out their hands in supplication. A barefoot woman with long dark hair and a flower in her sweater pushed a baby to us. "Porfavor, Senora," she begged at our window. Other people, wrapped in blankets, watched us from where they sat on pieces of cardboard. A blond woman handed out sandwiches from the back door of an old station wagon, and a group of Central American men climbed into the back of a truck. We drove slowly through the crowd. Maria Elena told me how she had tried to feed them.

Right before it happened, Pablo [her partner at the time] had bought a whole field of sweet corn that hadn't been harvested on time. It had got too hard for most people to eat it, so he bought it for us real cheap, and we ate corn for quite some time. Then the first time I drove with Pablo in his old truck past immigration and saw hundreds and hundreds of people just standing and sitting and waiting on the ground, including many children, I couldn't believe it. It was real awful. You could see men, their eyes, like crying. . . .

That day I cried, and I hollered to God, "Where are you? If there is a God, where are you?" Then I thought, maybe God is in prison. Maybe God can't come out of it. Maybe God is trapped someplace. I believe that God put a lot of himself into us, but there is also that evil part in us that is destroying ourselves. Whatever it is, it is some kind of very powerful evil that we have around us. It's so sad because the whole world is a beautiful paradise. But a lot of people have turned all the good powers that God gave us, and maybe that's where everything went wrong.

Then, that day, I thought, maybe I was meant to represent God. Maybe God divided himself into so many little pieces and gave each one of us a little piece of himself, so that we could carry on with something good. Maybe that's where he's at. In me, in you, in the people that he thought might be able to do something about it. 'Cause of that, maybe he can't do it without us.

So I started getting myself together, and I said, "Pablo, we've got to do something. We can take the corn, we can help them fill out applications, we can raise hell 'cause this is wrong! Then maybe when all these particles of

God come together, we can form one strong force of God and put him back
together again. So Pablo and I, we started working.[20]

That night I lay awake in Maria Elena's tiny trailer and stared at the ceiling.
I thought of the people we saw, Maria Elena's sharing of a field of corn, and her
idea about God. I wondered if God could be imprisoned in me. Maria Elena
gave so much. How could I not give a little? The next morning I transported
two Salvadoran women from the mesquite woods north to a meeting place
where they would get a ride. Two blocks after they climbed into the backseat,
Border Patrol officers began to follow us. I stopped at a stop sign, and they
pulled up next to me. I thought, "I'm going to be arrested. I don't have my
medicine with me. I know no lawyer or support group in Brownsville. What
will happen to the refugees?" The agents looked over at me, then the driver
listened to his radio and spoke into the microphone. They laughed, waved at
me, and pulled away. I turned back to the women sitting in my car. "It's okay," I
said in English. The blood flowed back into my face.

Maria Elena had seemed to reconcile the existence of a good God despite all the suffering her people experienced. She claimed God's presence
was with them and illustrated this idea through songs.

> *I have another song called "El Preso Pizcador." It means "The Harvest*
> *Prisoner." It also talks about a real situation but with a larger meaning. In*
> *it I'm a little child questioning my mom. "Mother, mother, where is God?"*
> *And she answers, "Well, God is by your side, el preso pizcador." Then the*
> *next verse applies to like Central America or Mexico or wherever the family*
> *has been separated or a parent has been killed or martyred. The child asks,*
> *"Why did my father leave? Why did he abandon us? I want to see his smile,*
> *I need his love."*
>
> *And the mother answers . . . "He died for our cause." Then she says,*
> *"There he is struggling by your side. The harvest prisoner."*
>
> *In the last verse, the child says, "Why, if God is so great and has so*
> *much power, there is war and hunger on earth and doubt about tomorrow?*
> *Then the child says, . . . "Why? Why? Mom, where is God to be found?"*
> *Then she answers, . . . "He's imprisoned in heaven, He's imprisoned in*
> *heaven, the poor farm worker."*[21]

Maria Elena thus answered her question: God is somehow imprisoned
within each of us, and God depends on humans to do the work of God.

A final aspect of these women's activism and spirituality is about finding God in communities. Pat Manning spoke to this.

I think God mostly reveals itself to me in community. When it hasn't been a personal mystical experience, which I had as a child, it was definitely in Nicaragua and in Guatemala working with different groups where I would feel very strongly that presence. Like the time with the Miskitos in their new village after they had been relocated.

Nicaragua, like a lot of countries that are resource-poor, depended on cutting down trees for firewood for cooking. In a lot of areas that were deforested, the rainy season could be dramatically violent. You have these tropical downpours on muddy slopes. So, in one particularly rainy season, I was out in an area in the middle of the country prone to flooding. It was in a resettlement area that had been rebuilt after their village nearby had been destroyed by the Contras.

The rivers nearby were rising and rising and rising. We had to get people out because it was threatening to wash away some of the lower-lying settlements. It was raining so heavily we could hardly hear.

In one area, we formed a line of people and passed swaddled babies over our heads. It reminded me of the best sense of communities pulling together, even when they're devastated, they're depressed, they're angry about the situation that they're in. It was, "Let's get the children and the elderly out first." It was like a communal baptism.

Mostly in Nicaragua God came to me not in worship experiences, although there would be some powerful ones where we would share with either Protestant or liberation theology Catholic base communities. I experienced God mostly in doing things. We would sit around at night and tell stories or sing songs. That was how people shared their lives. It could be women cooking together and singing and getting ready to serve the kids. It could be going in a group of folks from church to church in the really outlying areas on the giras, like circuit riding on horses with the priest. Some of the community would come with us, and we'd feel a very intimate camaraderie. They came both as guides and as our protection, because it was all in a deep, deep, deep war zone.

There was a sense of being in this together that was really important. We'd build structures after they'd been destroyed by the Contras. A lot of things are done in lines of us people. We set up lines to pass things like sheets of tin for the roofs. Or we passed cinder blocks or adobe bricks that have just been made by people and dried. We would do it in groups together, singing songs for picking coffee, songs for picking corn.[22]

It was therefore in communities, in "doing things" together, that Pat experienced God. The sense of being with each other further motivated her activism and gave her work meaning. Maria Elena experienced such a community through her work with undocumented immigrants. She recounted this event to me as if it were a dream.

I was helping some undocumenteds. It was still dark, in the very early morning, and I was supposed to pick them up in Matamoros and take them to the Mexican side of the river, out in the country. A man was supposed to be waiting for us. He was going to lead them across and then take them to a truck that was going to drive them north past la migra. There were six guys and a girl. . . .

It had been raining and, oh my God, it was muddy, and when we got to the river, the man who was supposed to take them wasn't there. We waited and waited and he didn't come . . . I thought, "I know the other side, maybe God is telling me that I have to do it." I've never crossed like that before, and I was scared that I'd get picked up as a coyote, so I didn't know what to do. And the river was high, 'cause of the rain, and it didn't look the same. We walked up and down the shore, and, finally, we saw footprints where other people had gone in. So I said, "I think this is the place to cross."

The men started to take off their clothes and put them in plastic bags to carry, but the girl looked at me like she didn't know what to do. So I turned my back to the men and opened my blouse and held it out like a screen for her to change behind. It was like I covered this girl with my body. She was very scared and shaking and started to cry and said, "You're not going to leave us alone, are you?"

So I told her, "No, I'm not. I'll go with you."

Then we started into the water, but it was terrible. The current was so strong, and the water was so cold, and for a few minutes, I was so scared. Then I made a promesa to God to keep on helping people in any way I can, and for the first time in my life, I felt like I was being baptized, and I looked around, and it seems like angels were with us.

When we got to the other side, we had to wade through mud almost up to our knees, and we lost our shoes. We fell many times, and the Huisache thorns covered our feet and legs, and we had to walk through three barbed-

wire fences. We got all cut up. Finally, we reached the truck that was sup-
posed to meet us. Then, when it was time for us to separate, the girl looked
at me and said, "I never had a mother." So I hugged her and said, "Don't
be scared, mija, [daughter] God is with you." And it was like I gave her my
blessing.[23]

Maria Elena's description of crossing the river takes my breath away. In the
two decades since I first heard this story, I am still profoundly moved by it.
Maria Elena's spirituality and actions were (and are) intricately bound.

The women's activism in various progressive causes is motivated and bound
by their spirituality. They addressed the meaning-of-life issues that were
deep in my heart. I felt I grew politically and spiritually by hearing each of
them wrestle with their profound concerns about human suffering and the
goodness of creation.

Conclusion

Probably the most persuasive use of oral histories, such as those I've collected in this book, is what the historian Michael Frisch has called the "capacity [of oral histories] to redefine and redistribute intellectual authority."[1] Oral histories give us a revised, often expanded vision of life, as well as alternative forms of knowledge. For example, farmworker and poet Maria Elena Lucas wrote a three-act play, which claimed the right to revision the Virgin of Guadalupe, who historically has been used as a symbol by the dominant religious tradition to keep women submissive. In her "rewrite," Maria Elena portrays the Virgin as a divine farmworker who delivers a political message. The Virgin tells the heroine, Rosamaria:

> Rosamaria, Rosamaria, don't cry anymore, please, Rosamaria. Look,
>   search for the man whom they call Cesar Chavez.
> You will find him
> where the sun sets and the beast falls,
> where a black eagle flies in my flag,
> in the fields
> where they sing "De Colores."
> There, reigning you shall find
> Justice, Peace, God and Cesar Chavez
> Fly, fly, black eagle,
> and when you return to these fields
> "De Colores" you shall sing.[2]

The new Virgin speaks with authority and is starkly political, calling upon the heroine to seek justice. In addition, Maria Elena's work on the Third

Testament, which she continues today, is a remarkable challenge to traditional biblical authority. When she was a child at school, she was given crayons and simply told to color by teachers who didn't want to teach her. Now she has the audacity to write a continuation of a document held sacred by her culture's most powerful elite. Maria Elena writes about the U.S.-Mexico border and the poorest of the poor. She longs to include them in the greatest text she can imagine.

Other women I've interviewed have made similar attempts to redistribute intellectual authority. Mary Tsukamoto, the Japanese American woman who spoke forcefully about the internment camps, claimed aloud a new, disturbing history of the United States. This counterstory included a radical denial of immigrants' and citizens' basic human rights. It contributed, as Frisch has called for, an essential challenge to the dominant history. Oral histories have the potential to "challenge the established organization of knowledge and power and the politics that rested on it."[3] Mary Robinson spoke about the importance of the deep moral community of her childhood. The African American residents had a vision of racial and economic justice, which they believed would prevail. If human actions didn't bring this justice about, God would intervene. The dominant culture of Mary's time ignored or repressed this community and its ideas. However, spiritual populations such as hers supplied many of the domestic working women who became the backbone of the Montgomery bus boycott and ultimately helped tip the balance of power in the South.

These counterstories confront an ideology that says nonelite people do not create history or change.[4] Even though she could not alter the systemic oppression of blacks in Mississippi, Sarah Jones (the nearly homeless old woman that I interviewed in the low-income housing in Milwaukee) lived long enough to testify about violence and lynching in her home community. Many college students and religious groups subsequently read her story. In this way, Sarah helped call into question both the sometimes assumed basic goodness of the southern system and the often easily dismissed homeless, who are perceived as inarticulate and unable to accurately describe their own social position. If we take seriously the challenge of these lived experiences from below and try to use their insights to question dominant positions, we will have what Shari Stone-Mediatore has called a "new lens through which we can organize our everyday experience and historical world." Through this lens we can "destabilize ossified truths."[5]

For example, we can fight any tendency to romanticize the past relationship between white housewives and their African American housekeepers. Josephine Hunter, who had been part of the Great Migration, told me that black domestics where she worked were not called by their real last names. If a woman worked for the Feinsteins, the crudest white people might have called the housekeeper "nigger Feinstein." The more considerate members of the white community might have called her "Josephine Feinstein." The white culture attempted to erase Josephine's real identity. Through Josephine's experiences, the dominant culture can begin to rethink and relearn its own history.

No cultural system is absolute. Each has contested, contradictory, and evolving aspects to it. It has cracks in its system, ruptures, and the women in these interviews have struggled to break through these openings. In these contradictions, the culture's vulnerabilities are exposed. For example, the belief systems of Maria Elena's parents and the dominant Anglo ideology of the growers required Maria Elena to work in the outside world to earn money, both as a child and as an adult. These forces required her to act submissively toward men and bear as many children as possible. This set up great contradictions within Maria Elena's heart. Personality strengths such as initiative and courage, which allowed her to survive working in the streets and fields during her childhood, led Maria Elena as an adult to flee her culture's expectation that she be submissive. These qualities helped her fight the oppressive structures of the economic systems of the Anglo growers. By paying less than subsistence wages, the farm structure caused cracks in its system of enforcement. Impoverished workers had to use their initiative and courage to survive, which helped many workers eventually rebel against the system.

In a similar way, Darlene Leache, the abused woman from the Appalachian mountains in Tennessee, was beaten down by both her husband and her religion, which taught her that the woman's role is submissive—no matter what. Like the migrant farm system of Maria Elena's past, internal colonialism had impoverished Appalachian men and women. In the process, dominant northeastern industrialists had expropriated coal and required mountain families, including women, to use resourcefulness and courage and develop tools for survival. These characteristics later helped them fight the system through, for example, union organizing. Radical nuns came from outside the community to try to help the women there improve their lives. As part of their own experience fighting oppression in the Catholic Church, these nuns carried with them a different vision of womanhood. They told Darlene that God valued women as well as men. They inspired Darlene and others to ask for more from life. I was stunned when I attended my first

Mountain Women's Exchange meeting and heard a group of women sing the old union organizing song, "We Want Bread but We Want Roses Too." Gradually Darlene learned bookkeeping and began to speak up about her own difficulties. Despite remarriage to the man who had abused her in the past, Darlene participated in the nuns' empowering movement.

Women can take these social contradictions and cracks in the system and birth new interpretations. Mary Robinson's love for the location and people of her childhood caused her to call for a redistribution of ownership. She spoke up for land for its workers and an accounting on God's terms, not those of mere humans. This claim came from within her own family's belief system and was not the result of outside political agitation. Likewise, the white reservation system for Native Americans did not seem to notice Irene Mack Pyawasit's grandmother, but she had studied that system and taught Irene to value education but not trust or fall victim to the thinking of white people. This led Irene as an adult to work against the dominant system and to advocate for indigenous education in the ways of whites and especially in the ways of her own Native people. Mary Tsukamoto, who had been part of the Japanese internment during World War II, learned to be polite and not confront authority, but she found that this method of living did not work for her. Eventually she confronted the government, the highest authority. Bernie Mueller had been taught to be an exemplary Catholic. As a mother and a nurse, she was told to confine most of her thinking to family issues. But when confronted with what she considered to be a government crime, she drew from the symbols of faith and went through a new conversion experience. Bernie dedicated the rest of her life to the cause and risked her liberty to help undocumented Central Americans.

The oral histories collected here are set within the meaning and symbol systems of each woman's community. As time has passed, and I have realized how deeply spiritual most of these women were, I have come to think that perhaps religion is the only meaning-making language available to some working-class women. Certainly, for many people in U.S. culture, to talk about God is to talk about what is ultimate meaning, although the quest for understanding uses different symbols and metaphors, depending on which group we're talking about. Maria Elena is a mystic in all she does. Her belief system was profoundly influenced by her grandmother's indigenous religion, which stressed a closeness to "Mother Earth," as Maria Elena put it. She also learned the folk Catholicism of her mother and other women in her community. As Maria Elena described it, this religion was the "direct product of the mestizo blend of forced Catholicism and native religions. This intensely spiritual belief system taught that faith and life are one, that health comes from harmony with the environment and other people, and that manifestations of the divine—the Saints, the Virgins, Jesus Christ, Mother Earth, and God—are accessible and immediate to the most humble of people."[6] Likewise, Mary Robinson's belief system drew from traditions of Africa, the form of Protestantism that had been taught to those enslaved, the visions and morality developed directly by the enslaved, and the profound beliefs of poor, struggling freedmen and—women. Her belief system was deeply moral: goodness would be rewarded and cruelty punished. Referring to behavior, over and over, Mary's mother had taught her, "God don't like ugly."

I agree with Shari Stone-Mediatore, who writes that a responsible thinker must not just listen to the narrators' stories or even present them to others. The analyst must also create oppositional knowledge and theorize about her own life in relation to the stories of others.[7] As oral historians, we bring "extra baggage" in terms of our own socializing to the interviews, and we somehow must begin to account for that.[8] It may be in the nature of the questions we ask or in our assumptions as we place the interviews in context. Sociologist Judith Stacey has written, "Ethnographic writing [such as doing oral histories] is not cultural reportage, but cultural construction, and always a construction of self as well as the other."[9] I might investigate the role of these statements by examining the contradictions in my life in relation to the women I interviewed. For example, Maria Elena and I both worked hard in our lives, although Maria Elena worked much harder than me. In many ways my relatively comfortable old age, compared to hers of poverty and illness, is simply a result of my good luck. I was born white and in an ownership economy where goods are partially allocated by a system of private inheritance. As a white girl, my whole world expected different things for me than did Maria Elena's. As an adult, I could rely partially on my husband's wages. He is also white. He was expected as a child to get a substantial education, and that education provided a reliable salary. In addition, he received a modest inheritance, which has helped us prepare for old age. None of these benefits was available to Maria Elena, a Mexican American farmworker. Plus the very ownership society that has benefited me was historically designed to make her a part of the desperate, nonowning, bottom-level workforce on which the dominant culture depends.

I could do a similar analysis with Mary Robinson, African American textile worker and union activist. Because she was awarded compensation in a lawsuit over deceptive insurance policies, however, her economic situation is not as dire as Maria Elena's. I was aware, at least somewhat, of my potential social, cultural, and economic biases as I worked with the women I interviewed. I have tried to contradict these tendencies by studying a class and economic analysis of history and the history of white domination in the United States. While I worked on the narratives of Maria Elena, Mary Robinson, Pat Manning, and the women on the U.S.-Mexico border, I did an extensive history of their living conditions. I began with an analysis of their material situations and examined the ways it fit into broad social hierarchies. I looked at the way the racial/ethnic situation had influenced that history and studied how it all was affected by gender. This multilayered approach, looking at each condition, ensured that I would not smooth over the basic class dimensions of each woman's problems.

With Maria Elena and Mary Robinson, we talked constantly about race, class, and gender, which helped us defuse many conflicts we might have had. Still, I view their situations from a white, now middle-class perspective. Perhaps Maria Elena and Mary thought about issues they did not discuss with me because they wanted to maintain our friendship. Ultimately, it was only by seeing myself as a "raced person" that I could see that we are all situated in different locations of the same power systems. By classifying myself as a raced person, I mean a person who is also considered to have a race. As a white woman, I have identity privileges in U.S. society, including assumptions of innocence and normality and the use of a language that considers "white" to be good. At the same time I was trying to view myself as a raced person, I was faced with the irony that in order to more completely understand the undergirding of the lives of my interviewees, I had to attend graduate school. Attending graduate school, however, increased the social distance between these women and me—another example of how power relationships are so insidious in the U.S. modern capitalist social system. As I learned more details about the underpinnings of social, economic, gender, and racial oppression, I was able to ask deeper questions and raise issues that Maria Elena and Mary Robinson had never talked about.

The scholar Daphne Patai has written that "[the] objectification, the utilization of others for one's own purposes . . . , and the possibility of exploitation, are built into almost all research projects with living human beings."[10] To study other people is to see them at least partially as a physical object that can be analyzed—to overlook their sense of integrity as a subject of their lives or, to use religious language, of their soul. Such research is often used for career enhancement, especially in the academy. Although Maria Elena received widespread approval when our book *Forged under the Sun* was published, her mother was outraged that she had revealed family secrets to an outsider. That conflict was painful to Maria Elena. Also I benefited from the research through the personal satisfaction of publishing books I had edited and compiled.

As oral historians, we need to ensure that others hear women's stories like these. The scholar Michael Frisch wrote, "Those truly interested in a history from the bottom up, those who feel the limits of the historical reality defined by the powerful, must understand that presuming to 'allow' the 'inarticulate' to speak is not enough. We must listen, and we must share the responsibility for historical explication and judgment." Frisch says we must bring to bear all our skills and abilities, our resources and privileges, to make sure the dominant culture hears what is being said "by those that have always been articulate but usually not attended to." What he calls the "arrogance of the powerful" must be challenged by the trustworthy records of another reality. The working-class women whose stories are compiled here are "history makers," and their records must be used to confront power.[11] I do not believe that simply recording their stories is adequate, however. It was only by attending graduate school that I learned the skills of historical explication. Perhaps other, more resourceful analysts might be able to develop those skills in another setting, but I was unable to. Placing these women's narratives in context is a really complex undertaking. After doing this, somehow we must confront the powerful with this redefined reality.

Frisch writes that what matters are the insights and questions that the historian brings to the task.[12] My basic assumptions and insights when doing the oral histories concerned my own experiences when I was poor and my interactions with other women at that time. From the beginning, I wanted my work to lessen the oppression experienced by poor and working-class women. With Jesusita Aragon, I had assumed that learning about midwives' traditions would empower other women to take more control over their bodies. In 1985, I had the naive assumption that by publishing my book *Dignity*, the stories of ten lower-income women, the middle-class people who read it would really understand the realities of poor women's lives, especially considering how hard they worked. Consequently, I thought, middle-class people would help the working class create more equitable situations. Back then, however, I did not fully understand the strength of the linkages among race, class, and gender in the modern capitalist system.

I soon realized that having their stories told made no difference in the material harshness of these women's lives. Since I had been poor myself, I assumed that poor women have agency, know the forces that are oppressing them, and will resist dominant powers. After I compiled the oral histories for *Dignity*, I realized that I needed to learn more about the underpinnings of dominant powers. This would allow me to write more complex introductions to set up the context of the women's lives and make my work more acceptable to intellectual powers. I knew, especially from my early work with Maria Elena Lucas and Mary Robinson, that I wanted to dedicate the rest of my professional life to telling the stories of activist working-class women. By sharing their stories with me, these working-class women had entrusted me with the responsibility to present their ideas in as forceful a manner as possible in the larger culture. Somehow, I felt, I must get them into the dominant public discussion.[13] "Information alone is not History," Frisch has written, but "what happens to oral history beyond the tape—how is it to be used and how is it to become, or be incorporated in, History?"[14]

In the past, it seemed to be enough for me to publish the books, to know they were being used as college supplemental texts, to try to publicize the conditions surrounding these oral histories by public speaking, to give the books to the women whose stories were told so they could use them with others as a consciousness-raising tool, and to teach about the complex social underpinnings and life conditions. When I was younger, I used to work politically to try to change the underlying structures. I've continued to do so, but my energy to undertake such actions has diminished as I have aged. Current social upheavals compel me to continue supporting progressive working or middle-class movements that rebel against the overarching system. We need to train more empowered, progressive intellectuals who can take on the social cruelties of the conservative political Right. These include anti-immigrant laws, voting restrictions, and the enactment of antiabortion rulings. It is my great hope that the work the women and I have done here will play at least a small part in this undertaking. These women have spoken clearly and forcefully, and their contribution to public debate must be taken seriously.

The oral histories I've compiled over the years have affected the lives of the women who tell their stories. For example, people traveled from all over the country to meet with Jesusita Aragon after *La Partera: Story of a Midwife* was published in 1980. Jesusita became even more renowned in her community and among public health and midwifery workers throughout the region. She received some financial help with the publication of the book, but it was not enough to make for an easy old age. Maria Elena Lucas traveled to conferences, spoke on panels, and told her story in many media after *Forged under the Sun* was published. She, too, received some financial help from the book, but it also was not enough to change the material conditions of her life. Both she and Jesusita live with the painful irony that they became modestly famous but are still without enough financial rewards to lift them out of poverty. Mary Robinson became locally famous, and since the publication of *Moisture of the Earth* she has spoken in different situations, but as of this writing she has made few financial profits from it.

When Jesusita was in her eighties, her daughter took over her affairs and decided I must be cheating Jesusita out of her money. The daughter reasoned that it was impossible that Jesusita could become so well known without making the same money as the authors of books sold in grocery stores. I tried to tell her that Jesusita was getting all the profits, that university presses do not earn much money, but I was unable to convince her that I was being fair. She cut off my contact with Jesusita during the final stages of Jesusita's life. For several years I grieved deeply for what had happened, and I still feel acute pain when I think of it. I was not informed of Jesusita's death. The anthropologist Ruth Behar, in *The Vulnerable Observer*, wrote, "This anthropology isn't for the softhearted."[15] Analysts are called to be vulnerable. Sometimes that vulnerability almost cuts out one's heart, but I know that we cannot really listen to others' stories on a deep basis without such profound involvement.

Coauthors Mary Jo Maynes, Jennifer L. Pierce, and Barbara Laslett have written that "alertness to the role of historical and institutional context is critical to the effective analysis of personal narratives, but it is not sufficient. To put our point bluntly: Individuals are shaped by their contexts but never reducible to them."[16] None of the women I interviewed stands only in her history or social system; all reach beyond. In today's harsh partisan political climate, we need a "debate-centered, participatory politics."[17] Such a politics would hold at least the possibility of justice for all those women and men who because of race, gender, economic status, and other social identities have been denied cultural resources and erased from cultural discourse. We need to encourage democratic communities where history is reinterpreted as we tell our stories to each other. In these communities we can find the clarity of vision necessary to reshape priorities or overcome our jointly inherited social system. The working-class women I interviewed were situated, embedded within their cultural, economic, and historical contexts. They and I have multiple identities, including race, class, gender, and country of origin. An examination of all these forces must be undertaken so we can analyze our social and cultural positions. These identities formed complex webs and structured the lives of the women I interviewed and in turn gave form to their resistance.

The women of color I interviewed were exploited in multiple ways, and the dominant culture often silenced their voices. However, they and the other women had agency, both alone and as groups. They worked enormously hard, but by themselves they were not able to break through some aspects of exploitation. Individually these women constructed memories that gave them strength and meaning, fueling their resistance and remarkable resourcefulness. They articulated their life situations and ideas, which often ran counter to the dominant discourse. Many of them have theories about the nature of their situation and their culture. These ideas are often strikingly different from those of the dominant culture, and, as knowledge from below, they have the potential to redefine intellectual authority. The dominant culture is extraordinarily powerful, and it will take alliances among multiple groups to confront it. Intersectionality, in turn, reminds us of its radical roots and calls for collective action and solidarity.[18] These groups must include women like those I interviewed in order to have depth and intellectual rigor. These conclusions have given me energy and focus, and I hope they embolden others to undertake similar projects.

Finally, I want to stress how hard the narrators worked when telling me their stories. They delved into old pains and ideas of which, perhaps, they were barely conscious before. Each woman probed her social system. As a whole, their work was creative, and they tried to tell stories and give the reasons behind these stories. They took their portrayal in this project seriously. In their resistance, many women tried to create documentation to influence broad political policies. Pat Manning, for example, who worked in war-torn Nicaragua trying to lessen the effect of the U.S.-backed conflict, went so far to maintain a collective memory of the Guatemalan victims that she smuggled documents containing records of specific attacks to the outside world. We need to create communities where we continually rethink the meaning of democratic participation and work toward politics grounded in each other's stories.[19] In this way we will help the women whose oral histories are compiled here in their quest to have their insights included in the evaluation of priorities that are part of the larger society.

Epilogue

In 2001, Maria Elena Lucas, a migrant worker who crossed the Rio Grande
with undocumented immigrants, and Mary Robinson, a civil rights worker
and daughter of sharecroppers, helped me work on my own oral history. The
tables were turned, and they interviewed me. One August afternoon in Iowa,
Mary accompanied me to the most painful location of my childhood. It was
the massive Independence Mental Hospital where my mother had been hospitalized when I was eighteen. My mother had hinted to me that her mother
also lived and died there. I had disobeyed Mom as a teenager. For days she
raged at me. Then, telling me it was my fault, she tried to commit suicide by
pouring a huge pot of boiling water over herself. My father eventually committed her to the state mental hospital because he could not afford private care.

During our work together on *Moisture of the Earth*, Mary and I traveled to the Alabama locations of her deepest pain as a child. Now, in 2001,
as she interviewed me about my life, I wanted her to accompany me to the
place in Iowa where I had hurt the most. I wanted a witness. At the time
of my mother's hospitalization, Independence Mental Hospital had been
crammed full with about eleven hundred often distraught patients. Kept in
locked wards with bars on the windows, they could not escape. Now Mary
and I walked through the dimly lit hospital museum, and a guide showed us
the equipment used for the shock (electroconvulsive) therapy. This form of
therapy broke the depths of Mom's catatonic depression but left her mentally confused, with twisted fingers. Outside the hospital after the tour, Mary
and I stood still, blinking in the sun. I massaged the creases of my forehead
with my fingers and breathed deeply.

"Do you know that quote from the New Testament, Mary, where Jesus says, when you leave an evil place, you should, 'Shake off the dust from your feet as a testimony against them,' and not turn back? I'm thinking of that phrase in terms of the hospital. You are with me. You witnessed. I think I can walk forward now. I don't need to look back." I glanced up at the sky. "Let's go to the hospital cemetery. It's peaceful." My sister and I had gone there before. Mary and I drove down a gravel road and parked. I carried an orange tiger lily I had brought from my sister's house. We crossed the road, climbed over a fence, and walked down a path made by a tractor through a soybean field. Cumulus clouds billowed in the brilliant blue sky. Insects flew up around us as we walked, and a warm wind blew.

Finally we reached a vast expanse of grass ringed by trees, bushes, and cornfields. A white wooden cross stood far to the left, and clumps of long grasses grew in the distance. We stepped onto the grass. The ground felt uneven. "These are all graves from the mental hospital, Mary. They're spaced only inches apart."

"All this?" Mary asked, incredulous as she walked forward. The wind blew across the grass, strange ripples, like little waves. "Where they at?" Mary asked.

"We're standing in them." I knelt to the ground. "See, there's a depression, then a ridge around the edge of a coffin, then a few inches and another ridge and a depression again. That's why the wind blows the grass like waves. It's different lengths, but even on top."

"But they ain't never put no stone here. That's so sad." Mary looked back and forth over what must have been hundreds, perhaps a thousand, unmarked graves. She stood in silence, then said, "God says one day he'll come back, and when he does, the sea'll give up its dead. That's what we have here. The sea." The grass was bright spring green, though it was August, but it sounded dry as the wind blew through the late summer leaves of the brush and trees that surrounded the cemetery. We walked farther onto the expanse.

"They just come here and dug a hole, like a potter's field. Nobody to mourn them. Probably just a caretaker," Mary said. I looked at a tall, wind-swept pine tree that grew along the edge of the field like a tree overlooking the ocean. An orange and black monarch butterfly fluttered in front of me and landed on Mary's shoulder. She stood still and turned her face toward it, but it flapped its wings and flew off. Two black butterflies flew with it.

We walked farther into the cemetery. "Look," Mary said. "On the far side, there's gravestones in the tall grasses." Perhaps two dozen small, light gray stones stood dotted among dark green, unmowed grass. Insects blew up in front of us, birds chirped, and our footsteps rustled the dry grass as we walked toward them. The sun warmed our shoulders. We reached the gravestones. The grass had gone to seed, like heads of wheat. Crickets trilled. Mary brushed the palm of her hand across the heads of tall grass, then stooped down and used both hands to separate the grass in front of one of the small lichen-covered stones.

She ran her fingers over the face of the graves. "There's initials carved in it," she said. "They kept something of the person. This one says, 'M.A.L.'" Mary moved to the next stone. J. R. She moved farther on. "Look, now they're only numbers." Then there were no more stones. Nothing marked the graves, but the late-afternoon light touched each blade of grass.

I watched the wind blow the grass into complex moving patterns. The rows of graves curved. A biplane flew above us, almost circling the field. "This must be what a battlefield feels like," I said.

"But these people be at peace," Mary responded.

"Maybe I'll leave my flower over at one of the gravestones," I said, "and I'll say prayers for the dead." I walked to one of the small limestone markers and placed my tiger lily on the grass. *God bless these people,* I prayed silently. *Wherever my grandmother is buried, bless her and help her be at peace. May the pain of all these people be gone.*

Mary called me from the edge of the field. "Look, it's a mulberry tree. Oh, this is a wonderful thing to be here." I joined her, and she reached into the tree and picked a berry. "And they be sweet too."

"Look," I said. "Blackberries, and they're ripe." Berries hung heavy, from deep green vines. I reached out and picked one. Juice ran along my fingers. The berry tasted succulent and sweet. We ate until our hands were purple stained.

I thanked Mary for coming to this place with me. I had wanted her to help me say goodbye to that part of my past. We began to walk down the path, back to the car. White butterflies blew up in front of us, marking our route. The pain that I had witnessed so intimately lifted from my shoulders. Never again did I agonize about my mother and grandmother as deeply as I had before. I thought of all the women I had interviewed, each one of whom had told me her deepest, most painful stories. Sometimes we formed what felt like profound bonds, but the bonds created when I shared my story with Maria Elena and Mary after they'd shared theirs reached even deeper. Oral historians must be open and forthcoming with the people we interview. We must understand how our own lives are situated. We must create communities of storytellers who not only help heal each other's lives but together challenge the structures of society.

Appendix
Profiles of the Women Mentioned

Jesusita Aragon

Helen Drazenovich
Berklich

Lupe Castillo

Josephine Hunter

Sarah Jones

Darlene Leache

Irene Mack Pyawasit

Maria Elena Lucas

Mary Robinson

Mary Tsukamoto

Jacky Turchick

Jesusita Aragon (1910–2005) was born in Las Vegas, New Mexico, where as a young girl she began practicing midwifery. She ranched with her two children on the plains of New Mexico, then moved back to Las Vegas, where she built a maternity clinic.

Rose Augustine was born in 1936 in Tucson, Arizona, where she lived in a largely Chicano neighborhood and her family drank water poisoned with TCE, a toxic chemical. As an adult, Rose became an activist in environmental justice campaigns.

Lilly Baker [pseudonym] was born about 1910 and lived in Kentucky, where her husband was a coal miner. She believed she was called by God to a healing profession and nursed the "sick and afflicted" in the mountains where she lived.

Helen Drazenovich Berklich was born in Duluth, Minnesota, in 1915. Her mother died, leaving nine children to live in an orphanage. Helen married young, to a miner on the Iron Range in Hibbing, to provide a home for her siblings. After her husband's death from miners' lung, she raised her siblings and four boys on wages from her restaurant job. She died in 1993.

Lucia Carmona was born about 1950. An undocumented Mexican with a large family, she was smuggled north locked in a crate. Reunited with her husband and most of her children, she worked in the agricultural fields around Onarga, Illinois, where she was a friend of Maria Elena Lucas. During a tense United Farm Workers demonstration outside a grocery store, Lucia raised her fist and started singing. Today she is legal.

Lupe Castillo is a Chicana activist in Tucson, Arizona, now in her sixties. Her father was a copper miner and union activist. She teaches humanities and Chicano history at Pima Community College.

Daisy Cubias (born about 1950) was a legal immigrant from El Salvador. Several members of her family were killed during the U.S.-backed government war against activists and peasants in El Salvador, but she smuggled her surviving family members to her home in Milwaukee, Wisconsin, where she spoke out publicly on these issues.

Cynthia Dakota (a pseudonym) was born in 1927, a Winnebago Native woman who lived near Black River Falls, Wisconsin. Like other Native children, she was forced to attend boarding school as a girl. Her older sister died at the school, and the family was prevented from seeing the child before her death.

Florence Davis (1930–2016) grew up on her grandparents' chicken farm in New Jersey. Her grandfather, a union member, influenced her to become a political activist. She was surrounded by the Ku Klux Klan when she visited black fish pond developers in the South and had her consciousness about LGBT issues raised by a young man abandoned by his father because of the son's sexuality. She campaigned actively for LGBT rights for the rest of her life.

Betty Dixon of Stearns, Kentucky, a friend of Irene Vanover, was born about 1950. Her husband was a striking coal miner. Betty was the oldest of ten children; the United Mine Workers strike split the family apart as siblings took sides.

Josephine Hunter (1907–87) was born in Memphis, Tennessee, and orphaned as child. She labored as a domestic worker and moved north to Milwaukee, Wisconsin. After she quit domestic work, she and her husband built a home for her grandchildren and foster children, a house that was later destroyed during an urban renewal initiative in Milwaukee.

Audrey Jones was born about 1950 in the mountains of Kentucky. Her young husband became a coal miner. When the union went on strike, he was sent to prison for dynamiting a field. The family was nearly destitute at the time of the interviews, and Audrey was in severe emotional pain.

Sarah Jones was born about 1910 in Sunflower County, Mississippi. Reared in a large, black sharecropping family, she was terrified by the ongoing lynchings in that violent county. She moved north to Milwaukee, Wisconsin, to escape but did not fare well there. She was illiterate, was evicted from her home, and probably died on the streets.

Darlene Leache, born about 1950 and the young mother of six, lived in the Appalachian mountains. Abused by her husband, she connected with a group of radical nuns who were organizing mountain women, put a stop to her husband's abuse, and was trained as a bookkeeper.

Mrs. Lewis was an elderly woman in the mountains of Kentucky. I was taken to her by Lilly Baker and tried to get her emergency care as she was apparently starving. She talked about her "company boy" and recalled that she and her husband had popped corn at carnivals.

Maria Elena Lucas is an artist, poet, and activist born in 1941. She was a farm worker and union organizer for the United Farm Workers and the Farm Labor Organizing Committee. The mother of seven children, she suffered the effects of pesticide poisoning and now lives on the border in Brownsville, Texas.

Pat Manning (born in 1956) is a poet and peace and border activist in Tucson, Arizona. In the 1980s she worked with Witness for Peace in Nicaragua, where she served in a war zone, hoping to help raise American consciousness about U.S. government complicity in the war against the Nicaraguan people. She also smuggled resistance documents into Guatemala.

Bernie Mueller (1925–2005) was a Catholic mother of eight. She was involved in the Sanctuary movement in the 1980s and said she experienced something like a conversion when she learned of the U.S. role in the wars of Central America. She was an activist in border causes for the rest of her life, traveling to Nicaragua, smuggling refugees north, and providing shelter for immigrants.

Irene Mack Pyawasit is a Menominee Indian from rural Wisconsin born about 1914. Raised by her grandmother, she rebelled against the boarding school she was sent to as a child. She eventually became a tribal leader and worked in Washington, D.C., as a lobbyist. At the time of the interviews, she was employed as a recruiter of Native students for the University of Wisconsin.

Lee Richards (a pseudonym), a mother of six from rural New Mexico, was born about 1923. She struggled with lifelong pain following the rape of her two daughters by their father and eventually dedicated herself to working with those accused of child abuse. She died in 1988.

Mary Robinson was born in 1943 near Montgomery, Alabama. The daughter of sharecroppers, she became active in the civil rights movement as a young mother, then worked in a textile mill, where she organized for the ACTU textile union. She retired from her job as a bus driver and is now an important elder in the Montgomery community.

Kat Rodriguez is a young organizer in Tucson who works with Latino activist groups, dealing with migrant workers and people coming north across the border. She talks about women's leadership issues in the Chicano movement.

Raquel Rubio-Goldsmith, born in the 1940s, was the daughter of a rural Arizona mining family. Dreaming of taking an active role in the struggle against social injustice, she earned a law degree in Mexico. She helped design and teach the curriculum in Chicano and Chicana Studies at the University of Arizona and Pima Community College in Tucson and is an activist on border issues.

Consuela Tafolla, (a pseudonym) was born about 1955, the daughter of Puerto Rican immigrants to Milwaukee, Wisconsin. When the family arrived, they were poor and discriminated against. At the time of the interviews, her husband, a war veteran, was suffering from post-traumatic stress disorder.

Mary Tsukamoto was born about 1920 of Japanese immigrant parents. Her large family worked in the strawberry and grape fields of California. She married a second-generation Japanese American, and they had a child. The entire extended family was imprisoned in internment camps during World War II. Mary became a leader in her community but dealt with the emotional and physical effects of that imprisonment for the rest of her life.

Jacky Turchick was born in Minneapolis, Minnesota, in 1942 at the beginning of World War II. A Jewish mother of four, she was haunted by thoughts of the Holocaust. Beginning in the 1980s, she defied the law to help smuggle Central American refugees into the country. Today she is an activist, artist, and writer.

Irene Vanover, born about 1920, was the leader of a women's committee of striking United Mine Workers in Stearns, Kentucky. Her coal miner husband suffered from black lung. The miners and their wives came to feel that the union had sold them out. She died in 1997.

Ana Maria Vasquez was born in Colombia in the 1960s. She is an artist and activist who paints large works on political subjects and sells them to raise funds for various resistance groups in the United States, Mexico, and Colombia.

Notes

Preface

1. Michael Frisch, *A Shared Authority: Essays on the Craft and Meaning of Oral and Public History* (Albany: State University of New York Press, 1990), 56.

2. Ibid., 85.

3. Ibid.

4. Mary Jo Maynes, Jennifer L. Pierce, and Barbara Laslett, *Telling Stories: The Use of Personal Narratives in the Social Sciences and History* (Ithaca, N.Y.: Cornell University Press, 2008), 6.

5. Martin Duberman, *Stonewall* (New York: Penguin, 1993), as described in Maynes, Pierce, and Laslett, *Telling Stories*, 53–56.

6. Hilary Cunningham, *God and Caesar at the Rio Grande: Sanctuary and the Politics of Religion* (Minneapolis: University of Minnesota Press, 1995).

Introduction

Epigraph: Quotation from Tineke A. Abma, "Powerful Stories: The Role of Stories in Sustaining and Transforming Professional Practice within a Mental Hospital," in *Making Meaning of Narratives: The Narrative Study of Lives*, ed. Ruthellen Josselson and Amia Lieblich (Thousand Oaks, Calif.: Sage Publications, 1999), 170.

1. See Alex Hulcochea, *Arizona Daily Star*, Wednesday, May 4, 2011, 1, 4.

2. Anthony Le Donne, *Historical Jesus: What Can We Know and How Can We Know It?*, foreword by Dale C. Allison Jr. (Grand Rapids, Mich.: Wm. B. Eerdmans Publishing, 2011), 21.

3. Mary Jo Maynes, Jennifer L. Pierce, and Barbara Laslett in *Telling Stories: The Use of Personal Narratives in the Social Sciences and History* (Ithaca, N.Y.: Cornell University Press, 2008), have described various ways to interweave the life history of the analyst of

the oral history with that of the of the narrator. For example, Ruth Behar, in *Translated Woman: Crossing the Border with Esperanza's Story* (Boston: Beacon Press, 1993), interweaves her own life story with that of a Mexican street seller in her sixties, whom she interviews. Maynes, Pierce, and Laslett also discuss Luisa Passerini's *Autobiography of a Generation* (Hanover, N.H.: Wesleyan University Press, 1996). Passerini interweaves her own diary entries and the account of her psychoanalysis with interviews she conducted with participants in the Italian student movement of the late 1960s and 1970s. She herself had been part of that movement.

4. Eric Alterman and Kevin Mattson, *The Cause: The Fight for American Liberalism from Franklin Roosevelt to Barack Obama* (New York: Viking, 2012), 109–26. These pages talk about fear in the United States of the "two Joes" of this era: Joe McCarthy and Joseph Stalin.

5. Ibid., 142–55.

6. Howard Zinn, *A People's History of the United States* (New York: HarperPerennial, 1980), 484–94.

7. Ibid., 539.

8. Betty Friedan, *The Feminine Mystique* (New York: W. W. Norton, 1963).

9. See Alterman and Mattson, *The Cause*, 1–14; and Martin Gilens, *Why Americans Hate Welfare: Race, Media, and the Politics of Antipoverty Policy* (Chicago: University of Chicago Press, 1999), 18–21.

10. See Alice Echols, *Daring to Be Bad: Radical Feminism in America, 1967–1975* (Minneapolis: University of Minnesota Press, 1989).

11. Jackie Pope, "Women in the Welfare Rights Struggle: The Brooklyn Welfare Action Council," in *Women and Social Protest*, edited by Guida West and Rhoda Lois Blumberg (New York: Oxford University Press, 1990), 57–74.

12. Shulamith Firestone, *The Dialectic of Sex: The Case for a Feminist Revolution* (New York: Bantam Books, 1970); Mary Daly, *Beyond God the Father: Toward a Philosophy of Women's Liberation* (Boston: Beacon Press, 1973); Rosemary Radford Reuther, *Liberation Theology: Human Hope Confronts Christian History and American Power* (New York: Paulist Press, 1972).

13. Gustavo Gutierrez, *A Theology of Liberation* (New York: Maryknoll, 1973).

14. Paulo Freire, *Pedagogy of the Oppressed* (New York: Seabury Press, 1968), 76–80.

15. Theodore Rosengarten, *All God's Dangers: The Life of Nate Shaw* (New York: Alfred A. Knopf, 1974).

16. Fran Leeper Buss, comp. and ed., *La Partera: Story of a Midwife* (Ann Arbor: University of Michigan Press, 1980).

17. Studs Terkel, *Working: People Talk about What They Do All Day and How They Feel about What They Do* (New York: New Press, 1972).

18. Fran Leeper Buss, comp. and ed., *Dignity: Lower Income Women Tell of Their Lives and Struggles* (Ann Arbor: University of Michigan Press, 1985).

19. Zinn, *People's History of the United States*, 573.

20. Gilens, *Why Americans Hate Welfare*, 21–22.

21. Fran Leeper Buss, comp. and ed., *Forged under the Sun/Forjada bajo el sol: The Life of Maria Elena Lucas* (Ann Arbor: University of Michigan Press, 1993).

22. Atkinson, Anthony B. *Inequality: What Can Be Done?* (Cambridge, Mass.: Harvard University Press, 2015), 18–24.

23. Ibid. Atkinson's figures are from the *Huffington Post*, February 3, 2016, quoting the Federal Reserve Bank of New York.

24. Fran Leeper Buss, comp. and ed., *Moisture of the Earth: Mary Robinson, Civil Rights and Textile Union Activist* (Ann Arbor: University of Michigan Press, 2009).

25. Shari Stone-Mediatore, *Reading across Borders: Storytelling and Knowledges of Resistance* (New York: Palgrave Macmillan, 2003), 64.

26. For examples of oral history programs, see "September 11, 2001, Oral History Narrative and Memory Project," Columbia Center for Oral History, Columbia University Libraries, New York. For more ideas, see the *Oral History Review: Journal of the Oral History Association*, Oxford Journals, Oxford University Press, online at www.oralhistory.org. For examples of scholars working together, see the editing relationship between Mary Jo Maynes, Jennifer L. Pierce, and Barbara Laslett in *Telling Stories*, vii–ix.

27. See the Center for Working-Class Studies at Youngstown State University, Youngstown, Ohio, online at http://cwcs.ysu.edu/

28. Kimberle Williams Crenshaw, "Demarginalizing the Intersection of Race and Sex: A Black Feminist Critique of Antidiscrimination Doctrine, Feminist Theory, and Antiracist Politics," *University of Chicago Legal Forum* 140 (1989): 139–67.

29. Gloria Anzaldúa, *Borderlands/La Frontera* (San Francisco: Aunt Lute Books, 2012); Audre Lorde, *Sister Outsider: Essays and Speeches* (Trumansburg, N.Y.: Crossing Press, 1984); Barbara Smith, "Introduction," in *Home Girls: A Black Feminist Anthology*, ed. Barbara Smith (New York: Kitchen Table–Women of Color Press, 1983), xix–lvi; Patricia J. Williams, *The Alchemy of Race and Rights* (Cambridge, Mass.: Harvard University Press, 1991).

30. Vivian M. May, *Pursuing Intersectionality, Unsettling Dominant Imaginaries* (New York: Routledge, Taylor & Francis Group, 2015), 3.

31. Ange-Marie Hancock, *Intersectionality: An Intellectual History* (New York: Oxford University Press, 2016), 33.

Chapter 1

1. See Sarah Deutsch, *No Separate Refuge: Culture, Class, and Gender on an Anglo-Hispanic Frontier in the American Southwest, 1880–1940* (New York: Oxford University Press, 1987).

2. Ibid., 46–48.

3. Jesusita Aragon's story, as told in Fran Leeper Buss, comp. and ed., *La Partera: Story of a Midwife* (Ann Arbor: University of Michigan Press, 1980), 17–18.

4. Ibid., 44.

5. Isabel Wilkerson, *The Warmth of Other Suns: The Epic Story of America's Great Migration* (New York: Vintage Books, 2010), 8–9.

6. Josephine Hunter's story, as told in Fran Leeper Buss, comp. and ed., *Dignity: Lower Income Women Tell of Their Lives and Struggles* (Ann Arbor: University of Michigan Press, 1985), 21–22.

7. Ibid., 56–58.

8. See Joan Wallach Scott, "A Reply to Criticism," *International Labor and Working Class History* (1987): 32.

9. Shari Stone-Mediatore attributes this idea to Eleni Varikas, "Gender, Experience, and Subjectivity: The Tilly-Scott Disagreement," *New Left Review* 211 (1995): 89–101, quoted in Shari Stone-Mediatore, *Reading across Borders: Storytelling and Knowledges of Resistance* (New York: Palgrave Macmillan, 2003), 102.

10. See Stone-Mediatore's discussion of Marx in *Reading across Borders*, 173.

11. Fran Leeper Buss, comp. and ed., *Forged under the Sun/Forjada bajo el sol: The Life of Maria Elena Lucas* (Ann Arbor: University of Michigan Press, 1993), 10.

12. Ibid., 11.

13. Ibid., 10–13.

14. Maria Elena Lucas's story, as told in ibid., 63, 65–66.

15. Ibid., 74–75.

16. Thomas E. Sheridan, *Arizona: A History* (Tucson: University of Arizona Press, 1995), 66.

17. Lupe Castillo's story, as told in Fran Leeper Buss and Josefina Castillo, comps. and eds., "Spiritual Visions/Border Lives: Progressive Women Activists at the U.S.-Mexico Border," unpublished manuscript, 29–30, 32.

18. Eileen Truax, *Dreamers: An Immigrant Generation Fight for Their American Dream* (Boston: Beacon Press, 2015), 185–202.

19. See Cesar J. Ayala and Rafael Bernabe, *Puerto Rico in the American Century: A History since 1898* (Chapel Hill: University of North Carolina Press, 2009).

20. Norma I. Cofresí, "Gender Roles in Transition and Professional Puerto Rican Women," *Frontiers: A Journal of Women Studies* 20, no. 1 (1999): 163. The issue focuses on Latina/Chicana leadership.

21. Author interviews with Consuela Tafolla, "Work and Family," Fran Buss Oral History Collection, Arthur and Elizabeth Schlesinger Library on the History of Women in America, Radcliffe Institute for Advanced Study, Harvard University, Cambridge, Massachusetts.

Chapter 2

1. Harriet Bjerrum Nielsen, "'Black Holes' as Sites for Self-Constructions," in *Making Meaning of Narratives*, ed. Ruthellen Josselson and Amia Lieblich (Thousand Oaks, Calif.: Sage Publications, 1999), 45–46.

2. Shari Stone-Mediatore, *Reading across Borders: Storytelling and Knowledges of Resistance* (New York: Palgrave Macmillan, 2003), 138.

3. Ibid., 139.

4. Mary Robinson's story, as told in Fran Leeper Buss, comp. and ed., *Moisture of the Earth: Mary Robinson, Civil Rights and Textile Union Activist* (Ann Arbor: University of Michigan Press, 2009), 86.

5. Mary Jo Maynes, Jennifer L. Pierce, and Barbara Laslett, in *Telling Stories: The Use of Personal Narratives in the Social Sciences and History* (Ithaca, N.Y.: Cornell University Press, 2008), 3, talk about the "subjective dimensions of social action . . . [offering] a privileged location from which to comprehend human agency."

6. Fran Leeper Buss, comp. and ed., *Dignity: Lower Income Women Tell of Their Lives and Struggles* (Ann Arbor: University of Michigan Press, 1985), 148.

7. Howard Zinn, *A People's History of the United States* (New York: HarperPerennial, 1980), 625.

8. Ibid., 524.

9. Irene Mack Pyawasit's story, as told in Buss, *Dignity*, 151–53.

10. See Stone-Mediatore's discussion of "narrative actors" in *Reading across Borders*, 135–38. 141.

11. John Alexander Williams, *Appalachia: A History* (Chapel Hill: University of North Carolina Press, 2002), 362.

12. Author interviews with Irene Vanover and Betty Dixon, "Work and Family," Fran Buss Oral History Collection, Arthur and Elizabeth Schlesinger Library on the History of Women in America, Radcliffe Institute for Advanced Study, Harvard University, Cambridge, Massachusetts.

13. Lupe's story is told in Fran Leeper Buss and Josefina Castillo, comps. and eds., "Spiritual Visions/Border Lives: Progressive Women Activists at the U.S.-Mexico Border," unpublished manuscript, 33–34.

14. Mary Robinson's story as told in Buss, *Moisture of the Earth*, 50.

15. Ibid., 68.

16. See Stone-Mediatore, *Reading across Borders*, 141.

17. Author interviews with Cynthia Dakota, "Work and Family," Fran Buss Oral History Collection, Arthur and Elizabeth Schlesinger Library on the History of Women in America, Radcliffe Institute for Advanced Study, Harvard University, Cambridge, Massachusetts.

18. Helen Drazenovich Berklich's story as told in Buss, *Dignity*, 61–63.

19. Ibid., 65.

Chapter 3

1. For a brief discussion of the history of using memory in a historical construct, see Mary Jo Maynes, Jennifer L. Pierce, and Barbara Laslett, *Telling Stories: The Use of Personal Narratives in the Social Sciences and History* (Ithaca, N.Y.: Cornell University Press, 2008), 39–42.

2. See Daniel L. Schacter, *Searching for Memory: The Brain, the Mind, and the Past* (New York: Basic Books, 1996). Schacter's book is an authoritative synthesis of scientific works agreeing that memory is a construction.

3. Edward M. Bruner, quoted in Norman K. Denzin, *Interpretive Biography*, Qualitative Research Methods, no. 17 (Newbury Park, Calif.: Sage Publications, 1989), 30.

4. Maria Elena Lucas's story, as told in Fran Leeper Buss, comp. and ed., *Forged under the Sun/Forjada bajo el sol: The Life of Maria Elena Lucas* (Ann Arbor: University of Michigan Press, 1993), 47–48.

5. Maynes, Pierce, and Laslett, *Telling Stories*, 148, emphasis in the original.

6. Anthony Le Donne, *Historical Jesus: What Can We Know and How Can We Know It?*, foreword by Dale C. Allison Jr. (Grand Rapids, Mich.: Wm. B. Eerdmans Publishing, 2011), 37.

7. Mary Robinson's memory, as told in Fran Leeper Buss, comp. and ed., *Moisture of the Earth: Mary Robinson, Civil Rights and Textile Union Activist* (Ann Arbor: University of Michigan Press, 2009), 72.

8. Michael Frisch, *A Shared Authority: Essays on the Craft and Meaning of Oral and Public History* (Albany: State University of New York Press, 1990), xxiii.

9. Jefferson A. Singer, "Narrative Identity and Meaning Making across the Adult Lifespan: An Introduction," *Journal of Personality* 72, no. 3 (June 2004): 445.

10. Dan P. McAdams and Ann Diamond, "Stories of Commitment: The Psychosocial Construction of Generative Lives," *Journal of Personality and Social Psychology* 72, no. 3 (1997): 678–94.

11. Ibid., 680.

12. Rose Augustine's story, as told in Fran Leeper Buss and Josefina Castillo, comps. and eds., "Spiritual Visions/Border Lives: Progressive Women Activists at the U.S.-Mexico Border," unpublished manuscript, 114–16.

13. Catrina Brown and Tod Augusta-Scott, eds., *Narrative Therapy: Making Meaning, Making Lives* (Thousand Oaks, Calif.: Sage Publications, 2007), xv.

14. Ibid.

15. Ibid.

16. Jonathan D. Sarna, *American Judaism: A History* (New Haven, Conn.: Yale University Press, 2004), 152.

17. Jacky Turchick's story, as told in Buss and Castillo, "Spiritual Visions/Border Lives," 196–97, 202–3.

18. Ibid., 207–8.

19. Helen Drazenovich Berklich's story, as told in Fran Leeper Buss, comp. and ed., *Dignity: Lower Income Women Tell of Their Lives and Struggles* (Ann Arbor: University of Michigan Press, 1985), 76.

20. Ibid., 82.

Chapter 4

1. Mary Jo Maynes, Jennifer L. Pierce, and Barbara Laslett, *Telling Stories: The Use of Personal Narratives in the Social Sciences and History* (Ithaca, N.Y.: Cornell University Press, 2008), 39.

2. Mary Robinson's story, as told in Fran Leeper Buss, comp. and ed., *Moisture of the Earth: Mary Robinson, Civil Rights and Textile Union Activist* (Ann Arbor: University of Michigan Press, 2009), 35–36.

3. Ibid., 39–41.

4. Michael Frisch, *A Shared Authority: Essays on the Craft and Meaning of Oral and Public History* (Albany: State University of New York Press, 1990), 61.

5. Lee Richards's story, as told in Fran Leeper Buss, comp. and ed., *Dignity: Lower Income Women Tell of Their Lives and Struggles* (Ann Arbor: University of Michigan Press, 1985), 196.

6. Maria Elena Lucas's diary entry, March 16, 1990, in Fran Leeper Buss, comp. and ed., *Forged under the Sun/Forjada bajo el sol: The Life of Maria Elena Lucas* (Ann Arbor: University of Michigan Press, 1993), 286.

7. Author interviews with Florence Davis, Fran Leeper Buss's personal collection, Tucson, Arizona.

8. Maria Elena Lucas's diary entry, January 24, 1990, in Buss, *Forged under the Sun*, 297–301.

Chapter 5

1. Author interviews with Audrey Jones, "Work and Family," Fran Buss Oral History Collection, Arthur and Elizabeth Schlesinger Library on the History of Women in America, Radcliffe Institute for Advanced Study, Harvard University, Cambridge, Massachusetts.

2. Jefferson A. Singer, "Narrative Identity and Meaning Making across the Adult Lifespan: An Introduction," *Journal of Personality* 72, no. 3 (June 2004): 445.

3. Alessandro Portelli, quoted in Mary Jo Maynes, Jennifer L. Pierce, and Barbara Laslett, *Telling Stories: The Use of Personal Narratives in the Social Sciences and History* (Ithaca, N.Y.: Cornell University Press, 2008), 73.

4. Paul Ricoeur, quoted indirectly in Harriet Bjerrum Nielson, "'Black Holes' as Sites for Self-Constructions," in *Making Meaning of Narratives: The Narrative Study of Lives*, ed. Ruthellen Josselson and Amia Lieblich (Thousand Oaks, Calif.: Sage Publications, 1999), 50.

5. Roy F. Baumeister, *Meanings of Life* (New York: Guilford Press, 1991), 9.

6. Jesusita Aragon's story, as told in Fran Leeper Buss, comp. and ed., *La Partera: Story of a Midwife* (Ann Arbor: University of Michigan Press, 1980), 27.

7. Ibid., 20.

8. Ibid., 22–23.

9. Ibid., 39.

10. Ibid., 44.

11. Ibid., 45.

12. Ibid., 44.

13. Ibid., 74.

14. Ibid., 84.

15. Ibid., 43.

16. Ibid., 78.

17. Ibid., 50.

18. Ibid., 59.

19. Ibid., 87.

20. Ibid., 77.

21. Ibid., 87–88.

22. Lee Richards's story, as told in Fran Leeper Buss, comp. and ed., *Dignity: Lower Income Women Tell of Their Lives and Struggles* (Ann Arbor: University of Michigan Press, 1985), 173.

23. Ibid., 173–74.

24. Ibid., 198.

25. Ibid., 169.

26. Ibid., 189–90.

27. Ibid., 194.

28. Ibid, 195.

29. Ibid., 198–99.

30. Mary Robinson's story, as told in Fran Leeper Buss, comp. and ed., *Moisture of the Earth: Mary Robinson, Civil Rights and Textile Union Activist* (Ann Arbor: University of Michigan Press, 2009), 31–32.

31. Ibid., 143.

32. Ibid., 139.

33. Ibid., 102.

34. Ibid., 90.

35. Ibid., 55.

36. Ibid., 87.

37. Ibid., 190.

38. Ibid., 69–70.

39. Ibid., 34.

40. Ibid., 106.

41. Ibid., 92.

42. Claudia Salazar, "A Third World Woman's Text: Between the Politics of Criticism and Cultural Politics," in *Women's Words: The Feminist Practice of Oral History*, ed. Sherna Berger Gluck and Daphne Patai (New York: Routledge, 1991), 95.

43. Mary's story as told in Buss, *Moisture of the Earth*, 125–26.

44. Ibid., 194.

45. Ibid., 129.

46. Ibid., 196.

47. Ibid., 193.

Chapter 6

1. Michel Foucault, *Society Must Be Defended: Lectures at the College de France, 1975–76* (New York: Picador, 2003), quoted in Colin James Sanders, "A Poetics of Resistance: Compassionate Practice in Substance Misuse Therapy," in *Narrative Therapy: Making Meaning, Making Lives*, ed. Catrina Brown and Tod Augusta-Scott (Thousand Oaks, Calif.: Sage Publications, 2007), 59.

2. See Shari Stone-Mediatore, *Reading across Borders: Storytelling and Knowledges of Resistance* (New York: Palgrave Macmillan, 2003), 162.

3. Lee Richards's story, as told in Fran Leeper Buss, comp. and ed., *Dignity: Lower Income Women Tell of Their Lives and Struggles* (Ann Arbor: University of Michigan Press, 1985), 175–76.

4. Darlene Leache's story, as told in ibid., 132.

5. Ibid., 136–39.

6. Ibid., 144.

7. Ibid., 44.

8. Ibid., 142.

9. Lauren J. Germain, *Campus Sexual Assault: College Women Respond* (Baltimore: Johns Hopkins University Press, 2016), location 1943.

10. Sarah Jones's story, as told in Buss, *Dignity*, 115.

11. Ibid., 117.

12. Ibid., 118.

13. Ibid., 120–21.

14. Mary Jo Maynes, Jennifer L. Pierce, and Barbara Laslett, *Telling Stories: The Use of Personal Narratives in the Social Sciences and History* (Ithaca, N.Y.: Cornell University Press, 2008), 9.

15. Mary Tsukamoto's story, as told in Buss, *Dignity*, 96–97.

16. Ibid., 99–100.

17. Ibid., 101–2.

18. Ibid., 108.

19. Ibid., 108–9.

20. Richard Delgado, "Legal Storytelling: Story Telling for Oppositionists and Others, a Plea for Narrative," *Michigan Law Review* 87 (1989), quoted in Alyssa Garcia, "Counter Stories of Race and Gender: Situating Experiences of Latinas in the Academy," *Latino Studies* 3 (2005): 261–73.

21. This poem is part of Maria Elena Lucas's diary entry of April 8, 1990, Domingo de Angustia, in Fran Leeper Buss, comp. and ed., *Forged under the Sun/Forjada bajo el sol: The Life of Maria Elena Lucas* (Ann Arbor: University of Michigan Press, 1993), 260.

22. Mary Tsukamoto's story, as told in Buss, *Dignity*, 108.

23. Josephine Hunter's story, as told in ibid., 39.

24. Ibid., 32, 39–40.

25. Garcia, "Counter Stories," 261–73, 272.

26. Author interviews with Lucia, Fran Leeper Buss's private collection, Tucson, Arizona.

27. Margaret Regan, *The Death of Josseline: Immigration Stories from the Arizona-Mexico Borderlands* (Boston: Beacon Press, 2010), xxiv.

28. See Stone-Mediatore, *Reading across Borders*, 94.

29. Ibid., 20.

30. Howard Zinn, *A People's History of the United States* (New York: HarperPerennial, 1980), 683.

31. Author interviews with Daisy Cubias, "Work and Family," Fran Buss Oral History Collection, Arthur and Elizabeth Schlesinger Library on the History of Women in America, Radcliffe Institute for Advanced Study, Harvard University, Cambridge, Massachusetts.

32. Ibid.

Chapter 7

1. Lupe Castillo's story, as told in Fran Leeper Buss and Josefina Castillo, comps. and eds., "Spiritual Visions/Border Lives: Progressive Women Activists at the U.S.-Mexico Border," unpublished manuscript, 42.

2. English translation by Maria Elena Lucas, in Fran Leeper Buss, comp. and ed., *Forged under the Sun/Forjada bajo el sol: The Life of Maria Elena Lucas* (Ann Arbor: University of Michigan Press, 1993), 80–81.

3. Rose Augustine's story, as told in Buss and Castillo, "Spiritual Visions/Border Lives," 120–21.

4. Ibid., 126.

5. Ibid., 122–23.

6. Mary Robinson's story, as told in Fran Leeper Buss, comp. and ed., *Moisture of the Earth: Mary Robinson, Civil Rights and Textile Union Activist* (Ann Arbor: University of Michigan Press, 2009), 149.

7. Maria Elena Lucas's story, as told in Buss, *Forged under the Sun*, 181–82.

8. Author interviews with Florence Davis, Fran Leeper Buss's private collection, Tucson, Arizona.

9. Pat Manning's story, as told in Buss and Castillo, "Spiritual Visions/Border Lives," 69–71.

10. Ibid., 73–74.

11. Author interviews with Ana Maria Vasquez, Fran Leeper Buss's private collection, Tucson, Arizona.

12. Mary Robinson's story, as told in Buss, *Moisture of the Earth*, 174–75.

13. Irene Mack Pyawasit's story, as told in Fran Leeper Buss, comp. and ed., *Dignity: Lower Income Women Tell of Their Lives and Struggles* (Ann Arbor: University of Michigan Press, 1985), 163–64.

14. Maria Elena Lucas's story, as told in Buss, *Forged under the Sun*, 226–27.

15. Ibid., 229.

16. Kat Rodriguez's story, as told in Buss and Castillo, "Spiritual Visions/Border Lives," 168–69.

17. Ibid., 180–81.

18. Lupe Castillo's story, as told in ibid., 42–43.

19. Maria Elena Lucas's diary entry of January 29, 1990, in Buss, *Forged under the Sun*, 269.

20. Irene Mack Pyawasit's story, as told in Buss, *Dignity*, 164.

21. Raquel Rubio-Goldsmith's story, as told in Buss and Castillo, "Spiritual Visions/Border Lives," 98–99.

22. Ibid., 105–6.

23. Pat Manning's story, as told in ibid., 77–78.

Chapter 8

1. For a fascinating look at how religion worked in the suffering nation of El Salvador during the 1970s and 1980s, see Anna Peterson, *Martyrdom and the Politics of Religion: Progressive Catholicism in El Salvador's Civil War* (Albany: State University of New York Press, 1997).

2. Irene Mack Pyawasit's story, as told in Fran Leeper Buss, comp. and ed., *Dignity: Lower Income Women Tell of Their Lives and Struggles* (Ann Arbor: University of Michigan Press, 1985), 153.

3. Helen Drazenovich Berklich's story, as told in ibid., 59–60.

4. John Alexander Williams, *Appalachia: A History* (Chapel Hill: University of North Carolina Press, 2002), 101, 123.

5. Maria Elena Lucas's diary entry of June 24, 1976, in Fran Leeper Buss, comp. and ed., *Forged under the Sun/Forjada bajo el sol: The Life of Maria Elena Lucas* (Ann Arbor: University of Michigan Press, 1993), 162.

6. Jacky Turchick's story, as told in Fran Leeper Buss and Josefina Castillo, comps. and eds., "Spiritual Visions/Border Lives: Progressive Women Activists at the U.S.-Mexico Border," unpublished manuscript, 202, 128–29.

7. Rose Augustine's story, as told in Buss, *Forged under the Sun*, 189.

8. Maria Elena Lucas's story, as told in ibid., 189.

9. Irene Mack Pyawasit's story, as told in Buss, *Dignity*, 164.

10. Lupe Castillo's story, as told in Buss and Castillo, "Spiritual Visions/Border Lives," 41.

11. Author interviews with Bernie Mueller, Fran Leeper Buss's private collection, Tucson, Arizona.

12. Pat Manning's story, as told in Buss and Castillo, "Spiritual Visions/Border Lives," 79.

13. Ibid., 92.

14. The original Spanish lyrics of Maria Elena Lucas's song, translated into English by Maria Elena, appear in Buss, *Forged under the Sun*, 192. She wrote the song on June 16, 1987.

15. Ibid., 290–91.

16. Mary Robinson's story, as told in Fran Leeper Buss, comp. and ed., *Moisture of the Earth: Mary Robinson, Civil Rights and Textile Union Activist* (Ann Arbor: University of Michigan Press, 2009), 195.

17. Raquel Rubio-Goldsmith's story, as told in Buss and Castillo, "Spiritual Visions/Border Lives," 107–9.

18. Pat Manning's story, as told in ibid., 74–75.

19. Ibid., 76.

20. Maria Elena Lucas's story, as told in Buss, *Forged under the Sun*, 271–72.

21. Ibid., 291–92.

22. Pat Manning's story, as told in Buss and Castillo, "Spiritual Visions/Border Lives," 79–81.

23. Maria Elena Lucas's diary entry of April 12, 1990, in Buss, *Forged under the Sun*, 301–2.

Conclusion

1. Michael Frisch, *A Shared Authority: Essays on the Craft and Meaning of Oral and Public History* (Albany: State University of New York Press, 1990), xx.

2. Maria Elena Lucas's three-act play, in Fran Leeper Buss, comp. and ed., *Forged under the Sun/Forjada bajo el sol: The Life of Maria Elena Lucas* (Ann Arbor: University of Michigan Press, 1993), 311–12 (appendix).

3. Frisch, *Shared Authority*, xviii.

4. See Shari Stone-Mediatore, *Reading across Borders: Storytelling and Knowledges of Resistance* (New York: Palgrave Macmillan, 2003), 113.

5. Ibid., 9.

6. Maria Elena Lucas, quoted in Buss, *Forged under the Sun*, 17.

7. Stone-Mediatore, *Reading across Borders*, 169.

8. Ibid., 76.

9. Judith Stacey, "Can There Be a Feminist Ethnography?," in *Women's Words: The*

Feminist Practice of Oral History, ed. Sherna Berger Gluck and Daphne Patai (New York: Routledge, 1991), 115.

10. Daphne Patai, "U.S. Academics and Third World Women: Is Ethical Research Possible?," in Gluck and Patai, *Women's Words*, 139.

11. Frisch, *Shared Authority*, 71.

12. Ibid., 13.

13. See Karen Olson and Linda Shopes, "Crossing Boundaries, Building Bridges: Doing Oral History among Working-Class Women and Men," in Gluck and Patai, *Women's Words*, 198.

14. Frisch, *Shared Authority*, 60.

15. Ruth Behar, *The Vulnerable Observer: Anthropology That Breaks Your Heart* (Boston: Beacon Press, 1996), 24.

16. Mary Jo Maynes, Jennifer L. Pierce, and Barbara Laslett, *Telling Stories: The Use of Personal Narratives in the Social Sciences and History* (Ithaca, N.Y.: Cornell University Press, 2008), 67.

17. Stone-Mediatore, *Reading across Borders*, 81.

18. Vivian M. May, *Pursuing Intersectionality, Unsettling Dominant Imaginaries* (New York: Routledge, Taylor & Francis Group, 2015), 6, 12, 48.

19. See ibid., 12.

Bibliography

Alterman, Eric, and Kevin Mattson. *The Cause: The Fight for American Liberalism from Franklin Roosevelt to Barack Obama.* New York: Penguin, 2012.

Anzaldúa, Gloria. *Borderlands/La Frontera.* San Francisco: Aunt Lute Books, 2012.

Atkinson, Anthony B. *Inequality: What Can Be Done?* Cambridge, Mass.: Harvard University Press, 2015.

Ayers, Edward L. *The Promise of the New South: Life after Reconstruction.* New York: Oxford University Press, 1992.

Brown, Catrina, and Tod Augusta-Scott. *Narrative Therapy: Making Meaning, Making Lives.* Thousand Oaks, Calif.: Sage Publications, 2007.

Buss, Fran Leeper, comp. and ed. *Dignity: Lower Income Women Tell of Their Lives and Struggles.* Ann Arbor: University of Michigan Press, 1985.

Buss, Fran Leeper, comp. and ed. *Forged under the Sun/Forjada bajo el sol: The Life of Maria Elena Lucas.* Ann Arbor: University of Michigan Press, 1993.

Buss, Fran Leeper, comp. and ed. *La Partera: Story of a Midwife.* Ann Arbor: University of Michigan Press, 1980.

Buss, Fran Leeper, comp. and ed. *Moisture of the Earth: Mary Robinson, Civil Rights and Textile Union Activist.* Ann Arbor: University of Michigan Press, 2009.

Christian, Barbara. "The Race for Theory." In *Making Face, Making Soul/Haciendo Caras: Creative and Critical Perspectives by Feminists of Color,* edited by Gloria Anzaldúa, 335–45. 1990.

Cobble, Dorothy Sue, ed. *Women and Unions: Forging a Partnership.* Ithaca, N.Y.: IRL Press, 1993.

Cobble, Dorothy Sue, Linda Gordon, and Astrid Henry. *Feminism Unfinished: A Short, Surprising History of American Women's Movements.* New York: Liveright Publishing, 2014.

Collins, Patricia Hill. *Black Feminist Thought: Knowledge, Consciousness, and the Politics of Empowerment.* New York: Routledge, 2000.

Combahee River Collective. "The Combahee River Collective Statement." In *Home Girls: A Black Feminist Anthology,* edited by Barbara Smith, 272–82. New York: Kitchen Table–Women of Color Press, 1983.

Conway, Mimi. *Rise Gonna Rise: A Portrait of Southern Textile Workers.* Garden City, N.Y.: Anchor Press, 1979.

Crenshaw, Kimberle Williams. "Demarginalizing the Intersection of Race and Sex: A Black Feminist Critique of Antidiscrimination Doctrine, Feminist Theory, and Antiracist Politics." *University of Chicago Legal Forum* 140 (1989): 139–68.

Crenshaw, Kimberle Williams. "Mapping the Margins: Intersectionality, Identity Politics, and Violence against Women of Color." In *Critical Race Theory: The Key Writings That Formed the Movement,* edited by Kimberle Crenshaw, Neil Gotanda, Gary Peller, and Kendall Thomas. New York: New Press, 1995.

Cruikshank, Margaret. *The Gay and Lesbian Liberation Movement.* New York: Routledge, 1992.

Cunningham, Hilary. *God and Caesar at the Rio Grande: Sanctuary and the Politics of Religion.* Minneapolis: University of Minnesota Press, 1995.

D'Angelo, Raymond. *The American Civil Rights Movement: Readings and Interpretations.* Guilford, Conn.: McGraw-Hill, 2001.

Davis, Joseph, ed. *Stories of Change: Narrative and Social Movements.* Albany: State University of New York Press, 2002.

Davis, K. "Intersectionality as Buzzword: A Sociology of Science Perspective on What Makes a Feminist Theory Successful." *Feminist Theory* 9, no. 1 (2008): 67–85.

Doss, Erika. *Memorial Mania: Public Feeling in America.* Chicago: University of Chicago Press, 2010.

Duberman, Martin. *Stonewall.* New York: Dutton, 1993.

Ferguson, Kathryn, Norma A. Price, and Ted Parks. *Crossing with the Virgin: Stories from the Migrant Trail.* Tucson: University of Arizona Press, 2010.

Frisch, Michael. *A Shared Authority: Essays on the Craft and Meaning of Oral and Public History.* Albany: State University of New York Press, 1990.

Garcia, Bedolla L. "Intersections of Inequality: Understanding Marginalization and Privilege in the Post–Civil Rights Era." *Gender and Society* 3, no. 2 (2007): 232–48.

Gilens, Martin. *Why Americans Hate Welfare: Race, Media, and the Politics of Antipoverty Policy*. Chicago: University of Chicago Press, 1999.

Gluck, Sherna Berger, and Daphne Patai, eds. *Women's Words: The Feminist Practice of Oral History*. New York: Routledge, 1991.

Gubrium, Jaber F., and James A. Holstein. *Analyzing Narrative Reality*. London: Sage, 2009.

Hancock, Ange-Marie. *Intersectionality: An Intellectual History*. New York: Oxford University Press, 2016.

Harding, Sandra, and Kathryn Norberg. "New Feminist Approaches to Social Science Methodologies: An Introduction." *Signs: Journal of Women in Culture and Society* 30, no. 4 (2005): 2009–15.

Harvey, Jennifer. *Dear White Christians: For Those Still Longing for Racial Reconciliation*. Grand Rapids, Mich.: William B. Eerdmans Publishing, 2014.

Hesse-Biber, Sharlene, and Gregg Lee Carter. *Working Women in America: Split Dreams*. New York: Oxford University Press, 2005.

Hill Collins, Patricia. "Toward a New Vision: Race, Class, and Categories of Analysis and Connection." *Race, Sex, and Class* 1, no. 1 (1993): 25–45.

hooks, bell. *Yearning: Race, Gender, and Cultural Politics*. Boston: South End Press, 1990.

Josselson, Ruthellen, and Amia Lieblich, eds. *Making Meaning of Narratives*. Thousand Oaks, Calif.: Sage Publications, 1999.

Kelley, Robin D. G. *Hammer and Hoe: Alabama Communists during the Great Depression*. Chapel Hill, N.C.: University of North Carolina Press, 1990.

Kendall, Frances. *Understanding White Privilege: Creating Pathways to Authentic Relationships Across Race*. New York: Routledge, 2006.

Kennedy, Elizabeth Lapovsky, and Madeline D. Davis. *Boots of Leather, Slippers of Gold: The History of a Lesbian Community*. New York: Routledge, 1993.

Kingsolver, Barbara. *Holding the Line: Women and the Great Arizona Mine Strike of 1983*. New York: IRL Press, 1996.

Lipsitz, George. *The Possessive Investment in Whiteness: How White People Profit from Identity Politics*. Philadelphia: Temple University Press, 1998.

Lorde, Audre. *Sister Outsider: Essays and Speeches*. Trumansburg, N.Y.: Crossing Press, 1984.

Lykke, Nina. *Feminist Studies: A Guide to Intersectional Theory, Methodology, and Writing*. New York: Routledge, 2010.

Marsh, Charles. *God's Long Summer: Stories of Faith and Civil Rights*. Princeton, N.J.: Princeton University Press, 1997.

May, Vivian M. *Pursuing Intersectionality, Unsettling Dominant Imaginaries*. New York: Routledge, Taylor & Francis Group, 2015.

Maynes, Mary Jo, Jennifer L. Pierce, and Barbara Laslett. *Telling Stories: The Use of Personal Narratives in the Social Sciences and History*. Ithaca, N.Y.: Cornell University Press, 2008.

McGuire, Danielle L. *At the Dark End of the Street: Black Women, Rape, and Resistance, a New History of the Civil Rights Movement from Rosa Parks to the Rise of Black Power*. New York: Alfred A. Knopf, 2010.

Mohanty, Chandra Talpede. *Feminism without Borders: Decolonizing Theory, Practicing Solidarity*. Durham, N.C.: Duke University Press, 2003.

Mohanty, Chandra Talpade, Ann Russo, and Lourdes Torres, eds. *Third World Women and the Politics of Feminism*. Bloomington: Indiana University Press, 1991.

Moraga, Cherrie, and Gloria Anzaldúa. *This Bridge Called My Back: Writings by Radical Women of Color*. New York: Kitchen Table–Women of Color Press, 1983.

Nash, J. C. "Rethinking Intersectionality." *Feminist Review* 89 (2008): 1–15.

Obasogie, Osagie K. *Blinded by Sight: Seeing Race through the Eyes of the Blind*. Stanford, Calif.: Stanford University Press, 2014.

Parker, Andrew, Mary Russo, Doris Sommer, and Patricia Yaeger, eds. *Nationalisms and Sexualities*. New York: Routledge, 1992.

Pawel, Miriam. *The Crusades of Cesar Chavez: A Biography*. New York: Bloomsbury Press, 2014.

Perks, Robert, and Alistair Thompson, eds. *The Oral History Reader*. London: Routledge, 1998.

Personal Narratives Group, ed. *Interpreting Women's Lives: Feminist Theory and Personal Narratives*. Bloomington: Indiana University Press, 1989.

Piven, Frances Fox, and Richard A. Cloward. *Poor People's Movements: Why They Succeed, How They Fail*. New York: Pantheon, 1977.

Roediger, David R. *The Wages of Whiteness: Race and the Making of the American Working Class*. London: Verso, 1991.

Rosengarten, Theodore. *All God's Dangers: The Life of Nate Shaw*. New York: Alfred A. Knopf, 1974.

Samuel, Raphael. *Theatres of Memory: Past and Present in Contemporary Culture*. London: Verso, 1994.

Smith, Barbara. "Introduction." In *Home Girls: A Black Feminist Anthology,* edited by Barbara Smith, xix–lvi. New York: Kitchen Table–Women of Color Press, 1983.

Stone-Mediatore, Shari. *Reading across Borders: Storytelling and Knowledges of Resistance.* New York: Palgrave Macmillan, 2003.

Welch, Michael. *Detained: Immigration Laws and the Expanding I.N.S. Jail Complex.* Philadelphia: Temple University Press, 2002.

West, Guida, and Rhoda Lois Blumberg, eds. *Women and Social Protest.* New York: Oxford University Press, 1990.

Wilkerson, Isabel. *The Warmth of Other Suns: The Epic Story of America's Great Migration.* New York: Random House, 2010.

Williams, Johnny E. *African American Religion in the Civil Rights Movement in Arkansas.* Jackson: University Press of Mississippi, 2003.

Williams, Patricia J. *The Alchemy of Race and Rights.* Cambridge, Mass.: Harvard University Press, 1991.

Index